DECENCY AND EXCESS

DECENCY AND EXCESS

Global Aspirations and Material Deprivation on a Caribbean Sugar Plantation

Samuel Martínez

Paradigm Publishers
Boulder • London

Paradigm Publishers is committed to preserving our environment. This book was printed on recycled paper with 30% post-consumer waste content, saving trees and avoiding the creation of hundreds of gallons of wastewater, tens of pounds of solid waste, more than a hundred pounds of greenhouse gases, and using hundreds fewer kilowatt hours of electricity than if it had been printed on paper manufactured from all virgin fibers.

All rights reserved. No part of the publication may be transmitted or reproduced in any media or form, including electronic, mechanical, photocopy, recording, or informational storage and retrieval systems, without the express written consent of the publisher.

Copyright © 2007 Paradigm Publishers

Published in the United States by Paradigm Publishers, 3360 Mitchell Lane, Suite E, Boulder, CO 80301 USA.

Paradigm Publishers is the trade name of Birkenkamp & Company, LLC, Dean Birkenkamp, President and Publisher.

Library of Congress Cataloging-in-Publication Data

Martínez, Samuel, 1959-
  Decency and excess: global aspirations and material deprivation on a Caribbean sugar plantation / Samuel Martínez.
      p. cm.
  Includes bibliographical references and index.
  ISBN 978-1-59451-187-5 (alk. paper)
  1. Sugar workers—Dominican Republic—Batey Monte Coca—Social conditions. 2. Sugar workers—Dominican Republic—Batey Monte Coca—Economic conditions. 3. Commercial products—Social aspects—Dominican Republic—Batey Monte Coca. 4. Alien labor, Haitian—Dominican Republic—Batey Monte Coca. 5. Batey Monte Coca (Dominican Republic)—Ethnic relations. I. Title.
   HD8039.S86D645 2007
   331.7'6336109729381—dc22
                                              2006035189

Printed and bound in the United States of America on acid-free paper that meets the standards of the American National Standard for Permanence of Paper for Printed Library Materials.

Designed and Typeset by Straight Creek Bookmakers.

11 10 09 08   2 3 4 5

Contents

Illustrations and Tables … vii

Preface and Acknowledgments … ix

1 Introduction … 1
2 A Place No One Calls "Home": The Plantation and Modernity … 21
3 Living in Nowhere … 33
4 Commodity Consumption in a Globalizing Age … 47
5 An Indecent Life … 61
6 Places and Flows … 93
7 High Times in Hard Times … 129
8 Material Passions … 143
9 The Hot and the Cold … 157
10 Conclusions … 195

Works Cited … 213
Index … 223
About the Author … 227

Illustrations and Tables

ILLUSTRATIONS

Figure 5-1. The prostitutes' quarters at La Yagüita.
Figure 6-1. Map of the Ingenio Consuelo.
Figure 6-2. Map of the Colonia Esperanza, Ingenio Consuelo.
Figure 6-3. Map of the transportation network surrounding the Batey Monte Coca.
Figure 6-4. Map of the Batey Monte Coca.
Figure 6-5. Map of "La Construcción."
Figure 6-6. Lean-tos and clotheslines, behind a cement barracks.
Figure 6-7. A partially built lean-to (lacking roof covering).
Figure 6-8. The kitchen of one of the batey's more prosperous households.
Figure 6-9. The kitchen of one of the batey's poorer households.
Figure 9-1. Opening the way for the *Rara* band, one man cracks a long whip.
Figure 9-2. *Banbou* players advance.
Figure 9-3. The *majò* in a display of footwork and dexterity.
Figure 9-4. A *majò*, dancing *gagá*.
Figure 9-5. The deaf-mute puppeteer.
Figure 9-6. A young woman dances in the style known as *gouye*.
Figure 9-7. Eroticized dancing on the perimeter of the *Rara* procession.
Figure 9-8. Woman, in trance.
Figure 9-9. The *sanba* (metallic rattle in hand) and a *majò*.

TABLES

Table 5-1. Distribution by Ethnic Group of Economically Active Women in Monte Coca.
Table 5-2. Distribution by Sex and Ethnic Group of Monte Coca Adults.
Table 5-3. Distribution by Sex and Ethnic Group of Conjugal Unions in Monte Coca.
Table 8-1. Rates of Ownership of Five Household Appliances, Batey Monte Coca, January 1986.

Preface and Acknowledgments

This book may well be one of holistic ethnography's "last hurrahs." Much of today's cultural anthropology inhabits archives, global networks, even cyberspace, examines texts or popular media, or, in a quite different vein, is guided by reductive bio-evolutionary theories and esoteric statistical methodologies. There is reason to celebrate if cultural anthropology has broadened its concerns and expanded its concepts regarding what counts as knowledge. Yet if, as a result of these trends, we lose touch with the kinds of people—pushed out of sight and hearing by the corporate media—whom our discipline has in the past excelled in bringing into view, then I think anthropology's current trends also give reason for regret. Today, neither the "scientific" nor the "post-modernist" wing of cultural anthropology places much trust in participant-observation-based, holistic fieldwork: the first camp dismisses it as too subjective; the second distrusts it for being implicated with Western global domination and wedded to realist narrative conventions. I believe that broad-ranging, community-based, empirical field study is not only still viable but should be assuming expanded importance in the present era of economic globalization. Only through this approach can cultural anthropology raise awareness of globalization's geographically and socially uneven outcomes and contribute to scholarly understandings of how local actors respond, when caught on the scissors of declining industrial production paired with rising consumer aspirations. Only by going to economically depressed communities—whether these be located in the under-developed or the excessively developed economies of the world—and talking to the people who live there, can we appreciate the human costs of today's accelerated capital restructuring. At the present global historical conjuncture, it would be ironic if cultural anthropology were to turn its back on the painstaking study of matters particular to localities around the globe. When critics and theorists join voices in raising concerns about the destructive effects of global economic forces and trends on local traditions and economic initiatives worldwide, should we not revitalize our fieldwork tradition sooner than abandon it?

While we should not give up on holistic ethnography, neither should we be uncritical of cultural anthropology's guiding concepts. I see particular need for greater critical scrutiny of anthropologists' all-too-frequent tendency to attribute all and sundry aspects of belief and behavior to *culture*.

Anthropologists have conventionally reified and "totalized" culture–not just studying it but seeing it as a thing, active in the world, and the primary cause of the social phenomena we observe. These ways of thinking about culture live on in our thinking and inevitably lead ethnographers into the interpretive trap of implicitly either idealizing or vilifying others' ways of life. Whether it bears a positive valence, signifying that a group's way of life is deserving of toleration, or a negative charge, implying that the group carries a social pathology (e.g., the "culture of abuse at Abu Ghraib"), culture is never politically neutral. Judgment, I fear, is built into the culture concept. Even eschewing the attribution of causality to culture, it may be that judgment is hard to avoid. I may unconsciously fall into it in other ways. Yet I think the people whose ways of life I have studied would not be well served by the positive or negative judgment inevitably connoted by characterizing all their beliefs and behavior as a product of culture.

Truth be told, were the way of life that I describe in this book to disappear tomorrow, no one, not even I, would much regret its passing. There is little that is whole, satisfying, and authentic, and not much very particular, great or of irreplaceable value, about this community's life ways. Monte Coca—the company compound for agricultural workers (*batey*) where I have done my fieldwork on a sugar plantation in the Dominican Republic—was enveloped by the rising tide of primary commodity export development that Europeans and North American business enterprises brought to much of the tropics in the late-nineteenth and early-twentieth centuries. The settlement was created in the process of converting the land around it into a massive for-profit agricultural industrial complex, and thus stripped clean of its place-specific cultural attributes. Amid the detritus of Western commodity culture, things unique, integral, genuine and enduring are hard to find. The existence in Monte Coca and other *bateyes* of a distinct system of spiritual belief and ritual, for example, centering on service to the gods of Haitian *vodou*, may be regarded as all the more precious for having been pieced together by settlers and sojourners from elsewhere. In past years, cultural anthropologists would look only at such genuinely particular aspects of culture, and turn their gaze away from the surrounding shops, bars, store-bought adornments, and work for wages; many an ethnographer would still. Yet, inauthentic, faddish and familiar though these circumstances of life might accurately be described to be, I am convinced it would diminish our understanding of people's lives in Monte Coca to focus primarily on things authentic, particular and enduring. Both things, the culturally authentic and the inauthentic, are means by which *batey* residents desire beyond adequacy, seek to transcend the limitations of the everyday, and in so doing tacitly affirm their humanity.

Largely, people in sugarcane worker compounds like Monte Coca do what they do because these are the things they have to do in order to survive, to find acceptance from their peers or to seek greater comfort and stimulation in otherwise hard and drab lives. Even more, the risky, illegal, abusive, and cruelly exploitative practices that very frequently take place on the Dominican Republic's sugar plantations make it seem even demeaning to say Monte Cocans possess a "plantation culture" or otherwise explain their behavior largely on cultural grounds. What would be learned by asserting that the physical and symbolic violence people in Monte Coca experience at others' hands, and commonly perpetrate upon others weaker than they, is "cultural"? Saying this would be tantamount to asserting that degradation is an immanent part and product of these people's character, hence blaming them and not the circumstances of their lives for the cruelty and prejudice at which I look squarely in this book. Therefore, I adopt, in my own way, Lila Abu-Lughod's (1991) advice to "write against culture." Important though it is to study the cultural implications of geographical uprooting and material poverty, you will search this book in vain for much mention of "culture." The concept is simply too judgmental and essentialist to be of much use to me here.

After I presented a condensed version of certain of this book's themes at a professional conference in 1998, the discussant for my panel, Bill Roseberry, said my paper delivered "words that make us wince." I have often since wondered what Bill would have made of the material that is the basis for my ethnography. What Roseberry was referring to, I think, are not just the appalling conditions of life on the Dominican Republic's sugar plantations. It makes me wince, too, to consider what people in Monte Coca have to do to survive. Degrading conditions of life, symbolic subordination and even physical violence are perpetrated not just by the sugar company but by workers who are themselves at times cruelly exploited by people higher up the capitalist "food chain." "Monte Coca" and the "Ingenio Consuelo" are the real names of the places where I have done ethnographic fieldwork. Bearing in mind that this book contains descriptions of many wrongs, including major human rights violations, no one will be surprised that the names of some individuals have been changed or concealed for their protection. My ethical obligations and scientific commitment to truth also lead me to point out even more insistently how my former neighbors in Monte Coca seek to transcend deprivation, degradation, exploitation and violence, and try to realize their own visions of what it means to live decently, against tremendous material obstacles. Aspirations to higher things are as much a part of the local scene as the acts of callous cruelty and exploitation that take place there.

The only unusual qualification I bring to researching and writing this book is perhaps a greater linguistic mastery than most ethnographers can claim. But even that is mainly dumb luck, for, of the two main languages spoken on the sugar plantations of the Dominican Republic, one (Spanish) I know from earliest childhood, and the other (Haitian Creole), I think, must be one of the world's easiest languages to learn the rudiments of. I first broached this topic—the search for dignity and meaning in degrading and alienating social environments—in the very first essay I wrote after returning to the United States in 1987 from my dissertation fieldwork in the Dominican Republic and Haiti. I set that essay aside during the years I spent writing my doctoral dissertation, thinking (correctly) that the issues it raised were simply best left for another project. In the intervening years, I have presented condensed versions in various public talks. During that time, I was often struck how the public mood in *the* United States and other industrially advanced nations of the world seemed to be swinging, pendulum-like, from post–Cold War euphoria to despair at the persistence of poverty and sectarianism. Over this time, increasing skepticism gathered as well around whether economic globalization is on aggregate a force for the good. Had I hurried my thoughts into publication in a post-fieldwork rush of enthusiasm, a book on the themes I present here would certainly have been regarded as prescient. Yet it would not have been as mature a work, nor would it have benefited from the long-term perspective I have gained from my subsequent stints of fieldwork in Monte Coca, visits during which I have also filled many a gap in my field notes. More importantly, I have seen, in the more than fifteen years since I completed my dissertation fieldwork, that things could get significantly worse than the already desperate state of poverty I witnessed on the Dominican sugar plantations in the late 1980s. Even then, I had the inchoate sense that these plantation workers were fated to be losers in the less fettered financial investment climate that was taking shape under free-market reform. Yet never could I have imagined how rapidly the country's sugar industry would decline nor how gut-wrenching the experience of that decline would be in Monte Coca.

Not just the passage of time has permitted me to develop a deeper perspective; I have also gained many valuable ideas from the friends with whom I have shared drafts and the audiences before which I have presented talks over this time. It is inevitable that my ability to assimilate all the thoughts they have offered falls well short of the quality of the comments and suggestions I have been given. For that I can only offer sincere apologies. All those who have presented criticisms in a constructive spirit, I thank from my heart. The time it has taken for my ideas to take shape in this book has been long and the intellectual debts I have accumulated in this process are many. As a result, there is a great risk of unjustly omitting some people from deserved individual recognition. There are, even so, a few particular debts that I would be particularly remiss in leaving unmentioned.

My postdoctoral appointments, at the University of Michigan's Center for Afro-American and African Studies and the University of Virginia's Carter G. Woodson Institute for African-American and African Studies, provided ideal settings for early development of the essays that would become part of this book. I thank the staff and my colleagues at both institutes, and their directors—Earl Lewis, at Michigan, and Reginald Butler, at Virginia—for their gracious and generous support. Funding for my field research was provided by the International Dissertation Field Research program of the Social Science

Research Council (SSRC), the Doherty Fellowship, the Carter G. Woodson Institute, the University of Connecticut Faculty Large Grant program, the William and Flora Hewlett Foundation, and the Program on Global Security and Cooperation of the Social Science Research Council. Authorship of the findings and opinions I present is my own, except where duly noted, as is responsibility for errors of omission or commission. I presented talks on the theme of "human difference and the material world" at the University of Michigan, the University of Virginia, the Johns Hopkins University, Colby College, the University of Connecticut, and at the 1998 joint AES/CASCA annual meeting in Toronto. I am grateful to all the participants and to the organizers of those colloquia for their comments and questions.

There is no chapter in this book from which the significant influence of Sidney Mintz is absent. In his role as my thesis advisor, he commented on that first essay I wrote after returning from the field. Even though this book was written without his guidance, his enthusiasm for that early essay has stayed in my mind as a source of strength and courage to persist in returning over the years to the themes that ultimately came together in this book. I am particularly grateful also to Lanfranco Blanchetti, who made me aware of the relevance to my concerns of Georges Bataille's writing. Even if my reading of Bataille lacks the subtlety that Blanchetti, among others, would bring to it, my readers will recognize what a debt I owe him for having brought the work of that great non-utilitarian theorist to my attention.

The rapidity with which I prepared the manuscript for review was as remarkable as the length of the book's gestation. I am grateful to all whose support enabled me to finish the bulk of the writing. Once I was determined that the book would be written, now or never, the provision of a spacious, comfortable and telephone-free office (read, "hideaway") in the University of Connecticut's Graduate School building was a boon. UConn Anthropology graduate student, Jennifer Telesca, went far beyond the call of duty, in her patient reading and detailed commentary on the entire book manuscript, as part of a tutorial course on Modernity and the Culture of Capitalism. Thanks also go to Benjamin Spaulding for map preparation, to the University of Connecticut Instructional Media office for scanning figures and photos, and to the SSRC Program on Global Security and Cooperation for the provision of publication support funds. Dean Birkenkamp, president and social sciences editor at Paradigm, has been close to my ideal for an editor, rapid and flexible when that has been needed, but always doing me the justice of assuming that I am as strongly determined as he is that this be a high-quality book. The two anonymous reviewers of the manuscript provided tough comments but were extremely generous in their praise and their suggestions for how to improve the book.

My greatest debt is to the people of Monte Coca. Without their patient tolerance and cooperation, my field research would have been impossible. I know they are aware how large the imbalance is between what I have gained and what they have gained, out of life and out of our relationship, over the years. I realize that, with the passage of time, their cooperation and hospitality are no more to be taken for granted today than they were the day I first set foot in Monte Coca. Their many kindnesses have made fieldwork there an activity I look forward to renewing. When I am with those who have remained there all these years, the interest they voice in who I am and what is new in my life helps make interviews seem like conversations, not interrogations. Among my former neighbors there, my greatest debt is to Francis Charles. Words can only begin to convey how much he, a former cane cutter, has been to me, personally as well as professionally: field assistant, guide, translator, bodyguard, confidante, friend, and *compadre*; solid and blessed with the gift of good humor in adversity. In the Dominican Republic, I feel privileged also to have friends and collaborators of a different sort in the Haitian-Dominican rights organizations that have become one focus of my field research since 2002. For their trust, friendship, and contributions to my knowledge, I wish to thank the staff members of the Movimiento de Mujeres Domínico-Haitianas and of the Centro Cultural Domínico-Haitiano, with particular recognition for the assistance given by these organizations' directors, Solange Pierre (MUDHA) and Antonio Pol-Emil (CCDH). Though she has not contributed directly to the findings I report in this book, there could be no more constant a friend and research collaborator than Glenis Tavárez María, Associate Director of the Museo del Hombre Dominicano. For their invaluable assistance in organizing and carrying out interviews with batey women in 2002, I thank Luis Cirito Carmelo and Ana Jiménez. The assistance of Sandra Vásquez, in transcribing interviews with Haitian-Dominican rights advocates, is also gratefully acknowledged.

To my family, I owe more than trite thanks but for them especially words seem inadequate. Here, I can offer little more than acknowledgment that my wife, Monica van Beusekom, and my children, Saskia and Nico, are the rock upon which all my life's endeavors are built. All the time that the preparation of this book has taken me away from them cannot be regained. It is my great joy to be in debt to them in perpetuity: being with them and loving them are gifts I gain so much from every day. With this in mind and with the hope for a better future, it is to the next generation—and particularly, to Saskia, Nico, and my Haitian-Dominican godchild, Franklin Charles—that I humbly dedicate this book.

1
Introduction

In common with people around the world, the residents of Monte Coca—a multi-ethnic sugar plantation community in the Dominican Republic—imbue the material world, of objects, space and time, with meaning. They interpret how others around them inhabit and make use of the material world, and on this basis they draw social boundaries between those people who are like and unlike them, thus making sense of the social domain with reference to the material. Yet the appeal of things material is never confined to sense-making alone. Another source of its fascination is the sensations people get from particular spaces, uses of time, and commodities. Though in principle distinct, sense-making cannot be divorced from sensation-seeking in people's interpretations of human difference in the material world. Judgments may be drawn, for example, about other people's identities and moral worth on the basis of what they consume, and when, where, and with whom they consume it. When that happens, then one person's seeking after novelty or an altered mood through distinctive consumption becomes evidence for on-lookers to process mentally into ideas about who that person is. Nor are such judgments confined to the social domain. I, as a cultural anthropologist, tend to give emphasis to social meanings. Yet the material and social worlds also have spiritual significance for the people among whom I have lived and learned from as I have done ethnographic fieldwork in Monte Coca, adding further density to the meanings of the material world. All this is my concern in this book.

Sense and sensation, the social and the spiritual: even in naked abstraction, these terms seem to oppose each other. Confronting contradiction, not evading it, is my main analytic strategy. One thing I have learned by living in Monte Coca—a company compound for sugarcane workers—for twelve continuous months in 1985–86, followed by several further stints of fieldwork over more than fifteen subsequent years, is that life does not come shrink-wrapped in neat theoretical packages. People behave in varied and inconsistent ways, and often do things differently than they say they do or should. Two contrasting anecdotes exemplify how contradictory my observations about life in Monte Coca frequently are. The first is an exchange that took place during one of the many partial life-history interviews I did with Haitian migrant workers in Monte Coca:

The gangan. We sat inside a shadowy room in a company barracks. The interviewee, a thin, middle-aged black man, dressed only in dark blue shorts, sat perched on the edge of one of the bunk beds with which the sugar company furnishes the seasonal migrants' rooms. A young woman sat on the ground with her back propped against the wall, wearing a white sleeveless dress. I was accompanied by my Haitian field assistant, Francis Charles. A few minutes into the interview, I asked, "What is your religion?" The interviewee shot out the word, *"Gangan!"* (which means vodou priest, in the Haitian Creole language). "Excuse me?" I asked. "I eat people!" he answered instantly. The young woman tittered. My heartbeat sped to a gallop. If his intention was to throw me off balance, he had succeeded. "Is that true?" I asked, for no reason in particular other than breaking the silence. "Well," Francis said quietly, grinning and raising his eyebrows with a wise look, "in Haiti there are people who have a lot of knowledge." "I can give you anything you want," the interviewee continued, in a matter-of-fact tone. "I can make you rich. I can give you any woman you want. I can turn this man into a rat," he said, pointing his chin without so much as a grin at Francis, who—to my surprise—was seized with laughter to hear this. "It is true," Francis said, still chuckling, "In Haiti there are people who know how to do a lot of things." "Well, if that is true, then what are you doing in this terrible place?" I regretted my impulsiveness the instant that question came out of my mouth but the gangan seemed not put out in the slightest. "I let the soldiers bring me here. I came to see if anyone here needed [spiritual] work done for them. But I will not stay long." Deciding not to press right away for further information on this point, I made a mental note to keep close tabs on the gangan and try to cultivate a relationship with him, remembering that some of my professors at Johns Hopkins had asked me to keep my eyes and ears open for signs of devil contracts like those Michael Taussig had studied among sugar plantation workers in Colombia. Yet, in spite of the company guard posted to keep the newly arrived migrants from leaving, the gangan and his companion were gone within a week.

A well-developed cultural anthropological line of interpretation, which Todd Sanders (2003) calls the "witchcraft-critiques-modernity thesis," has it that belief in supernaturally endowed persons, such as the gangan, constitute an important symbolic resource for people living in poverty and chronic insecurity, on the margins of the global capitalist system. Rumors of gain through contracts with the devil or other occult dealings are one way uprooted people make sense of being divided into haves and have-nots following their entry into an urban or industrial milieu. These beliefs may even be understood to constitute a tacit protest against market-driven social change, if rumors of the occult focus upon illicit enrichment and other negative consequences of the intrusion of money exchanges into livelihoods and social relations formerly governed by reciprocity and tradition.

Such an interpretation is immediately thrown into doubt by my second anecdote, much briefer than the first but with perhaps as much meaning distilled in it:

The portrait photo. It has been my custom to take portrait photographs for my neighbors in Monte Coca, as a way of thanking them for letting me take photos of them as they go about their everyday business in their tattered, less-than-flattering work apparel. A "pretty picture" for all the "ugly" ones, some people there say. One day, after one young man in a group of Haitian seasonal migrants struck a jaunty pose in the sunshine for his portrait with a simple transistor radio in one hand, every one of his roommates insisted on having their pictures taken with the same radio. It seems the radio had the power to grace its bearer's image in these portraits, regardless of whom it actually belonged to. An icon of modernity and a symbol of acquisitive power, the radio had allure, a magic quite different from the occult beliefs highlighted in the first anecdote. Done in the open, before an appreciative "audience," posing with the radio in hand conveyed nothing sinister about the desire for material satisfactions or the means of acquiring them. None of the men seemed to hesitate for a second to grab the radio when it came his turn to pose for the camera, much less express any fear that the sight of it might trigger the envy of later on-lookers. Anxiety about the encroachment of the capitalist mode of production was even further from the picture.

Importantly, the young men's decision to be photographed with the radio was far from unusual. Many other people in this highly impoverished community make a point of including prized possessions in their portrait photos. At times, men's motorcycles and horses and women's glass-fronted display cabinets push their owners to the margins of the picture frame. Where, then, is the collective suspicion of conspicuous consumption, of the kind many anthropologists have said is conveyed by the very kinds of beliefs in witchcraft that are rampant in Monte Coca and reflected in the words of the gangan? My neighbors' acts of display before my camera sooner suggest a belief that the desire to acquire even non-utilitarian consumer goods is a good thing. If cradling the radio for their portrait signifies anything, beyond pride in their own individual productive capacity, it is an unashamed embrace of the satisfactions that only advanced industrial society can make possible. In short, there could be nothing further from this than the notion that witchcraft critiques modernity.

In this book, I bring forward contradictions of this sort, between occult sanction and material satisfaction and, more broadly, between what people convey through rumor and ritual and what they do with objects in time and space. I look squarely at such contradictions and seek to understand what threads them together within a common field of meaning, rather than leaving these seeming contradictions out of my ethnography and hence tacitly defining them out of existence. I do this in part out of my taste for complexity and personal preference for giving headaches over prescribing easy remedies. Mainly, I wish to look straight on at messy reality because that is how I think the world is: contradictory, complex and hard to reduce to mottoes like "witchcraft critiques modernity."

Belief in the possibility of enriching yourself through witchcraft and belief in the power of commodities—to enhance beauty, define identity, and give purpose to life—have things in common. Both may be said to be forms of "enchantment": one attributes to spirits the ability to capture goods and the other attributes to goods an inherent life-enhancing quality. Beyond this, both sets of belief hold that identity—who a person is—is defined largely in relation to the command s/he exercises over objects, space and time. Both ways of relating to the world of goods tie in thus with my overarching concern, with how Monte Cocans construe human likeness and difference through the medium of the material world. Who you are, in Monte Coca, is defined by what your work is, how you take your leisure, what you eat, when and where you work, play, worship, and sleep, in short, by the who, what, when, where, and how of uncounted daily engagements with the material world. Through words and actions in a variety of contexts, people in Monte Coca ascribe occupational, ethnic, and gender differences to certain commodities, places of work and leisure, and times of the day and days of the week. Residents thereby project enduring social distinctions and hierarchies onto the uses given by individuals to commodities, space, and time. This book is, broadly conceived, about this dialectic between human difference and the material world, how each defines the other.

THE RESEARCH COMMUNITY AND ITS CONTEXT

Monte Coca is a "nowhere" place: in physical structure and appearance, it closely resembles hundreds of other sugar plantation workers' compounds in the Dominican Republic and elsewhere in the Caribbean. Compounding the visual aura of placeless-ness, Monte Coca is a company town. The land and most of the buildings in it are property of the Dominican state sugar consortium (Consejo Estatal del Azúcar, CEA), and the residents have only a tenuous claim to own any real estate. It is an environment built not to house families but to warehouse the single men and oxen who sustain the flow of cane to the nearby sugar-mill town of Consuelo. Add deep material poverty to this picture and it becomes understandable why everyone who lives in Monte Coca says they wish to leave it someday for a better place. Much of my motivation to write this book stems from wondering how people find means of resisting the alienation that would be expected to result from laboring to produce goods for the richer countries and being exposed to media images of consumer goods, while earning incomes that lag far behind their consumer aspirations. The search for dignity, on both material and spiritual planes, is a guiding concern in this book. Through the media of objects and actions in space and time, Monte Coca's permanent residents enhance the decency of their indecent surroundings and add novelty to their lives of dreary labor and poverty. Some behavior, such as weekend drinking binges, may elicit strong disapproval. There is no comfortable consensus among residents about what to consume or how to spend their leisure time or lead "decent lives" more generally. There is just agreement that the choices one makes are important, even if on reflection there may appear to be little or no room for choice at all.

What remains constant is that "decency" seems always to be defined by opposition with "indecency," and linked to enduring and even purportedly natural distinctions between men and women, Dominicans and Haitians, and permanent and seasonal residents. The following fieldwork vignette may make it clearer what I mean, by illustrating how distinctions between "decent" and "indecent" acts, places and people become a largely taken-for-granted part of their everyday surroundings:

A room of my own. Soon after embarking on my fieldwork in Monte Coca, I realized that my original plan, of sharing accommodations with a family, was just not working. I had learned a good deal about the residents' everyday routines and travails in the few weeks I spent with my host family, but I missed sleeping (the bed they had so graciously let me use had bugs) and I was obviously inconveniencing my hosts (a family of nine who occupied two sixteen-square-meter rooms). Worse, there was no space in their home for me to set up a writing table for my note-taking. When it was explained that a room could be assigned to me without evicting anyone else, I unhesitatingly responded, "Yes!" A widow of a former company boss was willing to cede one of the four barracks rooms in her possession, which was being used at the time just to store her surplus furniture. Once I bought an inexpensive bed and had ordered chairs and tables to be made, I moved in. My new neighbors immediately assured me, "This is a decent room. *Congoses* [seasonal migrants from Haiti] have never lived here." Perhaps noticing my raised eyebrows, one of my new neighbors quickly explained, "We could never live in a congó barracks. They [the migrant workers] are too rowdy. They make noise at all hours of the night and they stink up the place with garbage and smoke."

Residential segregation had been instituted by the company many years prior. It is likely this was done to facilitate keeping the seasonal workers under surveillance. Yet the permanent residents of Monte Coca give this segregation their own interpretation. They add it to the many oppositions that define their own decency by contrast with what they see as the inherent indecency of the poorer seasonal migrants who enter each year from the Dominican Republic's neighboring country of Haiti. The residents' own living quarters differ little in lay-out and are generally in worse physical condition than the seasonal migrants' barracks but are regarded as more "decent" places to live simply because these exclude those "indecent people" from Haiti.

Exclusionary language and actions like this would be repeated many times once the migrants began to arrive for the sugarcane harvest. Such acts of self-definition by opposition with the immigrants in their midst point to a second key concern: the very search for decency in the form of material attainments may deepen divisions based on ethnic identity and occupational/residential status. What is gained, and by whom, when the possession of material tokens of decency translates into perceived evidence of the superiority of one group over another? In *Black Reconstruction*, W. E. B. Du Bois argues that the "status and privileges conferred by race could be used to make up for alienating and exploitative class relationships: White workers could, and did, define and accept their class positions by fashioning identities as 'not slaves' and 'not Blacks'" (Roediger 1991: 13). Du Bois calls this the "psychological wage" of whiteness. I keep it for the concluding chapter to give this concept fuller discussion. By that point in the book, I think it will have become apparent that the concept of a psychological wage for in-group membership is applicable to ethnically divided working populations outside the United States and is not restricted to the white-black dichotomy of North American race relations. Suffice it here to add only that unity is made more elusive by the accretion of social distinctions, between Haitians and Dominicans and seasonal and permanent residents, onto the sugar company occupational hierarchy.

Of course people in Monte Coca are hardly exceptional today in facing the twin challenges of coping with material impoverishment and maintaining unity in the face of growing intra-community inequality. Today, there are few places in the world where being human, enjoying a decent existence, or being a good parent, child or neighbor are matters that remain unaffected by international flows of ideas, people and merchandise. Scarcely a page of this book can be read without finding signs that the people who live in Monte Coca are part of the same media-saturated world experienced by consumers in the United States, Western Europe, Japan and other advanced post-industrial societies. Yet Monte Cocans, in common with uncounted billions around the world, are consigned to be on-lookers at the global consumer feast. In large part, they experience advanced capitalism's panoply of goods vicariously, as recipients of advertising and other media images, possessing but very limited ability to acquire what they see. They have long lived in what Jean and John Comaroff (1999: 279) call the "Age of Futilitarianism," in which "postmodern pessimism runs up against the promises of late capitalism." Worse, the friction between declining material prospects and growing aspirations has only grown, over the fifteen years of repeated field visits on which I report.

Not just attitudes toward consumption but their entire way of life mark Monte Cocans as marginalized "moderns." The plantation and sugar mill they maintain through their work represent the underside of global industrial restructuring, the destruction of the old economy's smokestack industries that accompanies the construction of the new information and service economy. In the United States, the decline of long-established capital-intensive industries is commonly understood to involve a transfer of manufacturing jobs from "north" to "south" in the global economy. It is relatively under-appreciated that mining and other primary-goods producing and processing centers in lesser-developed countries, such as the Dominican Republic, have also been hit hard by de-industrialization. As world demand has declined for certain primary goods, such as tin and copper, heavy industrial plants have shut down in poor nations, such as Bolivia and Zambia, that depended heavily on these commodities (Gill 2000; Ferguson 1999). In the case of the Dominican Republic, world over-production of sugar has combined with international lender-demanded divestment in this sector, to weaken a formerly thriving industry that, even as it was home to many brutal injustices and inequalities, provided a livelihood to hundreds of thousands. How ironic, then, that many millions—in Africa, Southeast Asia, Latin America and the countries of the former Soviet Union—increasingly define who they are and what is of value to them through consumption. Even as their consumer aspirations rise, global economic integration and neo-liberal reform create upheavals that reduce and destabilize incomes for millions, and hence undermine their ability to realize these expanded consumption aspirations. Even as many gain, through new economic opportunities created by freeing up markets, many are crushed. In common with the Zambian Copperbelt residents interviewed by James Ferguson (1999: 12–13), Dominican sugar plantation residents have had their expectations of future prosperity yanked out from under them, leaving only "an overwhelming sense of decline and despair."

The United Nations Development Programme's Human Development Report of 1998, focusing on consumption, provides startling statistical confirmation that what has occurred in Monte Coca may be part of a global trend. Both consumption and economic inequality increased rapidly around the world in the twentieth century's final decades. The report finds that global consumption expenditures doubled in 25 years, to $24 trillion in 1998 (UNDP 1998: 46). Many benefits in human welfare have flowed from the increased aggregate prosperity that lay behind this dramatic increase in consumption. To an unprecedented extent, the spread of consumer products has reached even the poor, who own more "light" consumer durables such as bicycles, radios and wristwatches than ever before. The spread of consumption of industrial manufactures to every stratum of society reflects a global qualitative trend: "What was considered a luxury 20 years ago is now a necessity—a private car for every middle-class family in France, a wrist watch for every rural family in India, a refrigerator for every family in China" (ibid.: 60).

Even more striking, however, is the report's finding that "the poorest 20% of the world's people and more have been left out of the consumption explosion" (ibid.: 2). Deprivation among the poorest fifth is paired with over-consumption among the most affluent fifth. "Globally, the 20% of the world's people in the highest-income countries account for 86% of total private consumption expenditures—the poorest 20% a minuscule 1.3%" (ibid.: 2). Regional statistics also show important geographical disparities in consumption growth. Whereas consumption has increased steadily in the industrial countries and grown spectacularly in the high-growth economies of East Asia and Latin America, the average African household consumes 20 percent less than it did 30 years ago (ibid.: 1–2). The African data highlights the global reality: nations and communities are being divided into economic winners and losers.

There is now widespread agreement that global economic integration and neo-liberal reform have worsened inequality, both among and within nations.[1] Paired with the spread of global media and rising consumer aspirations, economic decline for the many million "losers" in the world economy creates a paradox: increased cultural integration goes hand in hand with heightened social exclusion. It is a kind of integration when the same kinds of employment, housing, life-styles, and expectations spread across the face of the globe. Yet when global consumer aspirations expand and grow more standardized at the same time as hundreds of millions sink deeper into poverty, the declining ability of so many people to add the items they want to their shopping baskets creates a recipe for a highly volatile kind of exclusion. In the cities of the global south, the disparities are perhaps most starkly visible: "Alongside the high-income gentrified housing are the homeless, and along with the high-earning finance and e-commerce sectors lie the vastly increased informal sectors of employment" (Munck 2005: 33).

The resulting disparities possibly deepen low-income people's subjective sense of deprivation and may even endanger gains in physical well-being brought about by higher standards of living. "Unequal income distribution translates into social exclusion if a society's value system places too much importance on what a person possesses rather than what a person is or can do. And if social standards are rising faster than incomes, consumption patterns can become unbalanced. Household spending for conspicuous consumption can crowd out such essentials as food, education, health care, child care and saving for a secure future" (UNDP 1998: 59). Neo-liberal reform, if it leads to continued public neglect of basic services, may worsen these possible adverse impacts of the boom in private consumption. Whether measured in housing, nutrition, education, or access to basic sanitation, clean water and health services, more than a billion of the world's people continue to be deprived of their basic needs for well-being (Sachs 2005).

It is striking that "social standards of consumption" and the unbalancing effects that these may have on needs provision even gain mention in the UNDP's primarily statistical assessment of the quality of life in all the countries of the world. But note the conditional phrasing: "conspicuous consumption can crowd out essentials ... if a society's value system places too much importance on what a person possesses." Inclusion of this issue in such conditional terms suggests that the existence of social needs is too important to be left out of a discussion of the global consumption boom but also implies that reliable information is lacking about the prevalence of these socially defined needs and of their negative effects. The phenomenon of social needs raises questions that statisticians and economists cannot answer without more field data: What are "essentials"? What might make a commodity seem essential to the consumer even if it is not necessary for physical well-being?

Awareness of the human costs of free-market reform and global economic integration has only grown since the publication of the 1998 Human Development Report, as a result of an upsurge in public protest against neo-liberalism around the world. Yet we still stand in need of more fine-grained studies of how market liberalization has affected work and consumption among low-income people in the global south. Seen against the background of anthropologists' increasing interest in global links and transnational flows, it seems remarkable how few ethnographers have paid much attention to global economic restructuring. Perhaps this oversight is less surprising if one considers that, unlike the transnational migrants who have been so often studied in recent years, the people who bear the brunt of restructuring's negative effects generally do not show up on the doorstep of Western Europe and North America. More often they are confined by poverty to squalid shanties, workers' compounds and other localities that are marginal locales even within the global periphery. It is my hope then that this book will be of value as a first detailed ethnography of the impact that poverty and heightened inequality are having on the social fabric of a small community of Third World primary-goods producers. I join a handful of other ethnographers in focusing on "the social experience of 'decline' itself" (Ferguson 1999: 15), among people who, far from riding transnational flows, are stuck in one of the global economy's stagnant backwaters.[2]

KEY CONCEPTS AND CONCERNS

In sketching out a distinctive ethnographic approach to understanding plantation dwellers' ways of making sense of human difference through the media of matter, space and time, four concepts are particularly salient: social meaning, social binarization, the material world, and "expenditure."

Social Meaning

In focusing upon the human distinctions that Monte Cocans "read into" goods, domestic environments, and work and leisure time, I subscribe to the idea that material culture is inherently meaningful. I am aware, nevertheless, how easy it is to slip into circular or superficial reasoning in substantiating the "meaningful-ness" of objects, space and time.[3] Therefore, my use of the term "meaning" immediately raises questions: How can students of material culture avoid uncontrolled semantic slippage around meaning's multiple meanings? What claim do I, an ethnographer, have to speak about matters that are so personal and so often implicit as the meanings of the material world? What phenomena determine meaning and are in turn affected by it or are effected in part through it?

One way to avoid being glib about the meaning of objects, space, and time is to be clear what type of meaning interests you. My concern throughout this book is with social meaning, concepts of likeness and difference between human beings. Social meaning, like other sorts of meaning, grows out of the universal human predisposition to dichotomize perceived reality and make sense of it in terms of binary oppositions. Social meaning springs more specifically from the act of perceiving people around us as being like or not like us. A moment's reflection is enough to appreciate that social meaning is "relative." It shifts according to who is being compared with whom and in what context. In some circumstances, gender may be the most salient aspect of difference and sameness: when a small group of women hurries through a "male space," say a village plaza in any number of small towns in Latin America or the Mediterranean, the gender difference between them and their male on-lookers is likely to jump to the awareness of all the people involved. Change the place and time and suddenly other human differences become salient. If, for example, the same group of women forms the nucleus of a private pre-nuptial ceremony, within the enclosure of a private courtyard, then other human differences, such as the greater experience and guiding wisdom of the older women in this group, come to the fore. What is constant is that people everywhere more or less constantly interpret observed behavior according to concepts of human likeness and difference, fashion bridges for desired social interaction with others like or unlike them, and build fences against intimacy with others still. All these are the stuff of social meaning.

What concerns me particularly is how space, time and matter enter into these perceptions of human difference in Monte Coca and in other sugar plantation communities like it in the Dominican Republic.[4] Monte Cocans draw conclusions about whether their neighbors are "decent" or "indecent people" and "live decently" or "scandalously"—judgments that express evaluations concerning moral character and quality of life—on the basis of how they relate to objects and space in time. More specifically, they draw such judgments on the basis of:

- Their neighbors' differing capacities to consume and the choices they make within their means about what and with whom they consume
- The size and location of their dwellings, whom they share living quarters with, and how the domicile is compartmentalized and adorned
- The kinds of work they do, and the amount of control they exert over their work hours and at their places of work
- How, where and with whom they spend their leisure

Through these means, Monte Cocans link themselves socially to some people and throw up walls against social interaction with others. Through the media of objects, space and time, they also perceive in each other's behavior markers of commonality and difference. By my observation (presented in detail in the ethnographic body of this book, chapters five through nine), the human differences that Monte Cocans most obviously and consistently draw onto the canvas of the material world pertain to gender, ethnicity, nationality, occupation, and immigrant residency status. These categories persistently take the form of binaries—male versus female, Dominican versus Haitian, manager versus field worker, and permanent resident versus seasonal migrant—comprising a texture of opposites.

Social Binarization

Social meaning seems never to be neutral but is always inextricably tied to positive or negative evaluations of other people and their actions. It seems that, at the very moment when we humans perceive and categorize a thing, we are always already evaluating it. Charles Osgood's (1976: chapter 2) systematic sample of semantic distinctions among thirty language communities yields evidence that emotion is a pervasive feature of meaning.[5] Of the vast number of value distinctions that the world's languages can express, people everywhere seem drawn to affective meanings of three types. Osgood calls these "evaluation, potency and activity" (ibid.: 88). "What is important to us ... about the sign of a thing," he writes, "is: First, does it refer to something good or bad for me? ... Second, does it refer to something which is strong or weak with respect to me? ... And third, ... does it refer to something which is active or passive?" (ibid.: 89). According to Osgood, cross-cultural studies do not exclude the possibility of considerable variation in the frequency and intensity of affective meaning. Some cultures, like some people, may be more judgmental than others. These studies even so suggest a universal disposition to accompany perceptions of other human beings with judgments about them. Is this person friendly, hostile, or indifferent to me? Am I pleased by what s/he is doing? Is s/he doing it well or badly? For most people in most places around the world, it takes a conscious effort to suppress such good/bad judgments. (You are probably making such a judgment now even as you read this.) Seemingly, judgments spring to mind virtually simultaneously with the act of observing other people and their actions.

In Monte Coca, it quickly becomes obvious also that prejudice and stereotype strongly influence the feelings that color residents' perceptions of human difference. These prejudices and stereotypes—as I highlight in chapter five, "An Indecent Life"—stretch beyond what social researchers commonly call an "ethnic division of labor," to involve distinctions relating not just to ethnic identity but gender and residence status. The very worst treatment—involving verbal disrespect, segregated housing, physically coercive forms of labor discipline, and at times mandatory labor during normal hours of rest—is meted out not to Haitians as a whole but to the seasonal segment of the estate population, the *"congoses."* Similarly, the women who in far smaller numbers accompany the seasonal migrants from Haiti are disproportionately targeted for sexual violence and exploitation. The seasonal migrants not only endure these degradations but embody the proletarian baseline condition of propertyless-ness. Both things convert the seasonal migrants into an emblem of a morally and physically indecent life in the eyes of Monte Coca's permanent residents, a "not I" by contrast with which they define a sense of self.

The Material World

Consumption, defined as the acquisition and use of commodities, is a centrally important matter but it is not the only dimension along which people in Monte Coca discern human similarity and difference. How and where people spend their time, for example, is not strictly speaking a question of "consumption"—they do things with their time other than consume commodities—yet time-use is too important an aspect of identity in Monte Coca to be ignored. As in any other industrial environment, material rewards and prestige go disproportionately to those who command the time of others. It should come as no surprise, then, that leisure—time when workers command their own activities—takes on an importance wholly beyond its utility as a time to recuperate the energy to work again. Leisure is the only time the worker fully possesses him/herself, and becomes fleetingly "sovereign." In chapter seven, I devote extended attention to two weekend gathering spots, Monte Coca's barroom and brothel and the open area surrounding its main dry-goods store, focusing on the wide range of leisure activities that take place there. Holidays, especially Christmas and Epiphany, are even more highly "magnified" times, for which people may save and prepare for weeks in advance. During hard times, people who are unable to meet the ceremonial needs associated with these holidays may experience acute emotional distress, as I witnessed in 1985 when a two-month delay in the start of the cane harvest ruined the Christmas celebrations of many.

Even as it relates to objects alone, commodity consumption is too narrow a concept to encapsulate my research findings. Caribbean sugar plantations have always been "spaces of flows" (Castells and Henderson 1987), designed to facilitate the movement of goods and profit to distant lands, the least possible consideration being given for the physical and social needs of their inhabitants. In chapter six, I examine how the residents of Monte Coca seek to superimpose a human, community-oriented logic of "places" onto this space of flows, through such practices as improving and adding onto company housing and planting yards for family recreation and daily tasks. Modifying their living environment gives the residents some level of mastery over a space designed to further management control. Intra-community inequality intrudes here, too: not all people have equal space or money to devote to home improvement, making domestic space one more dimension along which the residents of Monte Coca are divided into "haves" and "have-nots." These annexes are not commodities. Other than some nails, hinges and perhaps a latch, their owners purchase nothing to build them but throw up these structures using little more than cast-off materials and the unremunerated labor of household members. Nor are they likely ever to put the lean-tos up for sale or be able to find a buyer for them. Even so, their meaning is multiple and intense.

In short, my ethnography would be much the poorer if I had focused on commodities and consumption alone and not consciously organized my analysis also around time, space, and objects that are not commodities. I refer to humans' lived environment, of objects, space and time, as "the material world," and consider this to be a more appropriate conceptual frame for my study than the more conventional concepts of consumption or material culture, with their narrower focus on human-made artifacts.

What defines the material world as a frame of study is not just the addition of time, space and non-commodity objects to the study of commodity consumption. It is equally important to consider that these dimensions of the material world are inter-related, and relate in turn to social practice. Acts of commodity consumption assume sensible meaning only in relation to the times and spaces when consumption occurs and does not occur. Conversely, space means nothing independently of what human activities it makes possible or proscribes: as Henri Lefebvre (1991: 137) reminds us, the lived environment takes on its full meaning only in relation to social practice.

Thus it is that, in the ethnographic body of the work (chapters five through nine), I do not place the observations relating to any one topic—say, ethnicity or space—apart in its own chapter. To place consideration of space rigorously apart from information relating to people's use of time, for example, would do injustice to the inter-relatedness of these dimensions of the material world. Rather, each ethnographic chapter is a series of descriptions of places and moments, punctuated by detours into theory, history and comparative examples. Each chapter is organized around one of the topics of ethnicity, gender, space, time, and commodities but only loosely. Ethnicity, gender, space, time and commodities enter into every chapter, even as each successive chapter takes one of these concepts in turn as its focus. In a number of places where I have presented talks based on this material, people have told me that they enjoyed it because it was "like listening to a story," a response that confirms for me that this way of organizing the ethnography projects a satisfying verisimilitude.

Expenditure

I think there is at least one important message about consumption in my ethnography, namely, that any interpretation of consumption that emphasizes sense-making to the exclusion of sensation-seeking is flawed, and vice versa. I have already alluded to how consumption helps humans make sense of their world, when I refer to the projection of social meaning—in the form of judgments of human likeness and difference—onto the uses given by individuals to commodities, space and time. Creating social bonds with some people and barriers to others, through consumption activities, and otherwise discerning human likeness and difference against the backdrop of the material world, are ways people organize their relations with others and impose order on their perception of their social world. Yet, taking my lead from early-twentieth-century social theorist, Georg Simmel, I also hold that it is excessive rationalism to analyze consumption solely as a means for people to communicate messages to each other or otherwise make the world more meaningful. It may admittedly be impossible to document or otherwise "get at" sensations per se in a field research setting. Anthropologists gather information by observing and talking with people, not by hooking up electrodes to their skin to measure the neural activity inside. It is evident even so that many forms of consumption, uses of space, and leisure activities in Monte Coca derive a large part of their appeal from their sensation-creating potential. The consumption of alcoholic beverages, the omnipresent chatter and blare of radio-cassette players, the cool comfort of the plush furniture in the parlors of the community's more economically secure households all appeal to the senses or alter the user's mood or perception of reality. Any consideration of material culture in Monte Coca must ask why such non-utilitarian expenditures not only appeal to people but seemingly exert a pull too strong to be resisted, even by many who are at times too poor to afford adequate food. Omitting any consideration of stimulation and how it attracts people toward certain practices would therefore be to distort the realities that I interpret and theorize. With each successive ethnographic chapter of this book, I devote more attention to observations that pertain to the sensations elicited by certain uses of objects, space and time, and to practices that exceed the boundaries of the normal, the everyday and the necessary.

My main theoretical influence, in this, is the mid-twentieth-century thinker, Georges Bataille. Pleasure, according to Bataille, not only resists containment within the boundaries of social convention, it may even derive from or be heightened by exceeding the limits of propriety, frugality and necessity. Breaking from the cost-benefit rationality and the assumption of scarce means upon which conventional economics is premised, Bataille (1988 and 1991) defines a theory of "general economy." In this, "expenditure"—the using up of wealth, energy, power, matter, time—rather than the acquisition of resources, is the primary object of human action and measure of value. In his view, neither necessity nor scarcity confronts humankind with its most fundamental problems. Our main challenge, as humans and human scientists, is the allocation of the super-abundance of energy on the face of the Earth and in the body of each human being (Bataille 1988: 12, 28). A reflection of humans' more general ability and propensity "to conceive beyond reality, to desire beyond adequacy, to create beyond need" (Deren 1953: 138), non-utilitarian expenditure is for Bataille a defining attribute of humanity. The object of general economy is therefore to describe and analyze the forms in which the human organism's and human societies' surplus energy is expended.

The concept of expenditure, as Bataille defines it, again supercedes a narrow focus on commodity consumption, to encompass eroticism and ritual. Taking inspiration from the theory of "general economy," in chapter nine, I weave together ritual, social and economic forms. I make the argument that expenditure to excess is a common source of fascination in electronic media, weekend revels in the brothel, and the batey's most intense ritual occasion, the Easter *Rara* festival that became known as "*gagá*," after it was transplanted from Haiti to the Dominican Republic. All three gain heightened meaning through super-abundant, even frenetic, flow, whether of sensations, commodities, or human energy. Though ontologically distinct, each generates what Monte Coca residents approvingly call "heat," denoting spiritual energy or liveliness or health more generally.

METHODOLOGY

These research concerns imply an ethnographic focus that goes beyond the rituals and myths through which meaning has conventionally been examined by anthropologists. Paul Rabinow (1977: 58) points out that, unlike rituals and other human phenomena where "boundaries are easily discernible, symbols are neatly situated, and sequence is explicitly controlled," commodities hold meaning through "the less explicitly shaped and less overtly significant areas of day-to-day activity and common-sense reasoning." He adds that it is in these areas—the realms of "practice" (Bourdieu 1977) and "everyday life" (de Certeau 1984)—where "most cultural differences are embedded" and yet these realities are "disturbingly difficult" to observe, "for the phenomena are everywhere, thereby proving most opaque to the methodologies we have developed."

I base this book largely on information that emerged from my twelve months of continuous residence and ethnographic fieldwork in Monte Coca, in 1985 and 1986. Subsequent visits to the community have periodically updated my picture of life there, enabling me to supplement the main body of observations written in the "ethnographic present" with descriptions of important changes in the community's physical and social structure through time. Awareness of change more generally enriches my interpretation of the settings, events, and words that I made note of in my earlier fieldwork. The ethnography consists largely of written portraits of local events and settings, complemented by my recorded observations of people's actions and expressed reactions within these spatial-temporal contexts. Verbal statements and local terminology, gathered through my casual observations and interviews, are placed in the context of my descriptions of social organization and human activity. Maps and photographs supplement the written word as a source of information regarding the social meanings of space, time and commodities.

In keeping with Rabinow's insight, it must be said that people in Monte Coca do not often speak in general terms about how different people inhabit and shape their times and spaces of work, leisure and domestic life. Conscious knowledge of this kind is voiced at times, as when differences between occupational groups are cast in terms of ostensibly natural differences between the Haitians and the Dominicans who occupy different rungs of the sugar company job ladder. It is intrinsically important when distinctions of this kind rise to people's awareness and I therefore give considerable attention to the ways in which Monte Cocans so objectify cultural difference. Yet, much more often, these people articulate human distinctions less directly and elaborately, in fairly concrete ways relating to work, leisure and the use of domestic space. They speak about who does what, when and where, who does it well or does it badly, or they metaphorically transfer ethnic or gender-related terms to other social domains or to descriptions of the inanimate world. Such evaluations and extensions of meaning are fleeting, sporadic and require some linguistic fluency and cultural knowledge to catch but repeated observation reveals a recurring set of terms and distinctions, between men and women, Dominicans and Haitians, and permanent and seasonal residents, transcending the boundaries between activity domains.

Going beyond Rabinow's injunction to be attentive to the ephemera of day-to-day activity and common-sense reasoning, an ethnography inspired, as this book is, by critical social theory, urges consideration not just of fleetingly and sporadically articulated perceptions. Critical social theory analytically privileges things that are left entirely unsaid or critiques of power voiced in veiled or coded forms. Without listening to what is said by our teachers—the people among whom we live as we study their ways of life—ethnography would be worthless. What otherwise would be the point of going to live in such an uncomfortable, out-of-the-way place? My starting point is therefore what my neighbors in Monte Coca say about their own experiences and understandings. Yet this in no way implies that the ethnographer need restrict her/himself solely to what people say. Such a strictly positivist position would be death to any kind of critical analysis of society, for critical analysis hinges on placing the unsaid into interpretive tension with what is said. Not to look for silences and for topics only obliquely referenced in daily discourse is to capitulate to the silencing of the less powerful by the more powerful in any society. Therefore, this book is a methodological hybrid, in which ethnography, with its inescapably positivist features, becomes a vehicle for "reading" a range of statements, silences, and situations, observed in Monte Coca, "against the grain" of implicit power relations.

One set of contradictions I do not pretend to reconcile are the hoary dualisms that confront students of material culture—of positivist versus hermeneutic method, materialism versus idealism, and explanatory models that privilege either behavior or expression (more narrowly, what people do versus what people say). Rather, I aim rather to bring these—I think, inescapably distinct—analytic frames into productive tension at as many points as I can without shattering this book into a myriad of sub-texts. I prefer a restless holism, which involves always questioning my own simplifications of reality, over a settled reductionism. As James Ferguson (1991: 620) writes (about the approach taken in Parker Shipton's book, *Bitter Money*), "different theoretical approaches may be complementary, rather than opposed. Indeed, our truths are always partial, different theories do not directly contradict each other, but offer differently complete versions, which should be combined in illuminating ways rather than pitted against each other." Inasmuch as I aim to produce a more satisfying account by drawing in more empirical observations than would be possible through a more coherent theoretical line, my approach is characteristically, perhaps even traditionally, anthropological.

Theory in cultural anthropology stands in productive tension with empirical evidence, and at times ethnography thus confronts us with a choice between theoretical coherence and adherence to the truth as best we can determine it on the basis of our findings. "For the scientist and philosopher alike," Lefebvre (2002: 1) writes, "coherence is a basic requirement," but coherence, if extended beyond certain limits, "becomes system for system's sake." "Coherence," for Clifford Geertz (1973: 17–18), "cannot be the major test of validity for a cultural description.... [T]here is nothing so coherent as a paranoid's delusion or a swindler's story.... Nothing has done more... to discredit cultural analysis than the construction of impeccable depictions of formal order in whose actual existence nobody can quite believe." The twofold imperative of all social research is to search for coherence while remaining open to inconsistent and probably unforeseen empirical details. Openness to inconsistent details is, I believe, a more scientific approach than is certainty gained at the price of putting on blinkers against contradictory facts. Some of those who, like me, doubt we can know everything about humanity by its causes say that what they do is "not science." That may well be true, in many cases, but in phrasing the debate thusly—counterposing "science" and "doubt"—we anthropologists have lost touch with a basic truth. Doubt is the basis of the skepticism that stands at the heart of any scientific view of the world (Hecht 2003). My primary responsibility as a scientist is to the truth. As I see it, seeking the truth requires not concealing doubt where this exists, and beyond this, demands jeopardizing all significant findings with alternative explanations of what I observe.

More specifically, the hallmark of my methodological approach is to confront the unity of opposites that stands behind everything meaningful in human life, through what I call a "pendular synergism," a swinging back and forth between seemingly contradictory and opposing explanations of any significant phenomenon. This is not a willy-nilly eclecticism. It is more than just never settling for one explanation. Rather, I consciously seek out contradictory and mutually inconsistent explanations and juxtapose these, each one proving the limits of the other. My expository approach mimics the relentless dialectical logic of Haitian vodou and other polytheistic belief systems that key always on the duality of every meaningful object, idea, category or experience. As I discuss further in chapter nine, the power of vodou inheres neither in celebrating the beautiful and the holy and rejecting the ugly and the profane, nor in reconciling these, but in bringing irreconcilable opposites into collision. Bringing opposing life forces—death and fertility, mourning and gaiety, discipline and release, the holy and the profane—into proximity is never an entirely predictable diagnostic and therapeutic strategy. Yet, when done under the guidance of an experienced and knowledgeable ritual specialist, such juxtaposition of warring principles can generate a dynamic balancing of opposites that is productive of spiritual energy. In this book, my efforts to embrace contradiction, via a pendular synergism, is simpler. Embracing contradiction is, for me, to be true to the reality I observe in Monte Coca. Insufficient for my purposes here is any causal schema that considers the human to be either angel or animal, all rational cost-benefit calculator or all seeker after brute sensation. Rather than choose between or try to reconcile contradictory explanations, I put these into juxtaposition. Perhaps sacrificing some theoretical coherence (I leave that for the reader to judge), my aim is thusly to achieve a richer, more vivid and more convincing portrait of what it is to be human in a community bearing the brunt of massive economic upheaval.

Notes

1. See Munck (2005) for a cogent review of the data.
2. Ferguson 1999; Gill 2000; Nash 1994; Pred and Watts 1992: chapter 3.
3. I thank Jennifer Telesca for sharing this insight. As an example, Don Slater (1997: 132–33) asserts that "all consumption is cultural because it involves *meaning*" and then adds that "culture ... represents the fact that all social life is meaningful." Slater's unsurpassed erudition on the topic of consumption adds significance to this example, for, if even he can slip into circular thinking of this kind, then others, less steeped in the study of material culture, should be constantly on guard against overusing "meaning" and hence rendering the term meaningless.
4. "Difference," as Arjun Appadurai (1996: 12) points out, has taken on a "vast set of associations," largely traceable to Jacques Derrida's use of this term. Like Appadurai, I use this term in my own, non-deconstructionist, style, as "a useful heuristic that can highlight points of similarity and contrast between all sorts of categories: classes, genders, roles, groups, and nations." Defined in this way, a focus on "human difference" does not necessarily always give analytical primacy to the ways in which groups of people differ. It does, however, add other categories of sameness and difference to the menu of topics of ethnographic concern, alongside the more familiarly "anthropological" issues of "culture" and "ethnicity."
5. I became aware of the relevance of Osgood's research to my concerns through a talk presented by Roy D'Andrade (2003).

2

A Place No One Calls "Home"

The Plantation and Modernity

Arjun Appadurai (1986a: 357) has observed that the anthropological imagination tends to link certain places with particular substantive issues. In the extreme case, whole nations have come to be identified with particular topics of research: India has been regarded as virtually synonymous with "caste," Bali with "ritual," and Haiti with "voodoo."[1] Until the 1980s, New World plantation ethnography was equally narrowly defined. Exemplifying this metonymic thinking, Charles Wagley's essay, "Plantation-America: A Culture Sphere," identifies a huge swath of lowland North, Central and South America, plus the Caribbean, with this region's most distinctive social institution, the plantation. He defines this putative culture area in almost purely economic and social terms.[2] Only at the end of his essay does Wagley (1957: 9–10) make mention of common "cultural characteristics," which he rather superficially attributes mainly to the African provenance of many of this region's settlers. This discussion of plantation culture looks like an after-thought, seemingly tacked on after the main body of the essay and only weakly linked to the social and economic issues fundamental to his vision of "Plantation America." Wagley was hardly alone in his time in portraying the plantation as little more than a system of production with a collection of associated social problems. The ethnological vision of the plantation at mid-twentieth century gravitated toward "brass tacks" economic and social questions: How had supplies of capital, land, and labor shaped production regimes? What impact had poverty and dependence on wage labor had on community and family cohesion? Little of this literature is read today but—as I discuss further below—cultural anthropology has yet to rid itself entirely of the underlying premise that plantations have little to attract the serious student of culture.

Even while writing in a predominantly social and economic frame of reference, mid-twentieth-century ethnographers, Sidney Mintz and Eric

Wolf and later Chandra Jayawardena, made more lasting contributions to our understandings of the workings of culture on modern plantations. In writing about the manifestations and sources of solidarity and conflict among the plantation workers whom they had studied in Puerto Rico and Guyana,[3] they point to both divisive and unifying tendencies. The same workers who are capable of unquestioning unity at moments of confrontation with management are on ordinary days more or less constantly bickering, cutting each other down through gossip or petty vandalism or even engaging in overt physical or legal conflict. Their solidarity emerges not from strong leadership but from the workers' commitment to an egalitarian ideology, their shared sense of standing in a subordinate relationship to management and their view of themselves as being people of low status in the wider society. Plantation workers' shared commitment to the principle that they should treat fellow workers as equals enters into conflict with the significant inequality that does exist among them as well as with the striving for higher status that these workers generally share with people in the larger society. Against this backdrop of intra-community inequality and omnipresent status-striving, small slights or displays of ostentation are easily interpreted as signs of disrespect or a repudiation of equalitarian relations, generating the interpersonal quarreling for which Caribbean societies have something of established reputation in the anthropological literature (Wilson 1995[1973]). One larger lesson—that Mintz, Wolf and Jayawardena put forward in explicit criticism of the community-study approach that was in vogue at mid-twentieth-century—is that neither the divisiveness nor the solidarity are explicable solely by forces internal to the community. In tracing the roots of community solidarity and conflict, consideration should also be given to the simultaneous antagonism felt by the workers to the concentrated economic power that stood above them and their desire to imitate consumption norms prevalent in the rest of society.

Following Mintz and Wolf's path-breaking studies, considerable scholarly interest gravitated toward another seemingly ubiquitous divisive factor in plantation social life, ethnic and racial diversity, particularly as this relates to the entry of new laborers as migrants to take up the lowest-level rungs on the occupational ladder. Drawing inspiration from the concept of an "ethnic division of labor" and more specifically influenced by Edna Bonacich's (1972) theory that split labor markets are the primary ultimate source of ethnic antagonism under capitalism, historians and ethnographers have given detailed attention to the generation of ethnic rivalry among competing groups of plantation laborers.[4] The history of immigration to the Dominican Republic's sugar industry over the past century-and-a-quarter, for example, reveals that a new group of guest workers has been introduced every time cane growers have sought to break with established field labor practices and re-structure the work of cutting sugarcane (Martínez 1999: 63–67). West Indians replaced Dominicans in the cane fields in the 1880s and 1890s, just as employers switched from paying cutters by the task to ganged day labor. Haitians took the West Indians' place in the 1930s, as gang labor gave way to piece-rate wages. Each of these shifts reduced the workers' bargaining power. Resentment about these upheavals has been directed away from company management by granting jobs higher up the company job ladder to a few established workers, deporting many others, and letting the remainder find their way toward jobs in port cities. Plantation managers have thus not only circumvented resistance by replacing old laborers with new ones but have promoted ethnic divisions as a strategy of labor control.[5] In a mixed ethnic community, favoritism of a limited kind—setting aside some jobs or perquisites for one group, for example—almost automatically seems to generate perceptions of exclusion and feelings of resentment among competing ethnic groups. Through such ruses, the labor force is disunited, to the long-term economic detriment of each of its component ethnic groups.

The richness of plantation ethnographers' treatment of the issue of community conflict and solidarity contrasts with how little they have written about the cultural implications of commoditized plantation lifestyles and their even scantier attention to other domains of culture—e.g., myth, ritual and cosmology—that have been ethnographic staples elsewhere. There remains to this day an unspoken opinion that plantations are not good places to study how people attribute meaning to the spiritual, social and material worlds. This perception and the resulting ethnographic neglect of plantation culture are explicable in terms of the concerns that have guided anthropological research until recent decades. Betraying an inexplicit assumption that you must have a homeland to have a culture, anthropologists long held a suspicion that uprooted people—as plantation dwellers most often are—have taken the first step toward losing their culture.[6] The sense was that "de-racination" eventuates in "de-culturation," producing that ultimate freak, the "de-culturated native," neither Western nor Other, whose very ambiguity would for years be enough to make nearly all anthropologists turn their gaze away from rural proletarians and all other such non-natives, non-Westerners. This concern points to a second way in which plantation culture was long dismissed as lacking integrity and authenticity: the people are all "mixed up" culturally, being either a motley collection of diverse nationalities, languages and ethnicities or the "creolized" descendants of such a heterogeneous assembly. Studies of cultural "pure breeds," not hybrids—preferably of people not studied before by anyone!—were the preferred building blocks of academic anthropological careers. The prestige value that anthropologists have given to studying "uncontacted" groups raises a final problematic characteristic of plantation communities from a conventional anthropological standpoint: they are just too darn "westernized" to be of interest. Plantation dwellers have not just been contacted by Westerners. Their whole way of life is obviously *a product of* extended and intensive cultural and economic exchange with the rest of the world. On plantations, people earn wages and buy what they need from stores. They produce goods that they do not consume and consume mostly what distant, unseen others have produced. They might even live in rectangular houses with tin roofs, laid out in a grid! All these attributes have sustained the unstated conviction that plantations, like other industrial environments, might have some interesting "social problems" for ethnographic study, traceable to the very conditions of uprooting and hybridity that defined these places in the anthropological imagination, but do not possess a culture worth speaking of.[7]

The Devil and Commodity Fetishism, Michael Taussig's (1980) ethnography of myth, cosmology and ritual healing among Afro-Colombians on Cauca Valley sugar plantations, broke like a cannonball through this anthropological neglect of plantation culture. Taussig describes the role of the devil in folklore and rituals associated with proletarian production and illicit monetary gain among both sugar workers in Colombia's Cauca Valley and tin miners in highland Bolivia.[8] For Taussig, these occult actions counteract the Western capitalist fetish of the commodity, whereby the products of human labor are no longer seen in human relational terms but regarded as independent entities that stand over and control people. Further, he claims, rumors and accusations of dealing with the devil convey an almost instinctual aversion to the capitalist social order on the part of former peasants and semi-proletarians who have been incorporated into the bottom-most level of international commodity production chains. It is significant in this regard that, in the Cauca, compacts with the devil are never made by women or by wage laborers on small peasant farms but only by male workers on large, capitalist farms. The reproductive orientation of the female and the peasant household is inimical with money earned through devil contracts. That money, it is said, cannot be reinvested productively but can only be squandered on useless luxuries. The wealth is sterile and the men who make such contracts are doomed to an early and painful death.[9]

The lively debate occasioned by *The Devil and Commodity Fetishism* inspired further empirically grounded inquiries into the supernatural meanings attached to the cash nexus in Latin America and Africa. So many of these studies have emerged that "Devil-ography" seems poised to become a full-fledged sub-field of cultural anthropology.[10] More generally, *The Devil and Commodity Fetishism* presaged an even larger efflorescence of anthropological interest in spiritual and cultural forms of resistance to capitalist work routines in societies on the margins of the global economy.[11] A tenet of nearly all these studies is that phenomena such as spirit possession, accusations of witchcraft and rumors of devil contracts are not traditional, closed systems of belief that either thwart or are vanquished by a secular Westernized world view. They are rather highly adaptable responses to integration into the global economy and national politics. Occult beliefs conceptually counterpose and mediate the conflicting logics and demands of household reproduction, market production and individual status-striving.[12] This magical/moral economy literature contests earlier anthropological assumptions that beliefs in supernaturally endowed persons are destined to wane with increasing exposure to Western-style education, mass media and other secularizing forces. The exact significance of the persistence of these beliefs varies from author to author among the magical/moral economists.[13] Stories of witchcraft or devil-pacts are understood to respond to varying types of power and exploitation, not just wage labor (Edelman 1994). Every exponent of magical/moral economy analysis, even so, understands phenomena such as spirit possession or beliefs in witchcraft or devil contracts to be not just a holdover of pre-modern cosmologies but generally a dynamic response to the rapid social changes and value conflicts attendant upon entry into an urban or industrial setting. Concerning recent publications on African witchcraft, Todd Sanders (2003: 338) perceives "a striking degree of scholarly consensus" around the idea that witchcraft "is and indeed must be about modernity."[14] Sanders's generalization applies beyond Africa: the idea that supernatural beliefs offer forth a critique of modernity can be understood to be a defining theme of the magical/moral economy genre that Taussig pioneered.

To focus on myth, ritual, and cosmology was nothing new, of course: these have long been standard fare of anthropological research and introductory courses in cultural anthropology. Where Taussig broke new ground in *The Devil and Commodity Fetishism* was partly in *whose* cosmologies and subjective formulations of experience he studied—neither ritual specialists nor isolated tribal groups but people working at the bottom of international commodity production chains. The innovativeness of his analysis stemmed also from *what experiences* he argued their myths and rituals relate to—neither universal life passages nor exotic cosmologies but the process of integration into wage labor. Finally, his assimilation of the neo-Marxist dependency and world system theories is evident in *where in a global order* he situated Cauca Valley sugar producers and Bolivian tin miners—not as bearers of reified and bounded "cultures" but as people connected through trade to more privileged consumers in urban areas and capitalist core states. Taussig implicitly positioned South American primary-commodity producers as people who have something to say to the inhabitants of the global north about what effects their demand for cheap consumer goods is having on unseen millions in the south. He thus converted anthropology's implicit critique of expansionary capitalism into an explicit indictment. As Sanders (2003: 339–40) points out, many others have emulated Taussig's magic-critiques-modernity trope, according to which "peoples in faraway places" are understood to "offer unique insights into, and caustic critiques of, the workings of our contemporary world."

But does social indictment make good ethnography? While some of Taussig's many critics engage esoteric points of theory, it is telling that nearly all of them raise questions about his *ethnography*. One important detail that is particularly often questioned is the accuracy of Taussig's characterization of Cauca Valley sugarcane workers as "neophyte proletarians."[15] Certainly, the neophyte label seems less than fully accurate for the peasants of the Cauca, whose ancestors were brought in shackles from Africa, drank from the bitter cup of agro-industrial slavery, and seized the first opportunity to distance themselves physically and economically from plantation domination. More generally, Taussig's mischaracterization of the Cauca Valley sugarcane workers as neophyte proletarians points to an attribute of the entire magical/moral economy literature: it is premised upon an unambiguous and hence overly simple dichotomy between traditional and modern "spheres" or "logics." Economic and cultural dualism is an integral part of the magical/moral economy frame of interpretation. This is so regardless of whether "tradition" is viewed as Taussig understands it, as a single pre-capitalist world view, much the same the world around by reason of its being anchored in a use-value economy, or is held to be plural and diverse, as Jacques Chevalier (1982) insists, with perhaps as many modes of incorporation into capitalism as there are societies being incorporated. Whether "them" is monolith or myriad, it always comes down to "us" versus "them," in the magical/moral economy framework.

This dualism is to some degree justifiable and perhaps even inevitable. Even if the meanings of capitalist production and consumption for their lives are well-known to these part-peasants, part-proletarians before they set foot on the plantation, it seems hard to deny that there is an inherent tension between the peasant and industrial spheres. Yet much rides on how extreme the contrast is perceived to be. In Taussig's case, it is doubtful whether he could sustain the interpretation that satanic ritual, myth and rumor are expressions of a nearly instinctive revulsion to capitalism were he to have drawn a less absolute distinction between the peasant "use-value economy" and the industrial capitalist sphere.

Yet my main point of disagreement with Taussig and Devil-ography generally is not that its schema of history is inaccurate but that its portrait of the present is incomplete. Devil-ographers and others writing in a magical/moral economy mode generally do not give a full enough picture of the varied ways in which people find meaning in commodities and a proletarian life-style. Taussig and others for their part focus almost exclusively on ritual and folklore and fail to describe other domains of meaning in material culture, including the range of consumption activities engaged in by rural proletarians and semi-proletarians. Devil-ographers tend to base their accounts heavily on what people *say*, in myths and rumors, or on what people convey via rituals. Devil-ographers report very few direct observations of what people *do* with commodities.[16] I have no issue with relying primarily on evidence drawn from expressive culture as long as this does not come at the expense of recognizing that people derive some satisfactions from the modernity ostensibly critiqued by supernatural beliefs and practices. Yet every study in the magical/moral economy genre has a glaring absence of description of what people do with commodities. In driving home his point that Ihanzu rain magic does not represent a critique of modernity, Sanders (2003: 347) writes, "In many contexts, ... Ihanzu today actively covet rather than criticize modernity. Like peoples everywhere, they want 'the indigenization of modernity, their own cultural space in the global scheme of things' (Sahlins 1999: 410)". Having made this point, Sanders immediately drops any consideration of how Ihanzu inhabit the world of commodities and otherwise relate to modernity. Though unusual among Devil-ographers in opening the door to the seeming contradiction between what people do in the marketplace and what they convey through ritual and supernatural belief, he nonetheless reproduces one of Devil-ography's shortcomings in his failure to give that contradiction systematic attention. What matters here is that neglect of everyday practice is virtually a defining element of Devil-ography. The resulting emphasis on the exotic and anti-modernist makes it impossible for the critique of capitalist market relations that Devil-ographers read into myth, gossip and supernatural practices to be brought into comparison with how plantation dwellers *act* in their worlds of alienated land, wage labor and store-bought goods.

In theoretical terms, Taussig's failing is to have seen commodities as having use value and exchange value but turning a blind eye to commodities' "sign value." In other words, his approach relies solely on Marx and not at all on Weber, Veblen, Simmel, and more recent social theorists. These thinkers understood, in ways that Marx laid the conceptual foundations for but did not live to appreciate fully himself, that capitalist social hierarchies are based on symbolic distinctions as well as ownership of the means of production and other forms of wealth.

To concretize this point, I bring in the following pair of anecdotes from my fieldwork in Monte Coca. While similar to the stories with which I began the first chapter, these concern two women, who resided year-round in the *batey,* rather than male seasonal workers from Haiti:

Magical revenge. On a rainy October afternoon, I sat inside a room in a company barracks interviewing its occupant, a long-time Haitian resident of Monte Coca, about the cultivation of subsistence gardens on unused plots of company land. A gaunt woman in rags walked up, carrying a small child in her arms, and asked for money. I gave her a 25-centavo piece and she left, without further words. The man whom I was interviewing observed that she used to be a person of means but that others, out of envy, had made her mad through magic. Her husband left her and she became destitute. Even though she had grown children and siblings, none of these family members would have anything to do with her after she plunged into madness.

A portrait photo. Of the many gifts through which I attempted to reciprocate the tolerance and many kindnesses shown to me by Monte Cocans, the most popular by far were the portrait photos that I took for them. One photo that stands out in my memory is the one I took for Carmela Emile, a slim woman in her late 40s, born of Haitian parents in a settlement near Monte Coca. She occupied only one room, albeit in one of the most recently built barracks, inhabited entirely by permanent residents, with her Haitian partner, François, two of her children, ages 10 and 13, from an earlier union, and her two-year-old granddaughter. Her room was cluttered with electrical appliances and plush furniture. Framed pictures and shiny aluminum and enamelized metal bowls covered much of the wall space. In her photo, Carmela stands to the left side of the picture frame, wearing form-fitting slacks and a neat long-sleeved blouse. She holds her left hand up near her head, poised on top of a display cabinet packed with decorative porcelain figurines, painted glasses and fake crystal, a cool smile on her lips. Her right hand rests on her hip, wrist cocked so that her digital watch appears prominently. At her insistence, the photograph is framed with her off-center, to include a small television in the background, behind the cabinet to the right. When I gave her the photo some weeks later she expressed displeasure about my having caught her smiling (most people in Monte Coca prefer to keep an utterly serious expression when posing for their portraits). Two women neighbors who happened to be visiting heaped lavish praise on the picture, saying it was one of the best portraits they had ever seen, better even than those the professional photographers take.

What are we to make of the contrast between these two women, one, understood to have been rendered mad by magic, out of envy for her material prosperity, the other, almost crowded out of her own portrait photo by the goods in which she takes such unashamed interest (seemingly unafraid that she, too, might end up being so dreadfully envied)? My guess is that if Devil-ographers look as carefully at what people consume and how they generally engage with material things, they would in most cases find what I have found in Monte Coca. The very same people who whisper stories centering on supernatural acquisition or divestment of wealth can and do express a lively appreciation for the material satisfactions derivable from modern industrial society.

Contrasts such as these enliven ethnography but, more importantly, raise difficult theoretical and methodological questions. Which approach brings us closer to what commodities *really* mean to rural proletarians, expressive culture or observable behavior? Are we to attach greater evidentiary weight to the stories people tell or the uses they give to objects, and what they and others say about these uses? Or are these the right questions to ask? Should reducing the meaning of commodities and capitalism to one consistent philosophy or line of practical reasoning be the goal of an anthropology of the material world?

Whether such interpretations should be imputed unequivocally to our informants or should be admitted to be the ethnographer's best guess, recent ethnographies that pretend to tell us the meaning of commodities and the cash nexus too often hew exclusively to one or the other side of the expression/behavior divide. Among anthropologists who take a "magical/moral economy" line of interpretation, pioneered by Michael Taussig's monograph, *The Devil and Commodity Fetishism in South America,* there has been a bias toward considering solely "exotic" beliefs and rituals, leaving out description and analysis of how meaning may inhere in mundane and even seemingly "Westernized" practices and life circumstances. In order to create the illusion that the world corresponds neatly with theory, our attention is turned away from how Third World consumers may find meaning in even mass-produced commodities, by appropriating these for their own ends and consuming in distinctive ways.

New, more complex visions might be generated by trying to account for both things—the oblique critique of economic inequality voiced through supernatural idioms and the simultaneous aspiration for more of the satisfactions of modernity—among workers at the peripheral termini of international commodity production chains. I propose that plantation ethnography and the anthropology of consumption and globalization more broadly stand to gain by bringing these two approaches—the *cultural* focus of Devil-ography and the *social and economic* focus of the plantation ethnography that preceded it—into interpretive tension. Such an approach would juxtapose what people *convey* through myth and ritual with what they *do* at work and at leisure. This approach was hinted at by Wolf and Mintz (1957: 402), who observed—in an almost never-quoted passage from their very frequently cited article on haciendas and plantations in Latin America and the Caribbean—that "a pair of store-bought, two-tone shoes, or sunglasses, or canned goods are not merely new culture traits. They also represent participation in a larger social and economic system in which invidious comparisons are drawn between individuals, in terms of their capacity to consume." I build on Wolf and Mintz's insight by considering how the residents of Monte Coca discern human difference not just in consumption activities but with reference to the work that their neighbors do, the residential and recreational spaces that they occupy and the activities that they carry out when at leisure. To go beyond both the mainly social and economic analyses of an earlier generation of plantation ethnographers and the mainly cultural analyses of Devil-ographers, it is necessary to provide detailed descriptions of both the material culture of Monte Coca and its magical/moral economy.

Notes

1. Appadurai (1986a: 357) writes, "A few simple handles become metonyms and surrogates for the civilization or society as a whole: hierarchy in India, honor-and-shame in the circum-Mediterranean, filial piety in China are all examples of what one might call gatekeeping concepts in anthropological theory, concepts, that is, that seem to limit anthropological

theorizing about the place in question, and that thus define the quintessential and dominant questions of interest in the region."

2. He lists the region's "basic common features" as "monocrop cultivation under the plantation system, rigid class lines, multi-racial societies, weak community cohesion, small peasant proprietors involved in subsistence and cash-crop production, and a matrifocal type family form" (Wagley 1957: 9).

3. Jayawardena 1968; Mintz and Wolf 1950; Wolf and Mintz 1957.

4. Bourgois 1989; Chomsky 1996; Chomsky and Lauria-Santiago 1998; Moberg 1997.

5. Ethnographies and histories of the United Fruit Company's Central American banana plantations (see note 4) have shown that management has consciously played off new ethnics against old, by fostering invidious images of each group in the eyes of the other.

6. Appadurai (1988) and Gupta and Ferguson (1992), among others, have pointed out how closely linked territoriality is to the traditional-modern binary that has long stood at the heart of anthropological theory. A person or people not bound to a homeland and an exotic world view would quickly lose the interest of anthropologists, because such mobile cosmopolitans were regarded as too "modern," too much like the anthropologists themselves, to be worthy of serious study.

7. Sidney Mintz (1996) and Michel-Rolph Trouillot (1992) have observed that the entire Caribbean region shares the plantation's marginality in the eyes of the anthropological profession for its perceived lack of cultural authenticity, coherence and integrity. As Trouillot (1992: 21) puts it, "The entire corpus of Caribbean cultural anthropology from the early decades of this century up to the present can be read against the background of [the] basic incongruity between the traditional object of the discipline and the inescapable history of the region."

8. These proletarians employ spiritual beings to re-direct into their own hands some of the wealth they are systematically robbed of via alienated wage labor. In the cane fields of the Cauca, workers who out-produce their coworkers are automatically suspected of having made a secret contract with the devil to increase their wages. In the mountains of Bolivia, mining always involved ritual and magic but it was only after the Spanish conquest that this came to take the shape of evil, in the figure of Tío (uncle), the "devil" in the Christian idiom but understood by the workers to be the spirit who truly owns the mines. The tin miners leave gifts for Tío, which the spirit owner converts into ore and then leaves in the mines to be dug up by the workers who have performed the rites of gift exchange. The final step in the process is the sale of the ore on the international market by the legal owners of the mine. From the miners' perspective, reciprocal gift exchange with Tío sustains the production of the mineral wealth of the mountain, which is then converted into commodity form through the mediation of the miners.

9. Parker Shipton (1989: 60) describes similar beliefs, among the Luo of Kenya, about the sterility of "bitter money," which is earned through activities that repudiate ties to lineage and the ancestors, such as the selling of lineage land for profit or dealing in tobacco, traditionally a link to the ancestors. In the northern Guanacaste province of Costa Rica, according to Marc Edelman (1994: 71–72), belief in the sterility of ill-gotten capital explains the legendary squandering of a fortune in cattle, land and money alleged to have been accumulated by an immigrant Nicaraguan peon through a contract with the devil.

10. See, for example, the essays in these edited volumes: Comaroff and Comaroff 1993; Moore and Sanders 2001; as well as Behar 1987; Chevalier 1982; Comaroff and Comaroff 1999; Coombe 1997; Crain 1991; Edelman 1994; Geschiere 1997; Gordillo 2002; Kane 1994; Kapferer 1991 and 1997; Parish 2000; Sanders 1999 and 2003; Shaw 1997; Shipton 1989; Silverblatt 1987; D. J. Smith 2001; Wardlow 2002; West 2001; White 2000.

11. For John and Jean Comaroff (1987) and David Coplan (1987), the very words through which migrant laborers convey their experience encode the contrasts and contradictions between the alienated "labor" of the South African mines and the productive,

ever-developing "work" of the migrants' home places. Aihwa Ong (1987) interprets spirit possession among women factory workers as a language of protest mediating between the contradictory ideologies of Muslim patriarchy and modernity. Malay women workers, while able to challenge male authority in the home through the independence conferred by the wage, find it difficult to adapt to male supervision and intense capitalist discipline on the factory floor. Rather than a cultural relic, spirit possession expresses tensions arising from the workers' alienation from their own bodies, from the products of their work and from their own culture. More recently, the Comaroffs (1999) have discerned an upsurge in accusations and rumors of occult profit-making schemes not just in South Africa but in South and Central America, the Caribbean and elsewhere on the global capitalist periphery. They interpret this widespread upswing in anxiety about witchcraft, body-part theft, and ritual murder as a response to the rapid pace of change in the new global economy and the failure of this new order to deliver on its promises of greater prosperity for all. Nancy Scheper-Hughes (2002) makes the counterargument that rumors of body-part theft are not fevered products of the social imaginary of poor, Third-World people but respond to an illicit global traffic in organs for transplant, the existence of which she and others have verified.

12. As is suggested by the title of Peter Geschiere's (1997) book, *The Modernity of Witchcraft*, beliefs in the incidence of supernatural forces in mundane matters of political economy do not indicate resistance to change but its opposite, the rapid adaptation of such basic beliefs to changing social and economic circumstances. Geschiere focuses on the witchcraft beliefs of the Maka people of Cameroon, especially those beliefs concerning the rumored ability of Maka elites to eat their own kin as an avenue of power in the external political economy. Witchcraft rumors emerge in this light as an implicit dialogue about the need for local people to exert control over their kin who have left Maka territory in search of personal gain. Geschiere's analysis is echoed in two other recent studies from sub-Saharan Africa, one of the endurance of sorcery in rural areas of Mozambique, in spite of the hostility to this of FRELIMO'S scientific socialist modernizers (West 2001), and the other of the riot set off by a rumored ritual killing in Owerri, Nigeria, during Abacha's military government (D. J. Smith 2001). The authors of both articles see rumors of occult crimes (and in the Nigerian case, physical violence against their suspected perpetrators) as popular defenses against elite power, newly "derived from external sources and resistant to social redistribution" (West 2001: 122). Both also interpret rumor and popular justice as a protest against the emergence of forms of inequality unbound from "the moral obligations of kinship and patron-clientism" (D. J. Smith 2001: 805).

13. Geschiere (1997), D. J. Smith (2001) and West (2001) regard ambiguity and ambivalence as centrally important features of beliefs in supernaturally endowed persons, the supernatural realm being attractive to a few people as an illicit route to power but at the same time offering many would-be victims of evil-doing a means of protecting themselves from malevolent spirits.

14. Sanders (2003) contests the accuracy of this assumption on the basis of his ethnography of rain magic in Ihanzu, Tanzania. He points out more generally that "being *within* modernity and being *about* modernity are not, after all, logically equivalent" (ibid.: 340), so that "African witchcraft may well be a part *of* modernity, but by no means needs to be *about* modernity" (ibid.: 338).

15. Gregory 1986: 68; Gross 1983: 700; McEachern and Mayer 1986: 74; Roseberry 1989: 220–21; Trouillot 1986: 87.

16. Taussig's description of satanic rituals among the plantation workers of the Cauca, for example, is based not on his observations but on what trusted informants *told* him about actual people who had made contracts with the devil. Taussig is correct in saying that it matters more that the workers and even the managers of the plantation evidently consider these contracts to be real. Yet just what the workers believe beyond the question of reality or falsehood—what significance they attribute to contracts with the devil, for example—is another point where questions must be raised about Taussig's ethnography. As Christopher Gregory (1986: 67) points out, "what Taussig claims as peasant belief is for the most part

assertion: very little empirical evidence is produced to support this claim." Taussig (1980: 134–35) writes, for example, that the stories of Colombian plantation workers and Bolivian tin miners are "precise formulations that entail a systematic critique of the encroachment of the capitalist mode of production." Yet you will search *The Devil and Commodity Fetishism* in vain for words spoken by any Colombian or Bolivian suggesting that capitalism is evil. Much the same—"big assertion, unconvincing evidence"—can be said of a claim that is nearly universal in the magical/moral economy literature, that rumors and accusations of witchcraft and other occult dealings become more prevalent as people enter deeper under the domination of the state and the market economy. This claim is always backed up with evidence of a purely anecdotal nature. Virtually the only study of witchcraft to be based on quantitative survey data, Nutini and Roberts's (1993) volume on blood-sucking witchcraft in Tlaxcala, Mexico, comes to the opposite conclusion. Based on census material from over 1,000 households, involving more than 1,300 cases of death from witchcraft, as well as 50 in-depth cases, they report that the use of witchcraft beliefs as an explanation of local deaths has declined significantly since the 1960s, after commerce and the national school system made important in-roads.

3
Living in Nowhere

One of the most striking characteristics of modern sugar plantations is their visual resemblance to nearly all other modern sugar plantations around the world. While tramping the sugarcane fields of eastern Dominican Republic it often occurred to me how much alike all these fields were, along with the human settlements that dot them. Except for the nearby ridges and the more distant mountains, seen over the tops of the tall cane plants, you could be anywhere. If you consider that these agrarian landscapes are already almost a century old, an intriguing possibility is raised: what James Kunstler (1993) calls "the geography of nowhere" may have found some of its earliest manifestations not in the shopping malls, airport terminals, suburban housing developments, and high-rises of the modern West but in much humbler and earthier places on the capitalist periphery. "Nowhere" refers to built environments that, except for certain recognizable features of the surrounding landscape, could be anywhere. Kunstler specifies further that nowhere spaces are invariably designed and regulated to fit the needs of capitalist accumulation and, more specifically, laid out so as to optimize control over labor, goods or consumers. Defined thus, "nowhere" might include the sugar plantations of the Caribbean as early experiments.

As Mintz (1996: 295–96) points out, it may not be accurate to suppose that Europe's Caribbean colonies have always been in every way less "modern" than the colonial metropole. To the contrary, Caribbean sugar plantations were "landmark experiments in modernity":

> Workers were disciplined to work interchangeably, and by the clock. Caribbean industry was thought of as simple, since most of its labour over time was enslaved, and it was typified by few skilled categories.... Yet it was complex in so far as the unity of field and factory was an unvarying essential of labour efficiency. The system required overarching supervision to ensure that time schedules were met.... The large-scale use of furnaces and vessels was typical. Even steam was adopted very early.... These technical features, ... introduced more than just an aura of industrial modernity into what were operations which predated, in many cases by whole centuries, the Industrial Revolution.

> Modernity has to do not only with the organization of industry but also with the effects of such organization upon the labour force.... Accordingly, "modernity" as used here refers not only to the technological accompaniments to industry, but also to its social organizational sequelae: the circumstances for meeting and relating; to ways of socializing without recourse to previously learned forms; to an acquired matter-of-factness about cultural differences and differences in social style and manners; and to a social detachment that can come from being subject—while recognizing one's own relative lack of power—to rapid, radical, uncontrolled and ongoing change.

In this proto-industrial context, and recognizing also the enormity of the cultural upheavals set in motion by the capture, transportation and bondage of Africans, it is remarkable to note that on a number of Caribbean islands the enslaved actually developed feelings of *attachment* to their plantation abodes. Douglas Hall (1978) argues persuasively that, with emancipation in the British West Indies, former slaves did not so often leave the plantations willingly as they were *driven away* by proprietors intent on abridging rights to free housing, subsistence plots, and other small privileges formerly granted by custom to the enslaved work force. Feelings of attachment and even de facto ownership of their places of captivity surely flowed in part from the spiritual power that was often attributed by the Africans to the burial places of their ancestors. Yet it is also likely that this place attachment grew in part as an inadvertent consequence of the time-keeping mentality and market orientation that governed the management of the plantations, the very features partly responsible for making Caribbean industrial slavery so oppressive. One of the earliest lessons of life on the plantation for the newly arrived African must have been that time had a specifiable monetary value. The week was divided into the five-and-one-half or six days that were the "master's time" and the one day or one-and-a-half days of respite from alienated labor that was the captive's "free time" or "own time." The objectification of time implied in these terms is obvious but more concretely significant is that the enslaved seized this "free time" to work on their own account and partly for their own profit. They did this chiefly by cultivating "provision grounds"—subsistence gardens ceded to them by the estate owners—and by trading the produce of these gardens in island markets. The crops grown on the provision grounds during the slaves' "free time" improved the quality and security of their nutrition, and thus proved crucial to physically maintaining minimal well-being and survival (Mintz 1979). Beyond this, the provisions and money earned thereby served in general "to improve the quality of [the slaves'] lives beyond that of mere beasts of burden and toil" (Gaspar 1993: 114).

Some of this surplus was surely devoted to acquiring material goods that might make everyday life less trying and tedious. In his journal of 1816, Matthew Gordon (Monk) Lewis (cited in Higman 2001[1988]: 243) provides the following description of the houses in the "negro village" of his own estate in Jamaica:

> I never witnessed on the stage a scene so picturesque as a negro village. I walked through my own to-day, and visited the houses of the drivers, and other principal persons; and if I were to decide according to my own taste, I should definitely have preferred their habitations to my own. Each house is surrounded by a separate garden, and the whole village is intersected by lanes, bordered with all kinds of sweet-smelling and flowering plants.... The negro houses are composed of wattles on the outside, with rafters of sweet-wood, and are well-plastered within and whitewashed; they consist of two chambers, one for cooking and the other for sleeping, and are, in general, well furnished with chairs, tables, &c., and I saw none without a four-post bedstead and plenty of bed-clothes.

Descriptions of slave villages comparable to Lewis's are few and all are similarly lacking in fine-grained detail. Landscape artists of the era of slavery also were reluctant to depict the houses of plantation workers (ibid.: 243). Caution must therefore be taken not to overstate either the quantity or the importance of the slaves' material acquisitions, especially in light of Lewis's and other slave holders' presumable interest in exaggerating the material well-being of their own human chattel. Even so, it is striking that some slaves' material acquisitions were not limited to things of daily practical necessity. For example, former Cuban slave María de la Cruz Sentmanat remembered vendors of religious chromolithographs coming to the plantation where she lived as a child and selling to the slaves images of the Virgen de la Caridad and Santa Bárbara (corresponding to the deities, Ochún and Changó, in the Santería religion) (Pérez de la Riva 1975: 40). Even such modest items gain added significance against the backdrop of the total dispossession that was the primordial condition of the enslaved. In this context, even the simplest goods—a colorful scarf, a lamp and oil, a clay pipe, a simple wooden stool, iron cooking pots, utensils and tools—could significantly increase comfort, diminish monotony, enhance ceremony, and permit the enslaved to receive visitors with at least rudimentary hospitality.

With regard to the development of place attachment among the enslaved, it is important also to note that, for the greater part of the era of slavery and certainly before about the mid-to-late nineteenth century, sugar plantations were visually not as "nowhere" places as they are today. Prior to the turn of the nineteenth century, Caribbean slaves were largely left to their own devices to construct their houses in the style that they preferred, generally employing wattle-and-daub construction techniques of West African origin. Except for nails and sometimes hinges, locks and keys, the huts were fashioned out of materials found at hand and were built by the slaves in their own time (Higman 1998: 180). So the enslaved stocked their own houses with minimal material comforts and tokens of human dignity, which they crafted with their own hands or purchased with money earned through own-account labor. They built these houses themselves, largely from materials that they gathered. Taking into account the totality of what can be known about the uses given by the enslaved to objects, space, and time, then, it is easier to understand why they might have developed feelings of attachment to their places of captivity.

Plantations became more uniform in appearance and the workers' living quarters on them became more alienating environments with the introduction of barracks housing and the massive geographical expansion of sugar plantations over the course of the nineteenth and early-twentieth centuries. Barry Higman (2001[1988]: 244), based on his study of Jamaican plantation maps and surveyors' records, notes a shift toward a more regimented architecture and more compact, geometric lay-outs of slave villages, starting around 1790. The same trend is seen around the turn of the nineteenth century in Cuba, Puerto Rico and the French Antilles (Jopling 1988: 19–20). These spatially and socially more regimented settlements, rather than the quasi-autonomous spaces of earlier slave villages, are Monte Coca's direct historical predecessors.

The trend toward stricter attention and control over the lay-out and design of the workers' living quarters reached an apogee in the construction of fortified slave barracks in early-nineteenth-century Cuba. Juan Pérez de la Riva (1975) identifies the *barracón* (workers' barracks) as "perhaps the most typical edifice" of the second quarter of the nineteenth century in Cuba. This period left vivid signatures on the Cuban landscape, as a result of the most rapid expansion of slave-based sugar production in the island's history: ever larger fields of sugar cane and shrinking extensions of forest; the smoke-plumed high towers of the new, larger steam-powered sugar mills; and new railroad tracks, bridges, and docks for the transport of cane and sugar. Huts were replaced with barracks on sugar plantations in other parts of the Americas but the fortified barracks built in Cuba at this time seem to have been unique in their size, solidity and prison-like lay-out (ibid.: 23–24). The *senzalas* built in Brazil's Northeast, for example, resemble sugar plantation barracks of today in having several doors that open to the exterior. By contrast, the so-called *barracones naves* (nave barracks) of Cuba had an involuted lay-out, cut through by a central corridor onto which opened the doors of the many rooms that ran the extensive length of these barracks. Only two doors opened to the exterior, one at each end of the barracks, permitting stricter control over entry and egress than would have been possible in a Brazilian *senzala*.

In general terms, incurring the cost of building barracks and dictating the lay-out of the workers' settlements can be explained in terms of what the estate owners gained in labor control. Pérez de la Riva (ibid.: 26) reports that the earliest barracks in Cuba were built largely out of a concern to improve enslaved workers' productivity by curtailing truancy and keeping slaves from exhausting themselves in night-time outings. Toward mid-century, owners' concern seemed to shift toward avoiding insurrections. Barracks housing made it possible to keep closer watch on the slaves and lock them in at night, to prevent them from going out to meet with slaves on neighboring plantations. Building the barracks on a grid pattern also kept sight lines open and facilitated surveillance by concentrating workers' dwellings into smaller spaces.

Whatever the ultimate causes, it is striking to look at historical photographs of the late-nineteenth and early-twentieth century and note the sameness to the barracks, the mill works and the cane fields of plantations on a number of different Caribbean territories. Whether the setting be Guyana, Trinidad, Santo Domingo or Cuba, it appears to be the same place. The barracks of this post-emancipation period were clearly different from the *barracones* built in Cuba at slavery's apogee, being much cheaper and flimsier buildings, built of wood rather than of stone or masonry. With the doors to each residential cubicle facing out rather than in, these barracks also confined the workers less strictly. Yet the imposition of management control over the lay-out and construction of the workers' dwellings marked an enduring transformation of plantation residential space. As the sugar industry entered its multinational corporate phase at the turn of the twentieth century, management's interest in concentrating workers' residences into smaller and more closely supervised spaces would find expression in the construction of barracks and residential compounds of a monotonous sameness, establishing a de facto "international style" of plantation architecture. In common with other industries of the era and epitomized by Henry Ford's automobile assembly plants, the trend in sugar was to standardize not only the product but the space of production itself.

A Place No One Calls "Home"

Monte Coca is just such a nowhere environment. It is a company compound for agricultural workers (batey) on a state-owned sugar estate, the Ingenio Consuelo. The estate is a massive field-and-factory combine, situated in the midst of the Dominican Republic's primary region of sugar production, the rolling plain, about 150 kilometers long and 30 to 80 kilometers wide, which stretches along the southeastern coast of the island, from the city of Santo Domingo to the Mona Channel. It was here, in the east, where sugar production expanded most vigorously during the industry's formative period, 1875 to 1925.

Historically, the Dominican Republic differed from other Caribbean territories where sugar manufacturing underwent a contemporaneous transition to capital-intensive, factory-based production, in that its sugar industry did not emerge from earlier forms of plantation agriculture for export based on slave labor. Large, machine-driven sugar mills instead replaced independent cane cultivators and small-scale manufacturers, who produced coarse grades of sugar for domestic markets with antiquated grinding and boiling equipment. Transfers of technology, of management skills, and of capital from outside the island allowed modern mills to displace antiquated sugar producers in the east by the mid-1890s, less than two decades after the establishment of the first steam-powered mill (*ingenio*) in the region (Sánchez 1976[1893]: 34).

Each *central* (farm-factory combine) drew in cane from its own "company land" and from independent farms, for grinding and processing into raw sugar. To make room for planting sugarcane, the plantation owners uprooted thousands of peasant farmers and ranchers from the land, through purchase, litigation, intimidation, and even armed assault (Calder 1981). The Ingenio Consuelo was founded in 1882, and rapidly grew to become the nation's largest producer of sugar during the first two decades of the twentieth century.

Today, Consuelo controls about 20,000 hectares in sugarcane, divided about 60/40 between company land and private farms, with thousands more hectares being held by the company in pastures and forests. Before the establishment of the Ingenio Consuelo, the land surrounding Monte Coca was likely used for raising cattle, on extensive communal pastures. The gently rolling landscape must have looked quite different then, with many stands of trees interrupting the vistas that today stretch out on all sides from the highest hills on the plantation.[1]

The industry's rapidly increasing demand for labor initially attracted large numbers of displaced peasants to sugarcane work. Yet less than a decade after the first sugar estates were founded, Dominican labor began to seem neither cheap nor docile enough to please the country's (largely expatriate) sugar magnates. As early as the 1880s, sugar companies recruited cheaper and more easily disciplined seasonal workers from other Caribbean islands. The pressure of declining wage levels, coupled with the price inflation and currency devaluations that wracked Dominican consumers in the last decade of the nineteenth century, drove local seasonal proletarians away from plantation labor. The sugar companies have ever since recruited seasonal migrants as cane cutters, predominantly from the Leeward Islands, from the 1890s to the 1920s, and from Haiti, especially after 1915.[2]

After decades as a U.S. corporate enclave, scarcely interfered with by the Dominican authorities, the Ingenio Consuelo passed into Dominican hands in 1957, having been purchased, with the application of some heavy-handed pressure on its U.S. corporate owners, by the Dominican dictator, Rafael Leonidas Trujillo. At Trujillo's death in 1961, Consuelo became property of the Dominican state and in 1966 it was combined with the other nationalized properties of the former Trujillo sugar empire to form the State

Sugar Consortium (Consejo Estatal del Azúcar, CEA). Even after merger into this parastatal firm, the administrators and field bosses in Consuelo stayed effectively in control of the plantation's operations, while the CEA acted mainly as vendor of the sugar on domestic and international markets. When I did my dissertation fieldwork there in 1985–86, the estate was still a kind of quasi-autonomous fiefdom, with its own police force and dispute resolution mechanisms, where the National Police rarely intervened. Then as now, the residents were accustomed to a highly personalistic and top-down form of governance, in which all community services were delivered or coordinated by "the company," and currying the favor of local company bosses could expand the size of one's income and living space.

Monte Coca is a relatively large community, as befits its status as the "head batey" of one of the six agricultural sections (*colonias*) of the Consuelo estate. It is in most ways typical of bateyes of its size. As is common among Caribbean sugar industries, the yearly cycle of sugarcane cultivation comprises two periods, *zafra* (harvest) and *tiempo muerto* ("dead season"), coinciding respectively with the drier and wetter months of the year. The harvest runs four to six months, from December through June, and is the peak period of employment. Money changes hands freely, old debts are repaid, people eat a better diet and spend money in ways, practical and frivolous, that they could not afford during dead season. The dead season lasts six to eight months, and is, as its name implies, a time of reduced employment and, for many batey people, real hunger. The wages and quantity of work that the company provides during dead season are insufficient even for the reduced work force. During the final, hungriest two or three months of the dead season, the workers and their families subsist largely on loans, credit purchases and crops grown in their small, rain-fed gardens. During the dead season, ca. 1986, around 850 people lived in Monte Coca. During the harvest, the population would be augmented by about 300 people, including both seasonal migrants from Haiti and people who maintained residences in Monte Coca but worked elsewhere during the dead season. Both the permanent and seasonal segments of the population are surely significantly smaller today. Many people have moved out to escape the continuing deterioration in the quality of life. Smaller numbers of seasonal workers are needed today as well, sugar production at Consuelo and nationally having fallen by more than half since the mid-1980s.

Yet, just as it was when I first moved into a room in a company barracks in 1985, the seasonal residents are mostly men who come from Haiti as seasonal migrants (popularly termed *congoses,* in Spanish). The term *bracero* is also applied to the seasonal migrants, and I generally use this rather than *congó*, which has some pejorative connotations for both Haitians and Dominicans. I reserve use of *congó* and its plural (*congoses*) for those situations in which I think it is important to remain true to the local modes of reference, stigmatizing though these may be. Those Haitians who have taken up permanent residence on the sugar estates are termed *viejos* (old-timers), to distinguish them from the seasonal migrants.[3] The communications technologies and institutions that enable other international migrants to participate at a distance in the lives of people at home (Basch, Schiller, and Szanton Blanc 1994)—e.g., telephone, transfer houses, air travel, even regular postal service—are all inaccessible to Haitians in the bateyes. The majority of long-term Haitian residents of Monte Coca have effectively lost contact with their people in Haiti. Even so, about nine out of ten men in each year's cohort of migrants return to Haiti after the end of one harvest season (Martínez 1995: 81). Those who do not return to Haiti after a single harvest fall at risk of joining the majority of batey residents, who have no clear prospects of soon leaving the sugar estates. From the migrants' perspective, the batey can be likened to a vortex that one either only skims across and exits in short order or falls into too deeply to emerge from without much difficulty, if ever.

A recent survey of residents of CEA bateyes in the eastern province of San Pedro de Macorís, in which the greater part of the Consuelo estate is located, provides striking evidence of the geographical immobility of these plantations' permanent residents. Nearly a quarter of the respondents were born in the same batey where they now live and another 46.6 percent were born in nearby bateyes (FLACSO 2002: 28); 88 percent of these respondents have resided in their batey for four years or longer (ibid.: 30). Of the sons and daughters of the respondents who live apart from their parents, more than half reside in the same batey as their parents or in another batey in the province (ibid.: 41). Data on schooling and educational achievement also provide reason to worry that many children are inheriting the below-average jobs skills that have confined their parents to low-paid agricultural labor. In one-third of the bateyes of the province of San Pedro there is no school at all (ibid.: 19). Slightly more than half of batey residents nationally are illiterate (Méndez 2001: 62). The FLACSO (2002: 28) survey also confirms a point obvious to anyone who has spent any time in a batey, which is that the vast majority of people live there not out of preference but because they work for the plantation or have family there.

In the mid-1980s, the greater part of the braceros in Monte Coca and its surrounding bateyes were men who had been driven to cross the border by dire poverty and in full knowledge of the atrocious conditions that awaited them on the sugar estates. A relative few had been duped by unscrupulous recruiters in Haiti or forcibly rounded up in other parts of the Dominican Republic by the military. The officially backed use of forced and fraudulent recruitment lay at the heart of international human rights observers' repeated allegations that the employment of Haitian cane workers in the Dominican Republic was a "new system of slavery."[4] These practices were stopped by the government of President Leonel Fernández in 1997. As I had earlier predicted (Martínez 1996: 22), thousands of migrants still gravitate toward the sugar estates each year, drawn by unofficial recruiters but propelled also by rural Haiti's crushing poverty.

When a country meets the seasonal labor demand of its largest industry as the Dominican Republic does by importing braceros from a poorer country that neighbors it, even as its own people suffer increasing unemployment, the paradox excites the curiosity of social researchers and policy analysts. And when that country's civilian and military authorities join forces with its largest business firms to subject the migrants to inhuman conditions and severely limit their rights of mobility and association, the injustice cries out for condemnation by all who consider themselves to be advocates of human rights. These justifiable concerns had, until recently, drawn students of the Dominican sugar industry to give the plight of the Haitian braceros much greater attention than the situation of the bateyes' permanent residents, who make up the greater part of the population of these communities. A few studies have attempted to correct this imbalance by giving equal weight to the permanent and transient segments of the population,[5] but much remains to be understood about the survival strategies of permanent residents. What is certain is that communities like Monte Coca and its nearby bateyes are made up mostly of families who struggle to lead a decent life in an anti-familial environment.[6]

Batey housing is ceded to company workers free of rent but is woefully inadequate in quantity and quality. The typical family inhabits one or two small rooms, in barracks built for groups of single men to live in. Most of the time, these barracks rooms are shared by a woman and the children under her care, oftentimes in the absence of a male wage earner. In spite of there being large numbers of women living on the sugar estates, women rarely work in the cane fields but contribute to household incomes through petty commerce and domestic service. Prostitution, occasional or full time, is the biggest single source of independent income for women in Monte Coca and is by far the most common livelihood of single women. Prostitution in the bateyes differs from elsewhere in the Dominican Republic, in that the women are not shunned by their families and are thus less subject to exploitation by pimps than prostitutes are in urban areas. Many more women earn money through petty commerce. This said, women's incomes are generally even less adequate than men's to support a family, and most women depend heavily on what money their mates will share. More will be said about household survival strategies and women's roles in these in the ethnographic body of this book. Suffice it to add that, even though women make large and varied contributions to the reproduction of their households and of the plantation labor force, their work goes mostly unappreciated or is taken for granted by everyone, except perhaps by the women themselves.

It was already clear in the 1980s that CEA profits were declining. Late paychecks were the norm throughout the year I lived in Monte Coca in 1985–86. By the 1990s, privatization of the CEA had become a constant issue in the Dominican media. As the 1990s wore on it became apparent that some form of privatization was inevitable, and the company, as if economizing on social investment in people for whom it would soon cease to be responsible, increasingly neglected upkeep of Monte Coca's buildings and water supply. In the 1980s and 1990s, the government and one private philanthropy made sporadic efforts to deliver basic services, in the form of a consumer cooperative, a child feeding center, and a low-cost apothecary, but all these human services closed down after only a few years. It seemed that every visit I made to Monte Coca and every conversation by telephone with former residents in the 1990s brought news of the death of another former neighbor of the older generation and even some in mid-life. Late in 2000, the Catholic Church requested donations of coffins because batey residents were reduced to scavenging wood from their barracks to bury the dead (Tejada Yangüela 2001: 11). Monte Cocans interpreted the perceived spike in mortality as a product of hard times.

What human neglect had begun, natural forces brought to a finish. In 1998, Hurricane Georges flattened the greater part of the batey's rickety buildings. USAID provided zinc sheets to replace the roofing blown about for miles by the storm, but residents were otherwise left to their own devices to gather up the scattered pieces and rebuild their homes. Some barracks were never rebuilt but, when I visited the following year, I was surprised to see how many of Monte Coca's older buildings were standing just where they had always been. Worse for long-term morale, the storm knocked down the posts that carried electricity from the mill and destroyed the vehicular bridge that spanned the River Maguá, which runs between Monte Coca and Consuelo. The disruptions in electrical supply and transportation left residents feeling more isolated than ever. It took nearly three years, until the summer of 2001, for both the electrical link and the road bridge to be restored.

Developments on the national political economic front have left already poor and vulnerable sugarcane workers poorer and less protected than ever before. In the name of freeing the market and maximizing economic growth, the government of the Dominican Republic has introduced a set of economic restructuring and industrial privatization initiatives directly affecting the livelihoods of sugar plantation workers. These measures have included currency devaluation and deregulation of foreign exchange, the reduction of subsidies and price controls for food and other essentials, and cuts in government spending on health care and education. In this, the Dominican Republic has much in common with other countries that have enacted so-called neo-liberal reforms under pressure from the International Monetary Fund during the last two decades of the twentieth century.[7]

Surely the most important of these measures for people residing on state-owned sugar plantations has been the sale or private lease of state corporate properties, including the sugar plantation on which Monte Coca is situated. This process was set in motion in 1997 by the enactment of the Ley General de Reforma de la Empresa Pública (Public Enterprise Reform Law). The state commission set up by this reform has sought to re-capitalize the state-owned sugar plantations by leasing these properties to private investors. The financial decline of the CEA had already been hastened by a redefinition of national sugar policy, following the terms of an accord reached with the IMF in 1984 (Tejada Yangüela 2001: 5). The IMF agreement set the political and legal foundations for increasing the Dominican Republic's integration with world markets via the development of tourism and export processing zones, marking a shift from earlier policies, which favored the development of import-substituting industries. It was agreed that CEA lands would be gradually sold to private investors and planted in "non-traditional" export crops. Even though it was known at that time that the CEA was experiencing major economic difficulties, few could have predicted that its production would drop as rapidly as it did, by more than two-thirds from 1988 to 1997. The private lease of the state-owned sugar estates, finalized in December 1999, was in a sense merely an act of final surrender by an enterprise too weighted down with excess employees and too sapped by official corruption to continue functioning under government management for much longer (ibid.: 6–9).

During the privatization process, plantation residents were neither consulted concerning the negotiations between the government and the private bidders nor subsequently informed of what might be the new lessee's intentions regarding the housing that had always been provided free of charge by the sugar company. The re-capitalization process did not foresee the transfer of the social services that the CEA administered to the new management. The CEA's director, Manuel Báez, expressed the opinion that the lessees did not have to take on any of these responsibilities because they were capitalists, not social workers (Tejada Yangüela 2001: 11).

The lack of communication from above heightened plantation residents' apprehensions about the future but was entirely in keeping with the attitude of patronizing disdain with which the CEA and successive governments have regarded this population. The Dominican economy experienced impressive rates of growth in per capita GDP during the late 1990s, sending it into the ranks of the world's middle-income nations by 2002. Yet, on the sugar estates, the pain of national economic restructuring has mainly been followed by the aches that stem from sugar's continuing redundancy on world markets or, worse, the anguish of conversion to other export crops. Privatization and the preceding years of government neglect of the community's physical infrastructure and services have compounded declining levels of sugar production to worsen already extreme poverty and needs deprivation. It was estimated in 2001 that the cane cutters earn an average of 60 Dominican pesos per day (roughly US$3) (Méndez 2001: 59). This is better than the slightly more than one dollar per day that I found most cane cutters earned in 1986 but in real value, factoring in consumer price inflation, the increase is almost insignificant. A FLACSO (2002: 52) survey done in 2000 on former state-run estates found that more than a quarter of permanent residents earn less than RD$1,000 (US$50) per month. Almost one-fifth of the respondents who live in rural company compounds no longer work for the sugar company, two-thirds of these having been dismissed from their plantation jobs, surviving mainly on hand-outs and money earned through odd jobs and petty commerce (ibid.: 45–47).

Even more striking are plantation residents' opinions about privatization. In every aspect, except for receiving their pay more regularly and perceiving the private management to be less corrupt, the majority of residents sees the private lease of the state-owned estates to be unambiguously bad for them. They perceive their incomes to be lower, their hours of work, longer, and the returns from petty commerce and prospects for women's employment to be worse than before. Only 11.6 percent of respondents think life on the sugar estates has generally improved (ibid.: 58–60). Responses to the question, "What is privatization?" include: "The elimination of human beings," "The biggest disaster ever," "There is nothing worse," "The Devil!" "It makes you feel like a vagabond," "There is nothing good in it," "It has left us naked" (ibid.: 74, my translation). Monte Cocans, along with tens of thousands of their fellow sugar workers in the Dominican Republic, have thus joined millions of others around the world whose livelihoods and very chances of survival are being made not better but more insecure by free-market reform and increased global economic integration.[8]

Over the same period of time, the Dominican Republic as a whole, but especially its cities, have experienced a major spurt in consumption expenditures. In the Dominican capital of Santo Domingo, even people who live in the shanties that hug the River Ozama and perch perilously upon the city's surrounding hills have participated in this boom, largely by tapping illegally into electrical power lines and buying second-hand goods on credit. People, who in the early 1980s, would have counted themselves lucky to have an electric fan and a radio now commonly possess a color television set, refrigerator and propane stove. In this, Monte Coca has clearly been left behind. Exposure to media images of consumer opulence amid continuing poverty creates almost laboratory conditions for the study of frustrated consumer desire. Monte Coca's inhabitants are flooded with descriptions and images of a vast array of consumer goods, via the radio and television, but are largely excluded by their poverty from participating in global consumer culture. Yet even though Monte Cocans' desire for more of the material satisfactions of advanced industrial society is more often than not frustrated by their lack of disposable income, material standards of living have risen, in the sense that batey residents now possess more consumer goods than before. Long-time residents recall that in the days of Trujillo (Dominican dictator from 1930 to 1961) only company bosses could afford a bed. Today, it is not uncommon to see a mattress and box spring among other, more modest household possessions, in the cramped quarters of even some very low-income families.[9] The presence of color TVs in a handful of households (there was one in 1985) suggests that material aspirations like those commonly realized in the capital city are not entirely alien to them. The changes I have observed in Monte Coca over the last fifteen years continue processes set in motion over forty years ago, of rising material expectations, increasing social and economic inequality, and the gradual weakening of egalitarian ideologies.

As I write, Monte Coca is poised on the cusp between recent decline and a future more than ever uncertain. Luckily, the new managers have chosen for the time being to continue producing sugar in Consuelo's mill, thus sparing Monte Coca's residents the drastic downsizing of the work force that has accompanied conversion to citrus and palm oil on the neighboring Ingenio Quisqueya. The passage into private management has even so created a great deal of anxious uncertainty among Monte Cocans. They are caught between hope that the estate will be restored to full production and fears that sugar production will be discontinued or that the terms of work and residence will be redefined to their disadvantage. Monte Coca may thus be on the verge of disappearing. Were the plantation to be converted from sugar to another, less labor-intensive crop, the economic justification for its continued existence could vanish. Probably no one would regret the town's passing; life is so harsh there. Yet, perhaps even especially if the community ceases to exist by the time most readers pick up this book, it will be of value, I think, to have told the story of the beginning of this community's decline.

Notes

1. Both economic and technical imperatives dictated that the estates be so large. Rising production of sugar worldwide drove down prices over much of the nineteenth century. Declining prices in turn strongly favored larger, newer and more technologically advanced plantations, with lower unit costs of production, over smaller, less efficient plantations. Among the most important technical innovations of the late nineteenth century were transportation of cane by rail from fields to mill, more efficient, multi-stage rolling mills, powered by steam, and vacuum pan boiling. The new milling and refining technologies necessitated greater throughput of cane at each mill, and meant that each mill should command a larger area in order to operate at peak efficiency (Richardson 1975: 211).

2. Bryan 1985; Castillo 1978; Murphy 1991: chapter 3.

3. The terms *"congó"* and *"viejo"* can have subtly different meanings than seasonal migrant and old-timer, respectively. For example, *"congó"* may be used more restrictively to mean first-time migrant. Perhaps the only semantic constant is that these terms are always opposed to each other, with *"viejo"* always indicating greater experience and identification with things Dominican.

4. Americas Watch 1989, 1990 and 1992; Lawyers Committee for Human Rights 1991; Plant 1987.

5. Newton 1980; Sabbagh Khoury and Tavárez García 1983; Bobea and Guzmán C. 1985; Murphy 1986.

6. My census of Monte Coca households in May 1986 revealed that 92.1 percent of the batey's population (848 persons) lived in dwellings inhabited by groups of kin; 73.1 percent of dwellings (181 of 248) were shared by spouses or consanguines; and 26.9 percent (67 of 248) were occupied by solitary individuals. Slightly more than one-half of Monte Coca's permanent residents (428 of 848) were under the age of 15. On average, 3.41 residents inhabited each dwelling (248). Excluding the dwellings occupied by solitary men and women, the average household size was 4.29 persons. These figures are quite close to what has been found in other comparably comprehensive censuses, suggesting that the size and composition of Monte Coca's households are fairly typical of CEA bateyes nationwide. Also, both the national census of 1981 and a CEA-sponsored survey in 1983 found that around 22 percent of batey households were occupied by solitary adults and determined the average household size on CEA plantations to be 3.8 persons (Moya Pons et al. 1986: 456). In her survey regarding women's health in seven CEA bateyes, Annemieke Verrijp (1997: 110) found an average of 4.4 persons per household.

7. "Neoliberalism," Lesley Gill (2000: 3) writes, "like its older nineteenth-century variant, is an economic, political, and moral doctrine that posits the individual as the fundamental basis of society. More specifically, this ideology is rhetorically antistate and places unlimited faith in the 'magic of the market' to resolve all social problems.... Neoliberals see the state, in comparison ... , as a bumbling, inefficient, and frequently corrupt actor whose presence constantly encumbers the market's actions." Beginning with the stabilization and structural adjustment programs of the 1980s, the International Monetary Fund has more specifically been guided by the neoclassical economic mantra of "getting prices right." "The state was seen as too heavy-handed to get prices right, so it must withdraw from the economy as far as possible, for example, through the privatization of state firms. Another goal ... was to create a more 'open' economy. This entailed not only removing all tariff barriers and any other impediment, legal or otherwise, to the free movement of goods and services, but also, usually, export-oriented growth" (Munck 2005: 47–48).

8. Geographically and socially uneven outcomes of capitalist restructuring are nothing new, of course, even as I perhaps imply the opposite by applying the "new" term *globalization* to refer to the world economic system in which such disparities are taking shape. As Michael Watts (1992: xiii) points out, "From the inception of modern industrial technology to the present, the history of capital accumulation has been synonymous with processes of uneven development, with the constant emergence, realigned interaction, and transformation of local capitalisms."

9. In a sample of Monte Coca's permanent residents done in January 1986, only 4 of 67 households (6 percent) owned no bed.

4

Commodity Consumption in a Globalizing Age

Against this background of chronic poverty and inequality, it is perhaps surprising that little evidence points to a rejection of mass consumption and capitalism among Monte Cocans. Much suggests the contrary: that batey residents firmly embrace the enhancing potential of commodities and mass media. Non-utilitarian consumption has a high incidence and salience among all segments of the batey's population, except among the braceros who have the least disposable time and income and whose economic orientation—in common with guest workers around the globe—is to curb consumption in order to return to their home places in short order, with as much savings as they can accumulate.

What are we to make of evidence that people who live near the margin of subsistence hold an avid interest in distinctive consumption? Following Daniel Miller, I wish to avoid implying that these people are led astray in pursuing "artificial needs," deriving solely from a craving for higher status, when they consume beyond utility. Consumer research has debunked the idea that people form a mindless mass easily led to consume in new and useless ways by advertising (Gottdiener 2000: 16). Miller (1987: 14) prefers to ask how consumption may provide ordinary people a means of living with the contradiction between the greater material abundance made possible by modern industrial societies and the tendency of those societies to reduce the individual to an anonymous producer of goods. Consumption may assume heightened importance as a way for people to realize aspects of self-identity in social environments that, like Monte Coca, tend to submerge individuals within a mass of other, similarly alienated individuals.

The larger point is that distinctive consumption, leisure time activities and enhancements of living space of the kinds that I observe in Monte Coca can be fully explained only by taking into account not just social aims but a range of *personal* motivations. These include:

- Claiming personal dignity, by asserting control over one's surroundings,
- Reclaiming individuality, by consuming even mass-produced commodities in distinctive ways,
- Gaining momentary relief from monotony and drudgery, through the stimulating or soothing experiences created by certain types of consumption.

Though the greater part of my attention in this book is devoted to social meanings, these can never come close to accounting satisfactorily for people's fascination with things material. With Arjun Appadurai (1986b: 5), I therefore see a need to compensate for the anthropological "tendency to excessively sociologize transactions in things." In keeping with this corrective to excessive "sociologization," I begin this chapter by considering certain aspects of the individual's relationship to goods and later take on certain social and, ultimately, global dimensions of consumption.

THE POOR AND "EXPENDITURE"

It is now out of fashion for social researchers to suggest that low-income people should not spend their money on the lottery, cigarettes, drink, fast food, or other "vices," or at least it is understood that we should not say so directly and pedantically, in the manner of the Fish-in-the-Pot scolding the Cat-in-the-Hat. Yet, having correctly put aside class-biased judgments, social researchers have seemingly gone to the opposite extreme, of not paying any attention at all to low-income people's expenditures on things that go beyond basic physical needs. Having ostensibly put behind class bias about how the poor should spend their money, why have social researchers not returned to study what socially defined needs low-income people *do* spend their money on and what these expenditures mean to them?

Russell Belk's review article, on "Third World Consumer Culture," is an exception to social researchers' reluctance to look at non-utilitarian spending among the poor. He makes the case that the spending habits of people in the world's poorer nations deserve more attention. Belk (1988: 104–05) refutes the assumption that attaining subsistence security is a precondition for the development of a consumer culture. It might not even have been the case historically that people in Europe and North America deferred gratification of socially defined consumption needs until they had secured adequate food, clothing, and shelter (ibid.: 106–07). It is certain that, in the lesser-developed countries (LDCs) of the world, even people who lack secure access to these basic needs "are often attracted to and indulge in aspects of conspicuous consumption" (ibid.: 103–04). Belk finds evidence that non-utilitarian consumption is widely prevalent in the LDCs but he also notes the need for additional research before this "in some ways surprising and counterintuitive" phenomenon can be fully assessed (ibid.: 121–22). Nearly everyone who has done ethnographic fieldwork in low-income communities or worked in international development will recognize the reality of what Belk is talking about. Yet it is notable that his evidence regarding the distribution, prevalence and forms of non-utilitarian consumption in lesser-developed countries consists almost entirely of anecdotes.

The dearth of sample surveys and in-depth case studies on this issue is so absolute that I wonder if there is not also some sort of an aversion to this topic at play. Might not avoidance of the topic connote the same disapproval for working people's spending on "vices" and "low-brow" entertainment as was expressed by social observers in the Victorian and Progressive eras, with the difference that this disapproval is only implicit today? Is the hesitancy among social researchers, to look squarely at seemingly wasteful expenditures among the poor, rooted perhaps in an inexplicit but widely and deeply held middle-class belief in the virtue of frugality and deferred gratification?

Marxist theorists, for example, have conventionally either ignored or defined away the very possibility that proletarians could consume "luxuries." In *The Theory of Capitalist Development*, Paul Sweezy (1968: 109) defines "wage goods" as "commodities for which demand arises from wages, while luxury goods are commodities for which demand originates in profits and rents." The absurdity of this concept of the "wage good" is apparent if one stops for the briefest moment to imagine what it implies in the real world. For example, a packet of cigarettes is a "wage good" when bought by a worker but becomes a "luxury" when bought by his boss. What sense does that make? I can only guess what Marxists of the mid-twentieth century were thinking when they took such an idea seriously. Perhaps they were so wedded to giving primacy to production (as Marx himself prescribed) that they approved of putting conceptual stumbling blocks around the topic of consumption, lest any Marxist be tempted to study it in a serious way. Ironically, the wage good concept also echoes the Victorian moral precept that the poor, to be worthy of sympathy, should not spend their money wastefully. (This, of course, even as the Marxists rejected the corollary that the poor ought to be content with what little money they were being paid!) By defining away the very possibility that the poor might spend on luxuries, the wage goods concept tacitly accepts the Victorian ethical standard that the moral worth of the proletariat is reflected in its spending habits. Sweezy and other mid-twentieth-century Marxists arbitrarily turned that ethic in on its head by implying that the proletariat is always morally superior to the bourgeoisie, because proletarians cannot spend on "luxuries" but can only buy "wage goods."

While Marxist economists wove blanket apologies for the working poor's spending habits, cultural anthropologists set about vindicating the seemingly "irrational" behavior of tribal people and peasants. That they did so is understandable and arguably for the good of the people of the world's smaller and weaker societies, if we consider that the world order has been and still is dominated by individuals, institutions and nations that lay claim to being more rational and hence more deserving to rule. Yet problems set in when ethnographers take rationality to excess. In hyper-rationalizing non-market exchange systems—organized around reciprocity rather than direct payment or highly ritualized and oriented toward the accumulation of prestige rather than material wealth—ethnographers tend to reduce these institutions to one or another function or instrumental goal and hence narrow their meaning to the point of distortion. As I explain in chapter nine, recent anthropological interpretations of the Northwest Coast potlatch exemplify this reductionist tendency, by suggesting that this system of competitive, and at times, orgiastic, ritualized feasting, wealth display and gift exchange, existed in order to transfer surplus food from areas of seasonal glut to areas of seasonal dearth or promoted orderly visiting patterns and validated hosts' claims of higher status.

Utterly different, and infinitely more useful for my purposes, is the interpretation given to the potlatch by social theorist, Georges Bataille. Bataille focuses on that aspect of the potlatch least appreciated by the ethnologists who have interpreted it in a rationalist mode: the fascination that wanton, profligate expenditure holds for the human mind. Anthropological interpretations of the potlatch that see it accomplishing certain necessities lose touch with the source of its appeal, its symbolic banishment of necessity and its creation of a momentary illusion of inexhaustible wealth. Bataille looks squarely at and theorizes the profligacy of the potlatch, to which functionalist anthropology is blind. Borrowing from Marcel Mauss's *The Gift*, he observes that in competitive gift exchange, material loss is social gain and material gain is social loss. And, going beyond Mauss, he asks, *How* is it that the conspicuous ritualized giving away and even destruction of valuables confers honor upon the potlatch holder? The concepts of "expenditure" and "sovereignty," through which he approaches this question, are terms that I adopt to discuss sugar plantation residents' fascination with expenditure to excess. I will discuss the particulars in that context. Here I will just touch upon a few points, to situate Bataille's thought within the larger body of social theory on consumption.

Bataille suggests that much consumption appears to be done for its own sake in modern industrial societies, or more precisely, it is done for the fleeting glimpse at a world of unlimited abundance that flagrantly unnecessary expenditure opens in the mind of the consumer. This state of unlimited abundance stands at the core of Bataille's concept of "sovereignty." "What distinguishes sovereignty is the consumption of wealth, as against labor and servitude, which produce wealth without consuming it" (Bataille 1991: 198). Observing, specifically, that "states of excitation, comparable to toxic states" accompany the purchase of luxuries and other wasteful or impulsive expenditures of money, Bataille (1985: 128) suggests that the root appeal of non-utilitarian consumption is the awe-inspiring illusion of infinite plenitude occasioned by non-utilitarian expenditure itself. Instead of explaining it as an instrument toward some external end, he contends that flagrantly useless consumption is its own reward.

One of Bataille's aims is to attack the Victorian anxiety about the prodigality of the poor and subvert its moralistic underpinnings. Bataille, like Marx, begins from the intuition that capitalism has deprived humans of primordial freedoms. Yet, for him, the source of this unfreedom is not the alienation of the workers from the means of production but the bourgeoisie's usurpation unto itself of all legitimate forms of excess. Over the same nineteenth- through twentieth-century era of accelerated expansion in the consumption horizons of working class people, the owners of capital succeeded in restricting proletarian excess, to weak, time- and place-bounded modes of expenditure, such as sport, theatrical spectacles and drug foods. In common with other true "originals," Bataille overstates his case. Yet no one accounts more convincingly than he for why expenditure, and even destruction, of wealth may attract our interest more powerfully than production, acquisition and conservation. Destruction, of nature, of possessions, even of other human beings, *is* power inasmuch as it confirms more clearly than any other act that those things and people are powerless before us.

The insight that consumption is a form of power was not new even in Bataille's lifetime but was first developed systematically by social theorists of the early part of the twentieth century. Thorstein Veblen and Georg Simmel were not interested in the intrinsic appeal of expenditure so much as in pondering how consumption may be used as an instrument for achieving desired social ends. In his *Theory of the Leisure Class,* Veblen (1899) analyzes consumption as display. The "conspicuous leisure" of members of the upper class and their practice of "conspicuous consumption" testify to their superior social status. The "leisure class" is defined by its visible separation from the world of work. "All those in society who had to work yet engaged in forms of conspicuous leisure Veblen defined as 'vicariously' emulating the dominant class's life style" (Gottdiener 2000: 8). Consumption, for Veblen, similarly "has to do with the competitive achievement of status, power and hegemony" (Werbner 1990: 266). Simmel (1957[1904]), in his essay, "Fashion," is also preoccupied with the socially competitive uses of consumption. His "trickle-down" theory of fashion change holds that innovation happens as a result of the operation of two conflicting principles: "imitation," as status subordinates emulate the ways of status superiors, and "differentiation," as members of superordinate groups seek to regain social distance from those below, by adopting new fashions. Each act of imitation of people higher up is simultaneously an act of differentiation from people further below (McCracken 1988: 94).

In *The Philosophy of Money,* Simmel reaches beyond social effects, to explain the appeal of ever-increasing levels of consumption in psychological terms. He regards the urban money economy as a set of practices and institutions that corrodes the spirit and constrains the free will of the individual. Subordinated in an industrial or bureaucratic work setting, and reduced to an anonymous, inter-changeable consumer in the urban milieu, the individual seeks ways of reasserting her/his individuality. One way of doing this is by consuming in distinctive ways. Simmel (1957[1904], quoted in Gitlin 2001: 45) describes fashion as a means of expressing "the desire for individual differentiation and change (i.e., *I present to the world my unique self*)." Capitalist entrepreneurs pander to these desires for novelty and stimulation with entertainment spectacles and commodities. Repeated exposure erodes the distinctive appeal of these cultural products, generating a self-reproducing demand for novelty in more jolting and various forms: "ever faster and more colourful change of excitements ... are the ways in which the human soul ... seeks to come alive" (Simmel 1991: 120, quoted in Slater 1997: 105). "This search for stimuli," Simmel (1990[1907], quoted in Gitlin 2001: 39) concludes, "originates in the money economy with the fading of all specific values into a mere mediating value. We have here one of those interesting cases in which the disease determines its own form of the cure." While some doubt that money and the market really do tend so strongly to objectify all value (Parry and Bloch 1989), what matters more for my purposes is the way in which Simmel conceives of consumption as a form of power. There is power in the individual's ability to choose among goods and to revive her/his sense of individuality through the medium of goods. There is greater power still in manufacturing and selling commodity "cures" to boredom and alienation through the same capitalist production and marketing institutions as precipitated the "disease" in the first place.

Traceable also to Veblen but owing more to French structuralism is the concept of "sign value," associated primarily with social theorist Jean Baudrillard. Mark Gottdiener's (2000: 10) exegesis of the concept of "sign value" is useful to include here: "Commodities are not only the object of human alienation but they are also sign vehicles in the conveyance of social meanings.... Commodities or material artifacts *mean* something about status in addition to their intrinsically functional significance. In short, they are visible symbols of status and they connote meanings as sign vehicles about social positioning in a way that class relations cannot." Like Weber, Veblen and Simmel before him, Baudrillard begins by amending Marx's theory of value to account for the fact that capitalist social hierarchies are based on symbolic distinctions as well as ownership of the means of production and other forms of wealth. Yet he does not so much build upon as catapult beyond these earlier foundational thinkers by according sign value absolute primacy over use value. In the world's most economically advanced, post-industrial societies, according to Baudrillard, "the consumption of signs has replaced the consumption of goods" (Slater 1997: 146). The pace of consumption has gotten so hectic and the thicket of associations that surrounds each good, so dense, that no good is any longer just a functional object but assumes meaning primarily "in its differential relation to other signs," in a vast and largely autonomous system of objects-become-signs (Baudrillard 1981, quoted in Slater 1997: 146). Certainly, when you think about the image of Ché Guevara being emblazoned on skis, Swatch watches or bikinis, it is tempting to say that we have indeed plunged into a world where signs have gone wild. Yet the idea that signs have come completely unattached from either their social referents or use value is surely an overly one-sided and esthetic view of society, even in the contemporary West. When one thinks about the realities of people who spend long hours laboring in sugarcane fields, there is really no point to debating with Baudrillard's devotees whether use value really has disappeared into sign value (or ever could). Yet, considering it apart from Baudrillard's more extreme claims, sign value is a concept of crucial importance to the study of consumption, even, as the chapters to follow will show, in low-income communities of the lesser-developed world.

While recognizing that goods are used for making claims for personal identity, cultural anthropologists have taken the tendency to sociologize consumption further even than the sociologists. Ethnologists have mainly sought to describe how consumption plays a role in forging social relationships and is embedded in culture-specific regimes of value. For ethnologists, consumption is of interest as both a social and a semiotic domain. In *The World of Goods*, Mary Douglas and Baron Isherwood (1979: 12) observe, "goods are neutral, their uses are social; they can be used as fences or bridges." Consumption may fuse people into shared dialogues about value or provide occasion for cultivating valued social relations, even as it also sorts people according to their life-styles and capacities to consume. Other ethnological approaches to the "social life of things" owe much to recent critical theory that has enlarged the concept of "text."[1] These approaches conceptualize consumption as a channel of communication and identity formation. From this perspective, meaning is not so much possessed by physical objects as attached to them as goods are used in particular social contexts. Taking my lead from previous anthropological studies, I adopt the following principles as guide points:

- the meaning of physical objects is defined by their use;
- these uses are culturally specific;
- but consumption may in general terms participate in defining boundaries of human difference.

Sidney Mintz (1985) makes the point that anthropologists and other social theorists, in rightly making these micro-social points about the cultural and social-contextual determination of meaning, have too often lost sight of the macro-social power relations behind consumption. In *Sweetness and Power,* he chronicles the historical transformation of sugar from luxury to staple in Great Britain and along the way charts a more far-reaching transformation in how consumption sustains inequality. Over the centuries of history studied by Mintz, the power of consumption was revolutionized, eventually coming to inhere less in consuming distinctively than in molding the consumption habits of the great mass of people. In the older, premodern English social order, the primary diagnostic of power was whether one consumed the products of others (what Bataille calls "sovereignty") or produced for power-holders to consume. The creation of a mass market for sugar and sugared foods prefigured a social order in which consumption was to assume even greater power but less as a direct expression of social superiority than as an avenue to great wealth for the state and a relatively small number of producers, shippers, and merchants.

I follow Mintz's lead in seeking first to relate consumption habits to working people's micro-social life circumstances and then linking these in turn to other kinds of power (e.g., wealth and social control) on a macro-social level. What added complexities enter into this program of study as the macro-social level becomes increasingly global? As international market competition and economic liberalization increasingly differentiate primary goods producers and others on the global economic periphery into market winners and losers, what new meanings are taken on by consuming commodities? What connections can be drawn between closely observed, micro-level ethnographies of social inequality of the kind that I present here and academic debates about the nature and impact of economic globalization?

STUDYING THE GLOBALIZATION OF CONSUMER DEMAND

"Globalization," as Roland Robertson (1992: 8) aptly defines it, "refers to both the compression of the world and the intensification of consciousness of the world as a whole." Interdependence among people situated at widely scattered points of the Earth and consciousness of the global whole have both been increasing for centuries. Yet globalization, in both academic and common parlance, refers also to the observation that people, goods and ideas have been crossing international boundaries at an accelerated pace in recent decades. Increased popular awareness of these flows has surely also reinforced the rapid increase in academic interest in globalization since the 1990s. Contrary to the perception of certain critics (notably, Sahlins 1994), students of globalization have not forgotten about the diversity of humanity but have for some time now been grappling with questions concerning the endurance of diversity in humanity's globalizing phase (Robertson

1992: chapter 4). Is one world economy giving rise to one world culture or politics? Or is humanity now more cosmopolitan, more interwoven and mutually aware, but still highly diverse and often intolerant of the beliefs and comportment of culturally defined others?

Consumption and mass media are key concerns in this debate concerning the interaction of the global with humanity's diverse ways of life. Much of the controversy about cultural globalization consists of debates about the globalization of consumer demand. As Michael Rowlands (1996: 188–89) writes,

> The fundamental problem of modernity [is] the creation of a personal identity space in a world where no such spaces are preordained. It is also a fundamental anxiety of Western materialism that all other cultural resources have vanished except for the simulacra of preordained worlds energized by desire and "the wish to be."... Depending on taste, this state of affairs may evoke mournful nostalgia, joyful celebration, or both, but it also implicitly supports the equally classic notion that modernization is now of global cultural proportions and is no longer restricted to "the Western experience."

In common with James Clifford (1988: 15–17), many students of globalization today question the "destructive, homogenizing effects of global economic and cultural centralization," and give emphasis instead to the emergence of new orders of difference and meaning as people around the world find unanticipated uses for products emanating from the global economic core.[2] It can no longer be assumed that the spread of goods, practices and influential ideas around the world is making all people identical with one another. Recent ethnographies have instead tended to highlight peripheral societies' ability to adapt to uncontrolled outside pressures toward change, by picking and choosing among cultural imports and attributing new and distinctive meaning to these imports. As Arjun Appadurai (1996: 7) writes, "There is growing evidence that the consumption of the mass media throughout the world often provokes resistance, irony, selectivity, and, in general *agency*." Ethnologists no longer equate cultural difference with strict adherence to tradition but accept that participation in global markets may permit "far more diverse personhoods, social relations and communities than presupposed by the standard theories and terms of sociology or economics" (Miller 1995b: 290).

There is, in fact, nothing new about this: colonized peoples have selectively "indigenized" imported cultural products for generations before the present age of mass communication. Examples familiar to many anthropologists include the adoption of bowler hats—brought to South America in the nineteenth century by British railroad builders—as items of dignified dress by indigenous Andean women, and the transformation of cricket matches into occasions for community display and opportunities for gaining prestige in the early decades of the twentieth century, as documented in the ethnographic film, *Trobriand Cricket*. Such things were long familiar to anthropologists but, with few exceptions—such as the extensive literature on Melanesian "cargo cults"—these phenomena were largely topics for hallway chit-chat rather than scholarly publications. It took Immanuel Wallerstein's landmark book, *The Modern World System*, to awaken cultural anthropologists to the potential importance of their discipline's bodies of knowledge and characteristic methods for theories of global social processes.

Wallerstein (1974) holds that, since the sixteenth century, the entire world has constituted a single economic system, divided into a core, periphery and (intermediate) semi-periphery. Though only weakly integrated with the core at the system's advent, the peripheral societies of the non-Western world over time came to be organized increasingly around the economic demands emanating from the Western European and later North American core areas. Anthropologists took immediate exception to world-systems theory's consignment of non-Western societies to the role of passive recipients of political and economic penetration and internal reorganization by an expansionary Europe (Mintz 1977). Much of the ethnographic literature of the 1980s, such as that on peasant and proletarian accommodation and resistance and the magical/moral economy literature, placed consistent emphasis on how local social and religious institutions have adapted to or resisted capitalist encroachment. These bodies of research may therefore be understood as constituting one first wave of anthropological responses to world-systems theory. Even though debate has turned toward a new and distinct body of theory—globalization—the anthropological reflex still moves in the same particularizing direction as before. Anthropologists of the early twentieth century changed the face of Western intellectual and popular discourses about human difference by adding an "s" to the word, "culture," and speaking of many cultures rather than just one. Today, ethnologists in like manner draw attention to local culture's resilience in the face of the prevailing global political economic trends toward ethical universalization, technical standardization and space-time compression.

Certain of my field observations are in harmony with this turn toward greater optimism about local culture's adaptability in the face of political and economic globalization. People in Monte Coca and elsewhere in the Dominican Republic undoubtedly have become more like North Americans over recent decades, as a result of consuming more of the same things as their neighbors to the north. Yet they are not becoming so much more alike that their cultural differences threaten to disappear anytime soon. For example, people in Monte Coca are notably less inclined than North Americans to consume alone and they share more. Overall, the market has not yet *become* the culture to the degree it has in the United States (Rouse 1995). It is just as certain that their distinctive beliefs and attitudes are not being replaced wholesale by North American social and moral models.

Yet, even as fears of cultural "melt-down" and global homogenization may be exaggerated, concerns about commodification cannot be completely dismissed. Merely to observe that people of the global south have "indigenized it" does not make their increased dependence upon market exchange innocuous. Cultural survival—defined in either/or terms of homogenization versus differentiation—may be less cause for worry than the social impact of increasing internal economic disparities, paired with expanding consumer demand in the countries of the global south. Beyond imprecise and overly general questions regarding whether the "local culture" will survive or not, we have reason to be concerned if free-market reforms and the spread of global commerce increase the degree of inequality internal to many Third World countries, cities and villages, dividing these into acknowledged classes of winners and losers. Alongside these dangers, June Nash (1994: 7) succinctly summarizes a range of other large-scale trends that tend to undermine subsistence security and wear at the fabric of community solidarity in societies on the global economic periphery: "Global integration heightens the cyclical crises of capitalism by incorporating the subsistence sectors of advanced and peripheral economies. World trends show a contraction in industrial production, the rise of unemployment, an increase in military spending and decline in social welfare, a reversal of capital flows from developing countries to developed countries, and a worldwide drop in real wages." Cultural differences may survive this onslaught. Indeed, the rise of national particularisms and anti-materialist global philosophical movements—Islamic revival, for example—may be amplified precisely because they run counter to secular globalism. Yet, even if the world remains culturally diverse, the forces of the global economy may erode social solidarity and place the very survival of many at greater peril.

Anthropologists are particularly well situated to describe and analyze such local effects of the spread of mass markets but there have been few ethnographic studies of market-generated social differentiation in the recent context of globalization and economic liberalization. This may be both a product and a source of doubts about whether the conventional model of extended, first-hand, community-based fieldwork is up to the challenges posed by globalization. As George Marcus (1998: chapter 3) correctly notes in his essay "Ethnography In/Of the World System," anthropologists must recognize the importance of globalization and the need for anthropology to respond creatively to it. Marcus's prescription is for global ethnographers to surf the flows that link the global and the local, through multi-sited ethnography, tracing, describing, analyzing and hence de-mystifying the operation of global institutions and networks. I recognize and affirm Marcus's (1998: 20) contention that this mobile ethnography can bring us to a more ambiguous and hence more accurate (my term) depiction of power, by bringing about heightened awareness of "major fault-lines of the institutional exercise of power."

Marcus also claims that the multiplicity of perspectives opened up by multi-sited fieldwork can unsettle the moral certainties into which ethnography can fall all too easily, once making explicit judgments about justice becomes the ethnographer's accepted aim. I think that is a good thing, too: finding pure victims and paragons of virtue is certainly not one of my aims in this book.[3] Yet not everything is ambiguous and not everyone is equally to blame for observable injustices. One attendant danger of multi-sited fieldwork is that the ethnographer, as s/he comes un-anchored from fieldwork in one place, will no longer identify with any one particular group of people, leaving her/him without a toe-hold on the steep and slippery gradient of power that links the local and the global. Marcus (1998: 85) himself admits that through multi-sited fieldwork we tend to "lose the subaltern" and de-center "the resistance and accommodation framework that has organized a considerable body of valuable research."

For him, this sacrifice is worth it, "for the sake of a reconfigured space of multiple sites of cultural production in which questions of resistance, although not forgotten, are often subordinated to different sorts of questions about the shape of systemic processes themselves and complicities with these processes among variously positioned subjects." These goals seem to me a fair abstraction of just what I am striving to do in this book. Yet what if ethnography comes unanchored from its conventional aim of representing aspects of one particular community's perspective on the world, or can no longer portray the particularities of others' lives in convincing detail? In this case, I fear anthropology will be not only left without a moral compass but greatly dis-empowered in the world outside our discipline. Part of our claim to being given a hearing has always been that we can voice the concerns of the voiceless. Fraught though it is with the potential for misrepresentation, voicing the concerns of people excluded by the corporate media has more than sentimental appeal. It implies methodological, and hence, political claims. If we no longer claim to speak for anyone but ourselves through ethnography, then we leave ourselves more vulnerable to charges of bias and blatant subjectivity from representatives of the very interests toward which we wish to direct critical scrutiny.

I do not reject innovative multi-sited research strategies per se. Certain research projects, such as Nancy Scheper-Hughes's (2002) inquiry into the global black market reality behind so-called rumors or legends regarding body-part theft in Latin America, Africa and Asia, require tracing goods, ideas or practices as they cross international borders. My own dissertation research (Martínez 1995) was carried out in two rural communities, in Haiti and the Dominican Republic, and traced the connections between these sites forged by the Haitian peasant farmers who sojourn as seasonal agricultural workers in the neighboring country. And even though I have anchored the present book in my ethnography of one place and time, I have written it in a mode akin to Marcus's (1998: 11) recommended "multi-sited research imaginary," in that my explanations of local phenomena consistently look toward this community's relationship with the rest of the world. Like a hummingbird, I aim in this book to live small but see big.

Even as we structure ethnography around the big picture, we should not lose sight of the unique and in some ways privileged perspectives that localized fieldwork can open. Systematic, community-based, first-hand observation places anthropologists in a unique position to report upon and analyze the effects of economic liberalization and the expansion of global commerce in far-flung corners of the world. It would be ironic if we were to sacrifice our recognized strength in documenting the local and the particular, in order to study global financial, political and cultural flows, at the very moment when critics have joined voices to warn of globalization's threat to the particular life ways of human communities everywhere. Our developed methods for studying life in particular localities still work. We should not throw them out as we abandon the expediency of regarding our research communities as isolates and strive to encompass the global dimensions of a new set of research problems.

The study of globalization contributes to a major paradigm shift in cultural anthropology, the knocking down of the boundaries we always, at least implicitly, imagined stood between the world's societies (each with its distinctive culture). This advance in theory has yet to be fully and consistently concretized in our research: we still give emphasis to evidence of particular, place-specific constellations of belief and practice, and accord less interest and value to things obviously borrowed from "the outside." I think the emerging anthropology of globalization would do well to extend its concerns beyond those patterns of culture that are unique or particular, to include consideration of the demand for more of the satisfactions of modernity being voiced by people around the world. The meanings of people's uses of objects, space and time are, and will continue to be, shaped by culturally distinctive cosmologies, forms of social affiliation, and expectations regarding the life course, gender and conjugal and family life. At the same time, people in every part of the planet now aspire to have more of what modern industrial society has to offer. It is a natural extension of anthropology's preoccupation with the culturally particular that we should study how these aspirations conform to or rebel against established community norms and practices. But the major, uncontrolled changes that are taking place around the world today—in particular, the increasing commodification of livelihood and subsistence among populations on the global economic periphery—make it seem necessary to shift more of our attention to the sources and meanings of global consumer demand. A focus on global consumer demand is in keeping with another major recent theoretical shift in the discipline, the demotion of culture from the pinnacle of cultural anthropology's core substantive preoccupations. Anthropology today is less concerned than it once was with intra-cultural consensus and more concerned with human difference, broadly conceived. Virtually every page of this book reflects this de-centering of culture in current anthropological theory. Cultural differences still matter but are no longer assumed to subsume other aspects of difference, such as gender, age, class and race/ethnicity. Ethnography is still catching up with theory in this regard. Field workers, myself included, are still prone to base our generalizations on evidence of agreement, rather than patterned contention, among the people whose lives we study. Yet ethnography is as never before about dialogue, implicit negotiation, and veiled or open conflict among men and women, old and young, rich and poor.

It may seem paradoxical that greater attention than ever is being paid to intra-cultural fault lines at the same time as anthropologists have attributed unprecedented economic coherence to the whole world. Anthropologists in increasing numbers conceive of global research problems not as phenomena taking place in unconnected ways in different societies but as manifestations of a single dynamic of exchange between the highly developed core areas and lesser-developed peripheries of the world economy. Studies of commodity production chains, global merchandising and mass media are integral to scholarship on these "north-south" relations. Therefore, to study the material world in almost any part of the world today is almost inevitably to orient oneself toward global-systemic process, so strongly is people's relationship to space, time and objects in any locality shaped by external market forces, mass media and consumer goods.

NOTES

1. On the "social life of things," see Appadurai 1986b; also McCracken 1988; Rutz and Orlove 1989; Sahlins 1976: chapter 4. On "text," see Geertz 1973: chapter 1; Ricoeur 1971; Slater 1997: 140–47.

2. See, for example, the essays in Appadurai 1996; Friedman 1994; Robertson 1992.

3. It becomes difficult to sustain notions about proletarian virtue when you observe, as I have, Dominican workers abetting the subordination of Haitian workers, permanent residents of both ethnic groups collaborating to deny basic liberties to the seasonal migrants from Haiti, and all of the above being in some way in complicity with the sexual exploitation of Haitian immigrant women. Clearly, the chain of exploitation is not completed solely by linking consumers in the north to producers in the south.

5

An Indecent Life

> [H]ow comes it that men's importunate claims to humanity are cast in the accents of group pride?
> —Geertz 1973: 22

People's ethnic ancestry and gender strongly influence where they can find work in Monte Coca. The ethnic mix there is simpler than what is found in plantations in other parts of the Americas, yet as much as in any other place that mix is the historical product of the arrival of successive waves of immigrants over time. Sugarcane growers in the Dominican Republic turned to new sources of immigrant labor at two decisive moments in the past when they implemented major changes in how the work of cutting cane was to be done. The first to be brought were the *ingléses*, beginning in the 1880s, who came mainly from the English-speaking Leeward Islands of the Caribbean. They were followed a few decades later by the Haitians, crossing the land border that divides the island of Hispaniola into two nations. Each group was not only more desperately poor than the workers whom they replaced in the cane fields but also lacked any prior customary understandings with management about how the work was to be done. Both conditions permitted cane growers to impose new terms of labor with greater ease.

All these immigrants came to the sugar estates with the idea of staying only a few months' time. The vast majority did return to their home places in short order, whether with a small nest egg they could put to productive use at home or with their hopes for something better smashed under the brutal reality of cutting cane for starvation wages. Others stayed on, postponed their return home year after year, and thus little by little gathered into a large group of settled workers. These settlers and their children born on the sugar estates have added further complexity to the industry's ethnic division of labor, in many cases leaving fieldwork behind to take up jobs on the middle rungs of the company job ladder.

The purchase of the Ingenio Consuelo by Dominican dictator, Rafael Trujillo, in 1957, added a new ingredient to the ethnic mix, as ethnic Dominicans displaced North Americans at the top and in large numbers entered the middle echelons of the company hierarchy. Today, the best jobs are still reserved largely for ethnic Dominicans. The "men on horseback" (as they are termed by the Haitian cane workers) are the upper-level supervisors, who earn the best pay, experience little physical strain or danger at work, and have the privilege of carrying a firearm. It is rare for a Haitian immigrant, even of the second or third generation, to achieve this status. At each step down the job ladder, from the top local management posts to supervisory personnel—e.g., low-level foremen and watchmen—and skilled workers—e.g., tractor and truck drivers and railroad workers—there are progressively more Dominican-born Haitians (whom I call "Haitian-Dominicans"). Their pay, conditions of work and a multitude of small signs of social prestige place these middle-tier workers below the management and supervisory personnel but above the manual laborers. Important distinctions are drawn along these lines among the manual laborers, too, so that the closer you approach the bottom of the agricultural job ladder, the more Haitian nationals and seasonal migrants (braceros) you will find.

Physical proximity to the industry's raw material, sugarcane, is a key spatial marker of a worker's place within this hierarchy. The men who handle sugarcane at work, as cane cutters, cart drivers, and wagon loaders, are paid the lowest wages, do the most physically taxing labor, and the majority are of Haitian ethnicity. The lowest of these, in terms of pay and work conditions, are the cane cutters, who not only handle cane but are largely restricted to the cane fields when at work. The greater part of the cane harvest is usually brought in by the braceros, but enough Haitian and Haitian-Dominican residents cut cane that, in years when the supply of seasonal migrants from Haiti has been disrupted, the company has been able to get by with their labor and that of Haitian nationals forcibly recruited from other parts of the Dominican Republic (Martínez 1995: 45–50). It is, even so, exceptional to find a non-Haitian man who depends primarily on cutting cane for his harvest income.[1]

The gender-based division of labor on the sugar estates is at first glance much simpler than the ethnic division. As many residents of the sugar company compounds (bateyes) will tell you, the sugar company reserves employment for men and hires women only for office jobs, of which there are many in the mill but extremely few in the rural bateyes. Instead of earning incomes of their own, women stay at home with the children and live off their mates' wages. Yet stay a little while in any batey and walk in the surrounding fields and you will find that none of this is quite accurate. You will eventually come across women working in the cane fields and more importantly you will find that batey residents' gloss on women's work understates women's overall rate of remunerated employment.

Extended observation reveals another, less obvious dimension, that ethnicity and gender in Monte Coca shape each other to a certain degree. My impression, gathered from many conversations rather than a systematic poll, is that Haitians and Haitian-Dominicans will more often answer the question, "Do women cut cane?" in the affirmative than will ethnic Dominicans. It is obvious why this might be so: it is the Haitians' mothers and sisters, and not the Dominicans' womenfolk, who work in the cane, and overall more women of Haitian ancestry than of Dominican ancestry earn money (Table 5-1). The gender-based division of labor is inflected by the ethnic division, in the sense that not all the kinds of work carried out by Haitian women and Dominican women are the same. Symbolic weight accrues to these differences when one considers that Haitian women more often do work that is widely considered degrading, including not only cane work but sex work in Monte Coca's brothel (where all of the prostitutes are Haitian or Haitian-Dominican). Involvement in these branches of work not only marks the women as "indecent" but confirms widely held notions of Dominican superiority. The gender-based division of labor thus participates in shaping concepts of ethnic difference; Dominicans can consider themselves superior in large part because they think Dominican women have higher morals than Haitian women.

Insights like this take us closer to seeing the concepts of an ethnic and a gender-based division of labor for what they are, abstractions of more complex and variable sets of practices. The information presented in this first ethnographic chapter of my book casts ethnicity in particular in a new light. Looking at Monte Coca through the lenses of ethnicity can take us an important first step toward a deeper understanding of the social meanings of work but it cannot alone take us all the way to that deeper analysis. For, my ethnography reveals that the Dominican sugar industry's division of labor follows not just the lines of ethnic ancestry. Residence status—specifically, the line between permanent and seasonal residents of the batey—is, if

Table 5-1. Distribution by Ethnic Group of Economically Active Women in Monte Coca*

	Haitian-Dominican	Dominican	Haitian
No Independent Income	39 (52%)	27 (36%)	4 (17%)
Earns Independent Income	35 (47%)	47 (62%)	19 (79%)
Unknown	1 (1%)	2 (2%)	1 (4%)
Total	75	76	24

* Includes all Monte Coca permanent women 15 years and over.
Source: Census by author, March 1986

anything, a more salient boundary than ethnicity per se, both socially and at work. The very worst treatment—involving verbal disrespect, segregated housing, and physically coercive forms of labor discipline—is meted out not to ethnic Haitians or to Haitian nationals generally but to the braceros, those workers who enter the Dominican Republic seasonally and return to Haiti at the end of the sugarcane harvest. In the eyes of the batey's permanent residents, these degradations are interpreted as evidence of the innately degraded human character of the migrant himself. Unpunished physical and symbolic violence marks the line between "decent" and "indecent" women, too, inasmuch as even some women attribute sexual violence to the survivors' volitional association with bad men or their willing presence in inappropriate places for a "decent woman." The ethnic division of labor is maintained by violence as well as occupational segregation and ranking. Permanent residents can pummel and exploit seasonal migrants with impunity.

Consumption habits, domestic environments and work and leisure add further density to ethnic and gender differentiation. Here, too, behavioral differences may be shaped primarily by structurally determined limits—stemming from poverty or seasonal residence, for example. Yet these differences are often interpreted as outcomes of personal volition or evidence of innate character, as when permanent residents take the bareness of the braceros' rooms as a sign that these sojourners are *content* with a standard of living that should be unacceptable to any human being. Broadly conceived, I go beyond ethnicity and the gender-based division of labor, to consider how different locales of work and leisure as well as the treatment that a person receives at the hands of others attach a stigma of "indecency" to certain people and not to others. In this way, I also aim to give a more detailed account of what kinds of human difference I am looking at in this book.

THE PLANTATION HIERARCHY

The formal organizational structure of the plantation is highly centralized and hierarchical. Consuelo's sugarcane land is divided into six administrative units (*colonias*). Monte Coca is the "principal" or "head" batey of the Colonia Esperanza. Authority radiates outward from the plantation's head office in the mill town through successively lower levels of the company hierarchy in the bateyes. The head of agricultural operations (*jefe de campo*) has his office in Consuelo, in quarters snidely dubbed the "cold rooms" by the agricultural workers, for the air conditioners in constant use there. From this point, the *jefe de campo* manages the distribution of inputs to the six *colonias* and coordinates their production schedules. The top boss of each *colonia*, called the *superintendente*, will consult with the *jefe de campo* or with the *administrador,* the plantation's top administrator, if he has any doubt about what to do in a matter of importance, such as whether to permit a foreign anthropologist to live in a batey. In organizing matters that fall within the yearly round of activities, including even such sensitive operations as commissioning an employee to recruit migrant workers from Haiti, the *superintendente* is accorded effective autonomy.

The "*super*" is, with little exaggeration, a local superpower, who exercises limited police and juridical authority as well as economic decision-making power. Not only does he enhance the incomes of some of the workers under his supervision by granting them plum jobs, he also issues commands to the plantation's private police force in his *colonia* and even passes judgments and imposes settlements between workers and their families in property disputes. Even so, it is said that a *superintendente* who too obviously favors a few workers will quickly fall afoul of local gossip and may even be targeted for petty sabotage and destruction of his personal property.

Among the other local bosses who live in Monte Coca and work under the *superintendente*'s supervision, the most important is the *mayordomo,* who oversees the field workers and is the *super*'s de facto second-in-command. He is followed in line by the local *guardacampestre,* a man of much lower rank, really, than either the *super* or the *mayordomo,* who is the local representative of the company police and assigns living quarters in the batey. A range of higher and lower-level foremen work with different contingents of workers—e.g., cutters and cart drivers have different overseers—implementing the orders of the bosses above. Their standing in the plantation command hierarchy is determined by how far their responsibilities reach—e.g., whether they have authority over all the cane cutters generally or just one small group.

Company bosses and supervisors have their primary responsibilities to their superiors in this highly centralized, rationally managed and profit-seeking organization. Yet the plantation's priority on economic efficiency does not deter bosses at the level of the batey from also cultivating client ties with the workers below them and with the company's "higher ups." Indeed, important immediate goals, such as recruiting and retaining the core agricultural labor force that remains attached to the plantation throughout the year, seem to be facilitated by the cultivation of personal ties between overseers and subordinates. And even as they say some of their neighbors are poor because they shun hard work, Monte Cocans readily admit that the fastest and surest way to ascend the company hierarchy is with the backing of a company boss or a political entrepreneur. They tend to speak of such advantages more as a product of personal luck than of the social privileges that flow from connections of kinship and friendship. "Life is a lottery number," both Haitians and Dominicans will say, to explain why some people in the batey are wealthier than others. If you get an inside track to obtaining a supervisory position or one of the better jobs at the mill because you were born into a prosperous family or developed close personal ties with a local power broker, that is your good luck, regardless of the fact that such ties tend disproportionately to favor ethnic Dominicans.

Monte Cocans are not so fatalistic that they will not try to make their own luck. Many day laborers curry favor with company bosses in the hope of finding a patron who can help them find steady work. In the days when the Dominican state sugar consortium (CEA) managed Consuelo, there was something of a traffic in employment at the sugar mill, in which political activism could win or lose a man his job, depending on the fortunes of the party of his choice. Certain residents of the mill town also arranged for their friends to get jobs, in exchange for a substantial bribe. And, as elsewhere in Latin America, ritual co-parenthood (*compadrazgo*) was also and still is an important mechanism for establishing ties of solidarity. Godparents are solemnly sworn to provide whatever support they can for their godsons and daughters, and consequently choosing a godmother and godfather for one's child can be guided by strategy as well as by sentiment. Workers in Monte Coca seem more often than not to follow a two-track *compadrazgo* strategy, involving both status superiors and equals. Picking one godparent from among status superiors, such as a local business owner or the *superintendente* or the *mayordomo* or these men's wives, may open up important job assignments or sources of credit. Precisely because of this, company bosses typically have dozens of godchildren, which tends to limit the favors they are ready to grant. Also, company bosses can be and often are reassigned from one batey to another, diminishing their availability to provide assistance to the *compadres* they leave behind. Picking the second godparent from among status equals balances these risks by solidifying existing ties of trust with neighbors who are more likely to be available to the child's parents.

Not only company employment but also non-wage subsistence resources—such as the small plots of company land informally ceded to permanent residents for use as subsistence gardens—are distributed through ties of patronage and petty corruption and add to intra-community socioeconomic inequality. The subsistence gardens (*conucos*) supplement their holders' diets even when wage work is available from the company and are the main source of food security in times of scarce employment. As one *viejo* told me in 1985, regarding the three Dominican pesos then paid by the company for a half-day's work:

> But with that three *pyas*, Hhhh! [he laughs and shakes his head]. If you have a wife and children. Ha, ha! [laughs and claps his hands twice] You can figure it out. With those three *goud* you will make a little meal at midday [and then] in the evening, before you go to bed, there will not be anything! But if you have a garden, you go in, you go look for a little sweet potato, a little manioc, whatever you have in the garden, [and] you come [back and] you

say to your wife, "Here, boil up this thing I am giving you for the children. There is nothing [else]." Ha, ha, ha, ha! Because we cannot sleep like that. Ha, ha, ha! Because hunger is a thing that is really hard!

For this reason, this man added, "A person always seeks to care for their gardens before they do the work in the cane." Today, there are elderly Haitian men in Monte Coca who can no longer do the heavy labor of the cane fields but subsist largely off their garden produce and the wages they earn by working in other men's *conucos*. One reason why Monte Cocans liked the CEA better than the former North American corporate owners of the Ingenio Consuelo was that "the Americans" prohibited the cultivation of *conucos* on spare plots of company land. Whether Consuelo's residents will continue to enjoy the right of usufruct over unused plots of land is one of the many unresolved issues that has added to their anxieties regarding the recent transfer of the plantation's management to private hands.

Land for *conucos* is scarce and this scarcity is compounded by unequal access. Many of the neediest people can get gardens: of 135 *conucos* in and around Monte Coca, 60 are held by *viejos*, the Haitian nationals who have established permanent residence in the Dominican Republic. Yet the *conucos* vary considerably in size: in a sample of 13 randomly chosen *conucos*, the largest was 0.37 hectares and the smallest was less than 0.04 hectares. The larger and better-situated gardens—those that are far enough from the cane fields that they stand little risk of being wiped out by a company tractor or a drift of herbicide—are "owned" by bosses, supervisory personnel and skilled employees. Undoubtedly, most of the produce grown in the bosses' *conucos* is sold for cash rather than kept for household consumption.

An equally notable indicator of inequality is who works the land in the *conucos*. Few Dominicans will so much as lift a hoe in their own *conucos* but instead hire *viejos* to manage their gardens. The *viejos*, for their part, hire other Haitian men and women to help them clear and plant the *conucos*. Thus, some of the money from this parallel subsistence economy circulates even among people who are too poor or too recently arrived from Haiti to have obtained *conuco* plots for themselves. Yet there is also an element of exploitation in this sub-contracting of *conuco* wage labor, as when a savvy *viejo* profits by bargaining to plant a boss's garden for a sum of money substantially in excess of what he pays the laborers to do the work. Also, conflicts may arise when one man thinks another has outbid him for a day's work, especially late in the dead season, when work is least available and hunger is at its worst. Even so, payment of a wage does not necessarily signify exploitation. A *conuco* farmer who recruits another person to work for him will pay that person the going wage, even if they are friends who might on another occasion freely swap advice about farming or spontaneously lend a hand if one of them is not busy and sees the other working alone.

The judgments that people in Monte Coca make of each other are so closely linked to occupation and rank in the company hierarchy that it seems somewhat artificial to talk about ethnic identity as if it were a distinct and independent reality. Yet, at the risk of reifying "ethnicity," some words must be said about the categories that people employ and what these concepts imply about relations across ethnic lines. Monte Cocans recognize four basic ethnic categories among the people who live in the batey: *dominicanos, haitianos, arrayanos,* and *ingleses. Arrayanos* are people of mixed Haitian and Dominican ancestry, of whom there are many in Monte Coca. *Ingleses* are the second- and third-generation descendants of black immigrants from islands of the Lesser Antilles, whose ancestors were the first non-Dominican immigrants to be brought in large numbers to work in the sugarcane fields, from the 1880s to the 1930s. *Dominicanos* are ethnic Dominicans, people whose ancestors, back to their grandparents' generation, were all born in the Dominican Republic. As it is throughout the Dominican Republic, not only people born in Haiti but their Dominican-born children are referred to as "*haitianos.*" Thus, the category of *haitiano* lumps people born in Haiti and their children born in the Dominican Republic. Classified apart, Haitian-Dominicans make up a bit less than one-third of Monte Coca's population (Table 5-2). Counting all people of Haitian ancestry, slightly more than one-half of the batey's people are *haitianos.* Not only the inheritance of Haitian identity from one generation to the next but the yearly entry of hundreds of braceros from Haiti reinforce the line between *haitiano* and *dominicano.* Who is *haitiano* and who, *dominicano,* is common knowledge in Monte Coca but it is even so a distinction that is only so reliable as local memory. It is almost certain that the grandparents and earlier ancestors of some *dominicanos* in Monte Coca were in their own lifetimes known to be something other than "*dominicano.*"

The virulence of anti-Haitian prejudice in the Dominican Republic is reflected in the fact that Haitians are the only immigrant group whose children born in the Dominican Republic are not popularly considered to be *dominicanos* (Dore Cabral 1987). Haitian identity is not simply an unwanted label, imposed on Haitian-Dominicans by other Dominicans. When circumstances permit it, many Haitian-Dominicans express pride in their Haitian ancestry. Yet it is obvious to any person who has spent much time in a batey that their fluency in the Spanish language and their strong tendency to wish to stay in the Dominican Republic differentiates Haitian-Dominicans from the Haitian nationals on the sugar estates. In spite of the lack of a specific term for Dominican-born Haitians, their distinctiveness from their Haitian-born parents is implicitly recognized on occasion, as when one of my neighbors in Monte Coca would refer to someone as "a Haitian born/from here" ("*un/a haitiano/a nacido/a aquí*"). It is equally obvious that such phrasing conveys implicit acceptance that the Dominican-born children of Haitians are "Haitian," even to the third generation and

Table 5-2. Distribution by Sex and Ethnic Group of Monte Coca Adults*

Ethnic Group	Men	Women	Total
Dominican	97	75	172 (40.7%)
Haitian-Dominican and arrayano	59	76	135 (31.9%)
Haitian	67	24	91 (21.5%)
Ingles	15	7	22 (5.2%)
Unknown	1	2	3 (0.7%)
Total	239 (56.5%)	184 (43.5%)	423

* Includes all Monte Coca permanent residents over age 15.
Source: Census by author, March 1986

beyond, in spite of the right to Dominican citizenship that the Dominican Republic's constitution confers upon anyone born on the country's soil. The denial of this right to many thousands of Haitian-Dominicans has become an object of international human rights concern (Human Rights Watch 2002; MUDHA 2003).

By abandoning the sugar estates and passing as "*dominicanos*," uncounted numbers of people of Haitian ancestry have been assimilated into the Dominican mainstream. Among the larger lessons of this "passing" are that the ethnic boundary is permeable and at times ambiguous but also that the only way the children of Haitians have been able to gain social acceptance outside the batey is by denying their Haitian ancestry. I witnessed this in action early in 1986, at a point when the Dominican government had decided to post a squadron of Air Force recruits in Monte Coca for a time to lend a hand with the cane harvest, which was being hampered by a shortage of braceros from Haiti. A sergeant who came around to reconnoiter the batey before the troops' arrival stopped to converse with a woman who lived near me, and at one point he asked her, "There aren't any Haitians living in this batey, are there? Because the last place we were in was running with them!" "Oh, no!" answered my neighbor, whose own husband was a second-generation Haitian, "We are all *dominicanos* here!"

Racism exacerbates ethnic tensions even in the predominantly African-American communities of the country's sugar–producing areas. Monte Cocans are highly conscious of color. Even very dark–skinned *dominicanos* make racially prejudicial remarks against blacks and, in particular, against Haitians. *Ingleses* are keen to stand apart from Haitians and strongly resent being mistaken for people of Haitian ancestry. When I once absentmindedly hailed an *inglés* in Haitian Creole, the man grumbled, in Spanish, "That language should be banned from this country!" and added, in labored English (I paraphrase), "You saw I am black and you took me for something I am not. I am Dominican." I was struck speechless, and, after a moment's awkward silence, he admonished, "You may say 'excuse me,'" and angrily pushed down some stalks of cane to enter a field that he had been assigned to cut. Among both Haitians and Dominicans, there is a huge range of skin-color hues and facial features as a result of both nations being populated primarily by mixed race descendants of European and African colonizers (albeit with more very dark-skinned people and far fewer fair complexions among the Haitians). Yet, in spite of the overlap in physical appearance, it is widely accepted that Haitians differ visibly and are racially distinct from Dominicans. I once asked a Haitian-Dominican woman whether she considered herself Haitian or Dominican, and she answered, "Both." Then, after a moment's pause, she added, "You cannot hide that [being Haitian]. People see it in you."

In spite of their divisions and animosities, tension among the ethnic groups stays, for the most part, unspoken. This is in part due to how salient the ethnic distinctions are in people's minds: because pretty much everyone knows what group everyone else belongs to, they can and generally do avoid voicing prejudicial remarks until they are in a gathering made up entirely of their own ethnic group. It dampens tensions also that Haitians and Dominicans mingle almost constantly in their daily affairs in Monte Coca. Ties of reciprocal aid between households, cooperation at work and at leisure, and mixture of the two groups through intermarriage seem to have dulled the animosity against everything Haitian voiced trenchantly by Dominicans elsewhere in the country (Table 5-3).[2] You often hear batey children hurling ethnic insults at their Haitian-Dominican playmates — "*Haitiano bruto!*" (Stupid Haitian!) "*Paisan!*" (Bumpkin!) "*Haitiano del diablo!*" (Goddamn Haitian!). That the children mouthing these epithets are most often themselves Haitian-Dominican is disturbing in as much as it suggests these children have internalized anti-Haitian prejudice. Yet, considering the large number of Haitians in the local population and their generally low status on the sugar estates, it is remarkable that "*haitiano*" is, by my observation, said less often in an insulting manner by adults in Monte Coca than in poor neighborhoods in the city of Santo Domingo. The evidence is equivocal, but several writers confirm that the more frequently Dominicans interact with Haitians as neighbors and co-workers, the less likely they are to voice anti-Haitian sentiments.[3]

Much more often than "*haitiano*," permanent residents of Monte Coca, regardless of their ethnic heritage, use "*congó*" (a synonym of "bracero") as a term of abuse. "*Congó*" is typically directed against a person or animal

Table 5-3. Distribution by Sex and Ethnic Group of Conjugal Unions in Monte Coca

Ethnic Group for Women in a Union	Ethnic Group for Men in a Union			
	Dominican	Haitian-Domincan	Haitian	Other/Unknown
Dominican	34 (30.6%)	6 (5.4%)	5 (4.5%)	—
Haitian-Dominican	9 (8.1%)	19 (17.1%)	7 (6.3%)	—
Haitian	0	1 (0.9%)	18 (16.2%)	—
Other and Unknown	—	—	—	12 (10.8%)

Source: Census by author, March 1986

as an epithet or adjective denoting rudeness, ignorance, or ineptitude. A mother may, for example, reprimand her children for unruly behavior by warning them that they are getting *"demasiado congoso"* (too *congóish*). One hot and sunny afternoon, on a day when all the batey's water pumps were broken, I was typing up field notes when I recognized the voice of an elderly neighbor, shouting, "The people in this batey are worse than the *congoses!*" I rushed out to find him standing outside, looking on in disgust at a group of women shouting and jostling, buckets in hand, to be the first to reach the spigot of a water tank that had just been dropped off there by a company tractor. On another occasion an elderly Haitian man whom I was interviewing even referred to a frightened hen that flapped wildly around his room as a *"poul kongòs."*[4]

Beyond its metaphorical extension to unruly people and yard fowl, *congó* is a label that no one, particularly among Monte Coca's residents of Haitian origin, wants to be stuck with. Batey residents view the bracero as the archetype of a physically and morally indecent life. In their eyes, the braceros are the only people in the whole country who suffer a standard of living inferior to their own. This perception is on the whole an accurate assessment of the braceros' position. By any standard of comparison—housing conditions, incomes, work environment—the braceros represent the bottom of the nation's underclass and the poorest of its poor. The horrendous standard of living of the bracero, his lowly position in the company job hierarchy, and his social isolation from batey residents reinforce the racial prejudices that many Dominicans hold against Haitian people and tend to confirm the sense that the only form of social interaction that is possible between Dominicans and Haitians is as bosses and laborers. Even the *viejos*, though they are fellow Haitian nationals and were once *congoses* themselves, disparage newly arrived braceros as *"nèg bout pantalon"* (guys in cut-offs) after the tattered knee-length pants that are the stereotypical garb of the Haitian peasant man. An indicator of how little Haitians in Monte Coca wish to be identified with the braceros is that I only began to hear the term *"viejo"* used during the harvest, i.e., to distinguish the Haitians who resided there year-round from the braceros, once the latter began to arrive in large numbers. During the previous five months that I had lived in Monte Coca, I did not hear the term *"viejo"* used in this sense even once, causing me to wonder if it had passed out of usage or perhaps never had been more than a quasi-fictional bit of local color trotted out for gullible journalists and social researchers. Any doubt that I had about it being an active and potent term in everyday life evaporated once men, who had for months been simply *"haitianos,"* began to be referred to and to refer to themselves as *"viejos."*

Congó: Batey Archetype of an Indecent Life

Nearly every aspect of the bracero's material existence is understood by permanent residents of the batey to mark him as a model of indecency.

In Monte Coca, the company equips each room in the braceros' barracks with two or three steel-frame bunk beds, and issues each new arrival, man or woman, with a thin, old "mattress" of bare foam rubber. The braceros' rooms are otherwise almost bare. One or two plastic jugs for carrying water to the fields, perhaps a small stack of wood in a corner, and large tins blackened by use as cooking vessels typically comprise the sum of household items visible in the braceros' quarters. For the braceros, being able to pick up their belongings and move to another batey in response to unfavorable circumstances may mean the difference between starvation and returning to Haiti with enough savings to count their time among "the Spanish" as a qualified success. Poverty and frequent changes of residence tend to preclude acquisition of bulky consumer goods until the migrants receive their end-of-harvest bonus payment and ascertain that they will soon return to Haiti.

The braceros are housed in barracks of their own, apart from those of permanent residents, an arrangement that facilitates surveillance by company security personnel. Yet I have already observed in passing that permanent residents speak of this residential segregation as a question of "decency." A "decent" room is one no *"congó"* has ever inhabited, even if it is in a barracks that stands in worse need of repair than the braceros' barracks. Residents generally agree that living under the same roof with the braceros would expose them to assaults against propriety too constant and egregious for any decent person to tolerate. "You'll have no tranquility here once the *congoses* arrive," a woman in my neighborhood warned me in a jaded voice shortly before the harvest began. "They spend half the night up singing and making noise and they fill all this [yard] outside their barracks with trash." Few permanent residents set foot in the braceros' barracks, which they speak of as being too filthy and crowded to linger around during leisure hours. When I asked a group of *viejos* to explain why the braceros could not be housed in the same buildings as the permanent residents, some of the men grinned, looked down at their feet, and shook their heads. Others doubled over in laughter. Evidently, I did not understand even the most natural, obvious and correct rules of life in the batey. "They [the braceros] are just too piggish," one man finally wheezed, setting off a new round of guffaws.

Aside from brief contacts at work, it is only by seeking out the company of *viejos* in the *viejos'* own quarters that the exceptional bracero mixes with batey residents at all. The braceros do not often linger in the crowds of people that gather on weekend evenings in front of the *bodega*, Monte Coca's main dry-goods shop but prefer to make their purchases rapidly and return to their own barracks. All Haitian men avoid the barroom of the batey's brothel, La Yagüita, if they wish to visit a woman there. Haitians say they dislike the company of drunken Dominicans armed with pistols and long knives, and fear the possibility of a violent encounter there. The violent character of Dominicans is a subject of legend in the migrants' home places in rural Haiti. It is widely thought that Dominican courts of law do not harshly penalize the murder or assault of a Haitian. It worsens their apprehensions that La Yagüita draws in unfamiliar men from nearby towns and bateyes. Generally speaking, if a bracero seeks out social ties with local people, he does so by slowly extending relationships of trust to fellow cane cutters among the *viejos*. The more sociable men among the *viejos* may take on an informal role as social intermediaries, taking the trouble, for example, to introduce the bracero to passing acquaintances.

The braceros' isolation is institutionalized in their exclusion from the industry's labor unions (Murphy 1986: 362–63). For many, the bulk of their dealings with the company and the batey community takes place through the mediation of a company employee, called the "bracero foreman" (*capataz de* braceros). In spite of his title, the bracero foreman does not regularly supervise work but is instead responsible for an unspecified range of tasks involved in maintaining labor discipline among the seasonal migrants. The bracero foreman is typically a Haitian national or Haitian-Dominican, who has been rewarded with this job for recruiting a group of braceros in Haiti. "Given how deeply involved the *capataz de braceros* is in the company's practices of labor control," I have observed elsewhere, "it is perhaps surprising that joking and good-humored banter typifies relations between a *capataz* and 'his *congoses*'":

> Often, the relationship between *capataz* and bracero takes an aspect of informal patronage. In return for a small gratuity, for instance, the *capataz* may intercede

with a higher-ranking foreman, the *capataz de corte*, to secure an assignment to a "good" field of cane for one of his recruits. Yet no one holds any illusions about where the *capataz*'s ultimate loyalty lies. When push comes to shove, he will favor the interests of his employer, the sugar company. (Martínez 1995: 146)

The braceros' low wages and desire to save money to take back to Haiti also tend to isolate them from the permanent residents of Monte Coca. Ties of economic interdependence, like those that mitigate tensions between Dominicans and other Haitians in the batey, do not normally exist between residents and braceros. The braceros do not hire domestic labor nor do many take up residence with batey women. Rather, they do their own laundry as individuals, and as roommates divide the tasks of housekeeping, gathering fuel wood and water, purchasing shared foodstuffs, and preparing the main meal of the day (ibid.: 146–50). Dominicans especially regard the braceros as inscrutable figures. Even men who return to Monte Coca in several successive years may be perceived to have no more comprehensible needs and habits than migratory birds, who "seek out the same nest every year."

Batey people also voice strongly negative images of the paid work that the braceros do. They refer to cane work generally as *"struggling* with cane" *(bregar con caña)*. Many, though not all, Dominicans say that cutting cane is work fit only for Haitians. A young Dominican, who actively sought a job outside the plantation, told me, "If you grow up working in a batey, by the time you are 25, you will be old, you will look like a Haitian. The work here is too hard." Batey residents characterize cutting cane as a *"trabajo forzado,"* by which they mean not "forced labor" per se but work that taxes their endurance to its physical limits. It is simply not accurate to say that no Dominican will cut cane.[5] Yet the distaste for cutting cane is not purely symbolic at root. To ascertain this, you really need look no further than the physical toll the work has taken on the men who have worked most of their lives in the cane fields. The gnarled fingers, scarred hands and forearms, amputated toes, stiff, stooped backs, and deeply creased faces of veteran cane cutters attest to the severity of a life spent "struggling with the cane."

In the piece-rate wage system under which the company employs its cane cutters, the braceros are paid only according to the weight of cane that they harvest. These piece-rate wages quietly ensure that the cane cutters will work long hours even without direct supervision. After ten or twelve hours of labor, most only earn enough for one substantial meal a day. The company also shows disregard for the cane cutters' well-being by providing them with none of the safety equipment—boots, shin guards, heavy gloves, goggles—considered essential in other cane-sugar-producing countries (Murphy 1991: 116–17).

Nor does coercion take only economic form on the sugar estates. On a typical workday, company foremen awaken the braceros before dawn, barking insults at the men (*"Vámonos, vámonos, vámonos, congoses del diablo!"* [Let's go, let's go, let's go, Goddamn *congoses*!]) and making a great din by banging with the blunt side of machetes on the doors and window shades of the braceros' rooms to rouse them from sleep. The braceros rise from bed, step outside, shoulders hunched against the cool night air, wash the sleep from their eyes with a trickle of water, if there is any left in their plastic gallon bottles, then step back inside and put on their tattered and dirty work clothes. They then gather up their *mochas* (a kind of machete made especially for cutting sugarcane) and a plastic gallon or tin can to carry water to their assigned place of work. Before they leave, they may quickly eat whatever scraps of food are left from the night before or, if there is none, go to work without eating any solid food at all.

Besides these daily indignities, the braceros are at times ordered to go to the cane fields against their will. On some Sundays, for example, to avoid impending shortages of cane at the mill, company bosses require the braceros to leave their barracks to gather any cane they may have left lying in the fields the day before. The braceros condemn the denial of a weekly day of rest as being "like slavery" and a "shameless act" (*vakabôday*) on the part of the bosses. Norms of social propriety and concepts of health management, held by Haitians and Dominicans alike, define a weekly day of rest to be a human right and necessity. As one 18–year-old bracero put it, "Sunday is the day I remember Haiti the most." He explained that in Haiti he would spend all day Sunday relaxing with his pals, and complained that in Monte Coca there was no place to go for a swim nor even a spot where he could feel comfortable gathering with his work mates to drink and swap jokes. The braceros usually show the most reluctance to go out to work the Sunday after the biweekly payday. If they refuse to budge in spite of all attempts to cajole or intimidate them into obedience, the local *guardacampestre* may call in armed reinforcements from the company police in other bateyes to chase the men out of their barracks under blows. "On Sundays," Monte Coca's *guardacampestre* confided, "not even under *culatazos* (blows from the butt end of a rifle) do the *congoses* want to go out to cut cane."

The *viejos* are spared from direct physical coercion but they, too, must work long hours just to survive. The cane cutters frequently spend twelve or more hours a day in the cane fields, without any nutrition except the sugary juice they are permitted to suck from the stalks of cane. Their incomes are too low to afford enough nutrition for their long hours of physically exhausting labor. Hunger and fatigue force the cane cutters to take frequent breaks during the day. Walking the cane fields during the harvest, one commonly comes upon men sitting in the shade at the edge of a field, peeling stalks of cane with their *mochas* to chew out the juice inside. Cutting cane is heavy and dangerous work. In a series of rapid movements, repeated countless times over the course of a day, the cutter (1) stoops at the waist, grasps a cane stalk with one hand and chops the stalk at ground level with vigorous strokes of the *mocha*, (2) stands straight and cuts off the severed stalk's leafy crown, (3) scrapes off any leaves that adhere to the stalk using the blunt side of the *mocha*, (4) turns and cuts the stalk into two or three pieces, each about a yard long, and (5) tosses the remaining piece behind him into a pile. In the course of a typical harvest day, both hot Caribbean sunshine and sudden afternoon showers may pour down on the cutters' backs. Cane workers attribute many of their illnesses to sudden shifts between hot-dry and cool-damp weather. Sugarcane is cut green in the Dominican Republic, in contrast to many other sugarcane-growing countries where the cane cutter's work is speeded by burning each field immediately before it is harvested to rid it of excess vegetation. Cutting green reduces the amount of cane that a man can cut in a day and hence lowers the cutters' incomes. Yet bosses consider it impractical to burn most fields before harvesting, because burnt cane dries out more rapidly than green cane and the company's transportation system cannot be relied upon to carry the cane to the mill fast enough.

At the end of a long and exhausting day, the cane cutters trudge to their barracks, gather water with which to bathe, buy charcoal or gather dried out cane stalks to build a cooking fire, and set to preparing their only substantial meal of the day. The evening meal consists chiefly of cheap starches, high in calories but low in other essential nutrients. Even longer hours of work may be required of the braceros in emergencies, such as when an uncontrolled fire has burned several fields, which must be harvested rapidly, lest the burnt cane dry out completely. After particularly hard days, some men simply collapse onto their bunks and fall asleep in their work clothes.

As if their predicament were not bad enough, a many-branched system of pay reductions and petty corruption deprives the braceros of at least one-third to one-half of the income to which they are entitled. Part of this institutionalized theft is taken by the company and part goes into the pockets of local bosses and employees. Even employees low on the food chain cash in at the braceros' expense, such as the cart drivers who demand a small kickback from each cutter as a condition for bringing their carts around promptly to pick up their cane. It is also common knowledge that the fields with the lowest yields are generally reserved for the braceros. The batey's permanent residents know which fields have the best cane and spend time and small sums of money ingratiating themselves with the *capataces de corte*, who assign the cutters their tasks. When I did my fieldwork in Monte Coca in 1985–86, the only hope the braceros had of obtaining enough money to return to Haiti lay in the "incentive" the company would pay at the end of the harvest, based on the forced savings of RD$0.60 per ton of cane it withheld from each cutter's pay throughout the harvest.

In general terms, the indecency for which the bracero is reproached stems from conditions imposed on him by the company as well as other circumstances beyond his control. Yet batey residents tend to see the braceros as accomplices in the creation of their own substandard conditions of life. They blame the company for providing filthy, overcrowded barracks but fault the braceros for accepting these conditions. Dominicans insist that *they* would never be willing to work without a day of rest, like animals, but at no point stop to ask whether such awful conditions are necessary. No hope for improvement is ever discussed in the bateyes. Instead, the harshness of cutting cane is taken for granted and implicitly justifies the necessity of importing braceros from Haiti. With circular reasoning, some Dominicans explicitly interpret the degradations that the company imposes on the bracero as proof that the bracero himself is innately degraded. "The people in Haiti are nothing more than animals," a local pick-up truck driver explained to me. "Everyone knows that. Just look at the way they live here!" In the eyes of Dominicans in Monte Coca, the braceros' willingness to come from Haiti to work under such awful conditions stands as evidence of the degraded character of the Haitian people themselves. These rationalizations involve a twist of logic similar to what has been called "blaming the victim" (Ryan 1976). According to this line of reasoning, if the work the bracero does is dirty and brutish, and he is denied a day of rest and lives in conditions unfit for human existence, then his willingness to accept all that proves him to be inherently unclean and a brute.

Even though the bracero may be likened by some to an animal, there is no easy equation to be noticed in batey discourses between the bracero and natural, pre-industrial man. On the contrary, batey residents of all ethnic backgrounds tend to portray Dominicans as less amenable to industrial work discipline than Haitians. Even Dominicans who routinely work ten or twelve hours a day may insist that the great majority of their compatriots shun hard work. The Dominican's purportedly lower stamina and more ample need for leisure are defined by contrast with the Haitian, who is likened to a work animal in his capacity to do without rest or entertainment indefinitely. Even in his flaws, then, the Dominican appears more human than the Haitian. References of this kind also give the industry's ethnic division of labor the appearance of an inevitable, natural product of the purportedly innate national characteristics of the Haitian and Dominican peoples. In response to my questions on this topic, and in many other contexts where conversation turned to talk about work and ethnicity, batey dwellers would voice the opinion that it was the Dominican's character to take ample leisure and avoid hard work. People commonly invoke stereotypes of the "lazy *dominicano*" and the "hard-working *haitiano*" to explain why certain kinds of work are done by Haitians and rejected by Dominicans. I mentioned to a *viejo* who lived in Monte Coca that I thought it would improve the cane cutters' productivity if the company paid a separate contingent of workers to load the cane, leaving the cutters more time to cut. He responded that this would never work, because "the people [in the batey] are bad" and do not like to work hard. "To pay the Dominican more to do the same work that the Haitian does now would not give [good] results for the company," reasoned a local (ethnic Dominican) tractor driver and trade union representative, "because for every day the Dominican spent working, he would spend another day getting drunk on his pay." Even when such explanations verge on self-pornography, the stereotype of the lazy Dominican projects a certain kind of pride. It implies that the Dominican has not yet fallen as low as the Haitian, because he has the freedom of choice to reject a livelihood of heavy toil, all day, everyday, to the end of his days of life. He has the Haitian to do those jobs.

Haitians, too, seem never to tire of explaining the sugar industry's ethnic division of labor in terms that imply the superiority of their own group. As they see it, they do the heaviest and most poorly paid jobs not because they are poorer than the Dominicans but because the Dominicans are incapable of hard work, due to their innate laziness, feebleness, dishonesty and lack of pride. This opinion echoes a thought expressed by Trinidadian novelist Earl Lovelace, through the voice of the heroine of *The Wine of Astonishment*, that perhaps God made black people poor because they were the only ones strong enough to bear the burden of it. In a similar vein of thought, Haitians claim to be "the real bosses of the country" (*Se ayisyen ki chèf peyi-a*), because the entirety of the sugar industry depends on their labor and much of the wealth of the country depends, in turn, on sugar. *Viejos* speaking in Haitian Creole and out of earshot of any Dominicans, make it clear that they think Dominicans covet their hard-earned possessions and are rankled by the sight of a Haitian who owns something that the Dominicans lack and would like to have. That this perception has some foundation is confirmed by reports of household furnishings and livestock being pillaged after Haitian families have been deported or left the Dominican Republic in fear of being deported, as happened to tens of thousands of Haitian nationals in 1991 and smaller but steadier numbers of deportees since 1997.[6]

There is a grain of truth to these stereotypes. The braceros really are generally more tight-fisted with their money than the batey's permanent residents are and they are more willing to accept low wages for hard labor. Yet this is not just because they are poorer but because the goal that drives the braceros is to return to Haiti in short order with as much savings as they can amass. In common with millions of international migrants the world over, they do not care much what their hosts think of them. What matters is being able to return to their home country, their real home, with heads held high.

When batey residents observe the braceros' behavior and life circumstances and interpret these as evidence of the migrants' innate character, we see in action a tendency to confuse circumstantial constraint—poverty and the frugality of the guest worker—with free will. Monte Coca's residents see the braceros in their temporary role as seasonal laborers and mistakenly think they always live like they do in the batey or are perhaps even worse off in Haiti (otherwise, why would they cross into the Dominican Republic?). On the basis of this half-knowledge of the migrants' lives, Monte Cocans falsely reason that the braceros' seemingly infinite capacity to "do without" and willingness to accept unacceptable treatment at work reflect an essential aspect of the Haitian character. They thus fail to realize how their own evaluations of what it means to live decently converge with those voiced by the people whom they dismiss as indecent folk, as when both residents and braceros denounce mandatory labor on Sunday as an intolerable abuse.

WOMEN'S WORK

Batey gender ideology lays emphasis upon women's and children's dependence for survival on men's wages. The common wisdom is that women do not work in the cane fields at all but depend entirely upon their mates' earnings for subsistence. There is a kernel of truth to this, inasmuch as wage-labor opportunities on the sugar estates go overwhelmingly to men. Academic studies have backed this common wisdom with surveys revealing low levels of economic activity among batey women.[7]

My findings in Monte Coca partly contradict and partly support this picture, indicating higher levels of income-earning activity than have been found through surveys but confirming that women's incomes are mostly lower than men's. Most women (55 percent, or 101 of 184 females 15 and older) in Monte Coca do earn money and many work occasionally in the cane fields. I have never seen a woman cutting cane alone but I have seen Haitian and Haitian-Dominican women cutting cane in the company of their husbands or grown sons and even more often helping their menfolk loading piles of cane onto ox-carts to be hauled from the fields. The participation of women and children in planting and weeding cane fields is recognized by the sugar company in the form of wage rates lower than what men are paid to do these tasks. As a general rule, it would therefore be more accurate to say that women, in spite of residing in large numbers on the sugar estates, do much less work in the cane fields than men do but contribute to household incomes through petty commerce and domestic service.

Of the women who live in Monte Coca, the vast majority were born there or arrived there of their own volition. But company bosses also pay recruiters to bring Haitian women to the batey. These women have always entered the country entirely via unofficial channels; hence, their numbers are impossible to ascertain. Data from my genealogically based migration history census of two rural districts in southeastern Haiti (Martínez 1995: 80) suggest that about one of every ten emigrants to the Dominican Republic is a woman, which would add up to tens of thousands of women in the entire migrant and returnee population. Haitian-Dominican rights activists have told me that a certain number of women would even tag along, unrecorded, with groups of men entering via the bilateral guest worker program (suspended after President Jean-Claude Duvalier fled Haiti in 1986), which was officially restricted to men. More women still have crossed the border in small groups of undocumented entrants, at times comprised entirely of women but usually including men. When led by experienced migrants, who "know how to talk to" (and presumably bribe) the authorities whom they encounter along the way, these groups have often succeeded in traveling unmolested to their desired places of destination. Others, before 1997, were relocated involuntarily to state-owned sugar estates after either turning themselves in to the Dominican authorities at border garrisons or being arrested by soldiers or police at checkpoints further inside the Dominican Republic. Women have also joined large groups of laborers brought from villages in Haiti by Haitian recruiters (*buscones*), who generally work for a particular cane grower on the Dominican side. Today, the more flagrant coercive forms of recruitment have been abandoned but company bosses still pay the *buscones* the same fee per head for a woman as for a man, and issue each new arrival, whether man or woman, a food ration and a thin foam mattress on which to sleep.

The reason the company pays for women to be brought to its estates when it will not give them employment in the cane fields is, in a word, "control"—not over the women but over the braceros. Contrary to the image propagated by international human rights monitors (e.g., Americas Watch 1990; Plant 1987), the sugar estates have not been at any recent point in time and are certainly not today at all "like concentration camps." Even at times when the main roads are being kept under surveillance for departing braceros, the Consuelo estate is fairly easy to leave by walking out through any of the hundreds of alleys that crisscross the cane fields. Sugarcane growers not only think it inevitable that the braceros will change residence; they actively promote this mobility, by sending out agents to recruit Haitian laborers surreptitiously, even from other CEA estates, with tales of the good cane and high times to be had in the batey where they come from. Recognizing also that it would be absurdly expensive to maintain continuous surveillance over each bracero for the duration of the harvest, company bosses think women are one of the "carrots" that attracts braceros to their bateyes and then keeps them in place. As one of Monte Coca's top bosses once told me, "A batey without women will soon be a batey without men." Women's labor is crucial to the maintenance of a functioning social system in the bateyes, but this is not at all what this man was talking about. The many contributions that batey women make to their communities are more or less unappreciated or taken for granted by everyone except perhaps by the women themselves. Rather, the general opinion among men in the batey and people in Dominican society at large is that women live on the sugar estates for only one reason, to satisfy men's sexual desire.[8]

The one fundamentally important difference in how the company treats women versus men is that newly arrived Haitian women are not given living quarters of their own but must share rooms with people already living in the batey. A woman who has just arrived from Haiti for the first time must either stay with any friends, relatives or fellow villagers she might find in the batey or take up union with a man just to get a roof over her head. A number of women whom I have interviewed avoided having to become a total stranger's temporary wife, by making their first voyage with experienced migrants who guided them to the batey where they resided in the Dominican Republic and gave them shelter there. Those new arrivals who are not taken in by a host family are effectively forced by company policy to comply with the company bosses' preconceived roles for women in the bateyes, as prostitutes or cane workers' wives.

A handful of Haitian-Dominican men in Monte Coca have become particularly notorious accomplices to this traffic in women, by making special trips to Haiti to recruit prostitutes for the batey's brothel. A handful of women enter Monte Coca through this channel each year. Like the braceros, they arrive with the hope of returning soon to Haiti and many do leave the batey after the harvest is done, though a few have stayed for years. Like the braceros, these women do work that is dangerous (through exposure to violence and sexually transmitted diseases) and is despised by batey residents (openly entertaining paid sexual relations with men). As if in unspoken recognition of these parallels between the male and female seasonal recruits, the prostitutes' dwellings are shrunken imitations of the company barracks: a dozen small rooms, constructed in straight lines, out of cardboard, palm bark, cast-off pieces of wood and flattened metal cans (Figure 5-1). The bar's owners, a Haitian-Dominican couple, pay the recruiter a flat fee for each woman he brings to the batey. The same man who recruits the women in Haiti will generally also profit by renting them rooms. Each woman must also pay a steady fee to the owners of the bar but is otherwise free to keep her earnings and use these as she sees fit.

The complicity of Monte Coca's men in the sexual exploitation of Haitian women goes well beyond this. In the hours following the arrival of each new truckload of workers from Haiti, *viejos* from Monte Coca and various surrounding bateyes rub shoulders with the area's most renowned thieves, drunkards and good-for-nothings of all ethnicities as these men circulate around the braceros' barracks, to check out any women in the group. Seeing the hunger in the *viejos'* eyes on these occasions, I felt pity tinged by morbid speculation that it might be moments like this that these men lived for: preying upon women even hungrier and more desperate than they are might well be one of the few sources of satisfaction left in their lives. Haitian-Dominican women's rights activist, Solange Pierre, recalls seeing

Figure 5-1. The prostitutes' quarters at La Yagüita.

similar scenes each year, when she was growing up on a sugar plantation in the Dominican Republic's Cibao Valley:

> For example, in the batey where I was born and raised, a head batey on the old Ingenio Catarey, ... in the corral ... they would unload seven or eight trucks—the famous "Catareys," old flatbed Mercedes Benzes, that was the mode of transport!—there, four, six, even eight trucks would unload an enormous quantity [of people]. And then, after the boss and the authorities of the place picked their women, then ... the *viejos* would come by to pick among the ones who were left there to live with them. Many of those women, besides serving the guy, [he] automatically became their pimp.[9]

Saddening as this is, it is nothing compared to the culpability of various Dominican officials. It is unquestionably a violation of international human rights covenants when company bosses and other government authorities lead the way, by paying for this traffic in women and taking first pick among its victims. And, in years past, when the Dominican military organized round-ups of undocumented Haitians for involuntary relocation to the state-owned sugar estates, the immigrant women were in danger of sexual violence at every point in their journey from the frontier.[10]

In the country's more than 100 rural bateyes, the harassment not only continues but, worse, is commonly extended to the immigrants' Dominican-born daughters. As Solange Pierre says,

> We are a four-times-exploited group of women, for being Haitian emigrants or the descendants of Haitians, [for being] almost totally illiterate, [for being] black and [being] from the batey. But not only have we been victimized by outsiders but also, even more harshly, have we been exploited by the very people of our very own communities, [where] the boss of the batey feels he is owner of the women. Some years ago, during the 12 years of Balaguer [Dominican president from 1966 to 1978], it was common to see that, once a cane worker—who earned 50 cents a day—had a daughter turn 12 or 13, there would inevitably be a kind of blackmail, be it from the *superintendente*, the *mayordomo*, the *jefe de campo* or the *administrador* [all top plantation bosses], whoever might be interested in the girl at that moment. There would be a type of quid pro quo, "You loan me your daughter to have sex with me whenever I want," or the other option was, "we fire you and kick you out of the batey."

Immigrants with no contacts outside the bateyes or money to relocate to a nearby town and pay rent had little choice but to submit to this exploitation or move to another batey or to a rural proletarian camp in a coffee, rice or citrus growing area, where they might well encounter the same type of mistreatment. If the parents succumbed to the pressure, the boss would set up the girl in a room of her own, provide her with a bed and a little money to cook, and might even ask her to entertain his friends as well. When she became pregnant or ceased to interest him, she would simply be left to fend for herself, surviving initially perhaps through sex work at the batey's bar.[11]

Today, prostitution, occasional and full time, is the biggest single source of independent income for women in Monte Coca and is by far the most common livelihood of single women. Trusted informants indicate that, including the women who work at La Yagüita, 26 percent (48 of 184) Monte Coca women 15 and over are known to make recourse to sex work.[12] The only other category of female income-generating activity that comes close to it is petty retail sales, involving 22 percent (40 of 184) of Monte Coca's women. Rates of involvement in prostitution seem to correlate clearly with ethnic group membership: 50 percent of Haitian women, 34 percent of Haitian-Dominican women, and 13 percent of ethnic Dominican women engage in sex work either full time or occasionally.

In the sugar bateyes, prostitution is not as stigmatized as it is elsewhere in the Dominican Republic, inasmuch as sex workers are not shunned by their families and are less subject to exploitation by pimps. It is not that prostitution is tolerated if done openly outside the brothel. Prostitution generally is referred to in disapproving terms, such as "earning money in the bad [thing]" (*ganando dinero en lo malo*). I found it impossible to get women to talk about their personal involvement (I think a woman researcher with my level of local rapport and fluency in Spanish and Haitian Creole could easily elicit testimony about participation in sex work). When women broached the topic in my interviews, it was typically shrouded in euphemisms.

"My friends give me money, understand?" was how one woman termed it, looking me directly in the eye with raised eyebrows for just a second, as if to ask, "Can you blame me?" then casting her gaze downward at the floor. Another said, "If you are a woman, whether by the right hand or by the left (i.e., by hook or by crook), you get by." The euphemistic mode of reference reflects the fact that the sexual double standard is alive and well: women, not men, are regarded as culpable for engaging in extramarital sex. Sex work is therefore not so much condoned as tactfully ignored if it is done on the quiet and understood to be done chiefly to provide better for the children, under the extenuating economic circumstances of a disruption in household income or the chronic absence of a male wage earner. The women who are "in the life" and sell their sexual favors openly in the brothel, on the other hand, are spoken of with contempt. It seems an overstatement to say that prostitution is an "honorable alternative," as does the author of a batey development project pilot study cited by Gina Gallardo (2001: 74, my translation), but the justification offered for this characterization is entirely in keeping with my observations: "surviving is an honorable option, because no one has the right to opt for death when another road is possible."

For many in Monte Coca, therefore, maintaining a reputation as a "decent woman" and "good neighbor" depends more on keeping up appearances than absolute virtue. Being treated with respect by one's neighbors hinges on preserving an image of sexual propriety within the confines of the batey and especially within the home. "Creating a scandal" by carousing wildly *next door* would generate much stronger disapproval than any amount of misbehavior conducted out of the sight and hearing of the neighbors. The measures taken to preserve an image of propriety while engaging in sex work are numerous. A small number of Monte Coca women have discreetly "traveled" or "taken trips," working as prostitutes, it is rumored, in neighboring cities and even other Caribbean islands. Other women are known to visit nearby bateyes to engage in sex work, under the pretext of visiting friends or family. Others still arrange to meet men in rooms owned by their pimps or even in the cane fields. Restricting themselves to a steady clientele and arranging rendezvous through their pimps (cane workers who do not take a cut of their women' earnings but can demand sexual intercourse from them free of charge) are other means by which women may keep their involvement in sex work quiet. These women are objects of gossip. By contrast, a woman would be shunned if she were observed shutting herself into her home with a man who is not her husband or if she started keeping hours at La Yagüita.

In sum, the opinion of many in the batey seems to be that sex work is improper but has its justification—dire poverty and the need to feed and clothe the children—and its place—it must be done outside the conjugal household, if a woman is to receive the courtesy due a "good neighbor" and a "decent woman." Other kinds of behavior in and around the home can and more often do lead neighbors to label a family "indecent people" (*gente indecente*)—for example, frequent loud quarreling or domestic violence, slovenly housekeeping or improper disposal of household waste. All these underscore the primacy of the home environment as a nonverbal medium for the communication and evaluation of moral reputation. The batey's brothel is the socio-spatial antithesis of the proper domestic environment: the brothel is a place of "scandal" and "vice." No decent woman would set foot there. Even though there are few limits on women's movements and occupations outside the home, the brothel's status as a "no-go" area for decent women confirms the existence of a sexual double standard, in which a woman's public behavior much more than her man's is understood to be the index of her family's moral decency.

Contrasting with the bateyes of the American-owned estate at La Romana, where no single woman not employed by the company is allowed to keep a room for herself and her children, a woman who has lived in a CEA batey for several months may obtain a room of her own, in exchange for the payment of a small gratuity to the local company police officer (*guardacampestre*). Unlike the situation in La Romana, the breakup of a conjugal union in Monte Coca therefore does not force a woman to seek a new mate immediately just to keep a roof over her head. An unethical *guardacampestre* may, however, seize this situation as yet another opportunity to obtain a sexual favor. The contradiction therein characterizes many aspects of life in Monte Coca: the workers and their families are victims of the neglect and corruption that characterize the day-to-day administration of the batey but they are often exploited in a highly personalistic rather than a rational, bureaucratic or rigid, *apartheid*-like manner, and in small ways they can also make the system work in their favor.

In 2002, I organized a series of life history interviews with Haitian and Haitian-Dominican women in bateyes in three different regions of the Dominican Republic. Through these interviews, I sought to elicit first-hand testimony of abuses against women committed by company bosses or government officials. I recruited female interviewers, thinking that women interviewees would speak more freely with other women about "shameful" experiences, such as sexual exploitation, but even so the interviews failed to bring forward the kind of information I was seeking. I suspect that a number of the interviewees had experienced or witnessed such abuses but chose not to share their knowledge of misdeeds by the local men in power. Even under assurances of anonymity, it is understandable that an impoverished Haitian woman might be reluctant to say anything that could implicate Dominicans in criminal actions, at the request of interviewers with whom they had no previous acquaintance. The lack of trust was probably compounded by the lead interviewer being a Dominican woman who spoke no Creole.

It is also likely that the worst abuses have diminished in recent years, as the company's grip weakened over the cane workers and their families. During the 1990s, international human rights pressure on the Dominican government made itself felt in the bateyes, not through specific reforms so much as a general sense that company bosses should curtail the worst excesses. More livelihood spaces have opened up for Haitians outside the sugar industry, particularly in construction, maintenance work, domestic labor and petty commerce in urban areas and tourist resorts, diminishing the number of Haitian and Haitian-Dominican families who can easily be coerced into accepting degrading treatment under pain of losing their homes and livelihoods. Of lesser immediate effect but holding out greater hope in the future, many more Haitians and Haitian-Dominicans now know that they can find support among Haitian-Dominican rights organizations and the Haitian consulates, the Haitian government's having become more involved in advocating for immigrants' rights after Jean-Bertrand Aristide's return to the presidency in 2000.

One type of response was elicited repeatedly in the interviews of 2002, and bears importantly on both the possible reasons for the interviewees' seeming reticence and my larger concern with the ways in which lines are drawn between "decent" and "indecent" women. A handful of the women interviewees seemed annoyed even to be asked whether they had ever experienced or witnessed sexual abuses, and responded to this question by suggesting that sexual violence and exploitation only happen to "bad women." The following exchange was recorded in an interview conducted in Batey Bermejo, Ingenio Haina, División Guanuma:

> Q.: For how many years did you say you have lived in the batey?
> A.: I came here at the age of seven and now I am 42 years old.
> Q.: During all that time, has anything ever happened here in the batey to you in particular, which you could say perhaps was an abuse that had been committed against you, by someone in the batey?
> A. [rapidly and with some agitation]: No, because I am a person who is not like that. I am not in the middle, wandering in the middle. I don't drink. I, nothing. Sitting here at home! So I can't find myself in a problem. A person who is like that does not run into problems, almost. No![13]

During my 1985–86 fieldwork, I was shocked to hear once that a 14-year-old Haitian girl in Monte Coca was flogged by her mother in punishment for objecting when the batey's *guardacampestre* placed his hand on her waist, which seemed to me appropriate boundary-maintaining behavior for a girl concerned with keeping her virtue. That even survivors of rape can be judged culpable for the wrong done to them is suggested by the example of one conjugal union that broke up in Monte Coca when the girl revealed to her partner that she was not, as he thought, a virgin but had once been raped by a man who forced himself upon her as she walked in an alley between some cane fields. While some of my neighbors expressed sympathy for her, and others, for him, no one voiced any doubts that in principle he had the right to send her back to her parents. I happened to be present when a woman neighbor confronted the man and told him he should take the girl back. He insisted he was right to have broken up with her because she had lied to him and now he had no way of knowing "how many men have passed through her."

The 2002 interviews with Haitian and Haitian-Dominican women did yield an out-pouring of accounts of domestic violence. Almost all of the 20 interviewees told of one or more recent incidents of wife beating or child abuse they had seen or heard of in their communities. All agreed that many men beat their wives in the bateyes. It is impossible to determine with any certainty whether the incidence of spouse and child abuse has increased. I certainly heard of many instances of violence in the family during my year-long stay in Monte Coca in 1985–86. Yet other observers concur that there has been a sharp upswing in domestic violence with the hard times brought by the precipitous decline in the CEA's sugar production during the 1990s and the subsequent quasi-privatization of the state's sugar plantations.[14]

None of this necessarily indicates that overall rates of sexual violence have diminished, just that these wrongs seem to be less often taking the form of a flagrant abuse of power by a company official. Worsened poverty in the bateyes may, to the contrary, be obligating more women to engage in survival sex and to put up with abusive domestic situations, in order to stave off the threat of starvation. Some batey women might not regard being obligated to exchange sex for food and shelter as an "abuse." Yet, as certainly and remorselessly as the most impudent figure of authority ever could, poverty and economic uncertainty are still forcing women to compromise their basic freedom of control over their sexuality. Though there may be room to argue about degrees of culpability, coercion is coercion, whether it be exerted physically, psychologically or economically.

Nor has the opening up of the plantations to greater outside oversight brought entirely positive consequences either. With the recent lease of the CEA's estates to private corporations, for example, the size and power of the sugar company's private police force have declined, and contingents of the Dominican National Police are now stationed for the first time in a few rural bateyes. Unfortunately, reliable sources indicate that certain police officers have seen their placement in these remote communities as an opportunity to exploit and prey upon their vulnerable hosts, with greater impunity than the *guardacampestres* ever did (who, after all, maintained their family residences in the bateyes and hence were more controllable by locals via gossip, shunning, witchcraft, and vandalism of their personal property). This is but one outcome, of limited relevance, but I think it is illustrative of the dangers of introducing apparently liberating reforms with total disregard for the underlying social and economic subordination of the victimized population. Without accompanying social and economic uplift, purely legalistic reforms may simply eventuate in abuses of authority being shifted from one group of officials to another.

Another example of the inter-connectedness of political/civil rights with economic, social and cultural rights may be observed in the negative health consequences of women's subordination. Solange Pierre and her co-workers in the Haitian-Dominican women's rights advocacy group, *Movimiento de Mujeres Domínico-Haitianas* (MUDHA), have had ample opportunity to gauge the health effects of poverty, sexual exploitation, and spouse abuse, as they have sought to organize batey women to demand their own rights. On the basis of MUDHA's research and experience, she remarks, "The mortality rate [among batey women], resulting as much from disease as from violence, is much higher [than in the population at large]. The incidence of prostitution among adolescents, after having been used by the bosses and then abandoned, and the rate of adolescent motherhood is extraordinary. All those problems were always there [among] the women of the bateyes, always were worse and still are worse than the situation of the men." A recent epidemiological study finds that the rate of HIV infection is significantly higher in the bateyes than in the immigrants' rural Haitian places of origin, suggesting that it is the immigrants and not the host population who are coming under increased risk of STD infection as a result of immigration from Haiti (Brewer et al. 1998).

A Woman's Place

One overarching theme of this book is that, in spite of living in alienating and dispiriting circumstances, few people in Monte Coca seem alienated or without hope. If this is so, it is chiefly women's doing and especially an outcome of women's particular involvement with raising offspring and building ties of reciprocity with neighbors and co-religionists.

Even though the incidence is high, most women in Monte Coca do not engage in sex work but contribute to their households' reproduction through other forms of paid work as well as their unpaid domestic labor. Women's primary commitment to childcare and keeping house does not prevent them from contributing to household incomes through a range of petty commercial activities. Some women walk out to the cane fields to fry dough and sell home-baked bread, cooked spaghetti, or chilled, sweetened drinks to the men working there. Even these women do the greater part of the preparation work at home. Other petty income-generating activities, such as making occasional sales from a wayside stand or family store, do not take women away from the home at all, except for the days they go into town to restock, nor do these tasks usually distract them for long from tending to children, cooking and other household chores. A second-hand refrigerator may be bought mainly as a domestic convenience but it can also pay back a part of its purchase and running cost through the sale of bottled water, soft drinks and home-made flavored ices. These commercial activities also reinforce women's identification with the home in that they are virtually all extensions of women's unpaid domestic tasks. Cooking and laundry are obvious examples but even running a family shop is in a sense the opposite side of the same coin as the responsibility for managing their households' consumption budgets.

Any consideration of the sources from which the immigrants from Haiti draw hope would be incomplete without mentioning the ultimate fruit of their struggle to make the batey a more family friendly environment: the new generations of people brought into adulthood in the batey. In my earlier book on the circulation of men and women from rural Haiti to the sugar plantations of the Dominican Republic, I conclude that the women, much more often than the men, leave home in response to highly adverse and at times desperate social and economic circumstances. The women have less land or other income-generating resources to return to in Haiti than the men, and in some cases they have more to run away from, in the form of abusive parental or conjugal relationships or attacks perpetrated against them via witchcraft. It is partly for this reason that women are more likely than men to settle and raise a family on the Dominican side. Of the 21 female interviewees in my sample who had spent more than one year in the Dominican Republic, *all* had either borne or adopted a child there (Martínez 1995: 128).

These children, more than anything else, are the source of hope for a better future for the men and women of Monte Coca, especially among the Haitians, who are disproportionately poorer and face discrimination in the society at large. Examining the extended family of one Haitian woman, Charitable Charles, confirms that even in the material poverty of a batey, it is not necessarily unrealistic to pin at least modest hopes for respect, emotional support and freedom from dire want on one's progeny. Charitable lived in Monte Coca for almost 65 years, from her arrival in the Dominican Republic from Haiti sometime in the late 1920s until her death there in 1992. In 1986, when I did a census of Monte Coca's households, she was widowed and had recently lost a brother in a work accident but had five living children, all of whom were born in Monte Coca and still resided close at hand, one son living in the very same barracks room where he was born. She counted twenty-one grandchildren, between seven months and twenty-one years, and four great-grandchildren, ages one through eight.

Not only did Charitable enjoy the social benefits of a large extended family but her children and grandchildren gained small economic advances over her generation. Her children had all had hard lives, including involvement in prostitution by the three daughters. Yet her sons and daughters' husbands had all moved out of work in the cane to take up less physically debilitating and marginally better-paying jobs: two were lower-level foremen, and one each was a night watchman, railroad operator, and mechanic. One son gained added income by renting out accommodations to the prostitutes at Monte Coca's brothel, including at least one woman who bore children for him. These children and grandchildren provided Charitable not only with material security in her final years. A fervent believer in the ancestral spirits of Haitian vodou, Charitable could also feel reassured knowing that she had many descendants to remember her and feed her soul after death. Unlike so many single men from Haiti who have died without progeny in Monte Coca, she would not become a wandering, hungry soul without anyone in this world to serve her spirit. Charitable Charles's extended family was unusually large and closely gathered. Yet her story and those of a handful of other elderly Haitian women in Monte Coca, including two whose stories I summarize in my earlier book (ibid.: 128–30), confirm the wisdom of the Haitian aphorism, "Children are wealth" (*Pitit se richès*).

Notes

1. In my census of Monte Coca's permanent residents in March 1986, 10 percent (10 of 97) of ethnic Dominican men and 8 percent of Haitian-Dominican men (5 of 59) listed cane cutter among their occupations.

2. Of the conjugal unions that I recorded in my census of Monte Coca in March 1986, 18 percent (20 of 111) paired a person of Haitian ethnicity with an ethnic Dominican, with no apparent bias shown toward or against women of Haitian ancestry (nine of whom were in union with an ethnic Dominican man). Looking at Table 5.3, there is nonetheless a notable tendency for "like to marry like," Haitians tending to form unions with Haitians, and Dominicans with Dominicans, only Haitian-Dominicans showing a slight preponderance of unions with the other two groups.

3. Howard 2001: 35; Murphy 1991: 139–40; Newton 1980: 94. Some social researchers sustain the opposite or say there is no clear positive correlation between greater tolerance for Haitians and familiarity with them. David Howard (2001: 39) cites one social scientific study indicating that expression of anti-Haitian feeling neither diminishes nor increases with frequency of contact with Haitian immigrants. Carlos Dore Cabral (1995) reports survey data supporting the idea that lower-class Dominicans are more anti-Haitian than upper-class Dominicans.

4. The vowels in the Haitian Creole orthography that I use in this book are pronounced approximately as in French. The "n" in "an" and "on" is silent, these digraphs indicating nasalized "a" and "o" sounds.

5. In the mid-1980s, even some Monte Coca boys as young as nine or ten would earn pocket money on occasion by banding together to cut cane during school rest days (since the 1990s child labor has been restricted, in response to international human rights pressure). Monte Coca's top boss, Don Ricardo, claimed with evident pride to have at one point or another done every type of field labor there was to do on the plantation, including cutting cane.

6. Author's interview with Antonio Pol Emil, Director General, Cento Cultural Domínico-Haitian, 4 July 1997.

7. Báez Evertsz 1986: 311; Bobea and Guzmán C. 1985: 126; Moya Pons et al. 1986: 443. Jansen and Millán 1991: 98 is an exception.

8. Though erroneous, word that women only go to the Dominican sugar estates to engage in sex work seems to have reached rural Haiti, too, contributing to the Dominican Republic's atrocious reputation in the major migrant source areas of southeastern Haiti. Of 29 migrant women whose life histories I have recorded on either side of the border, *none* ever left her conjugal partner behind in Haiti, but she either traveled after having broken up with her mate or to rejoin a conjugal partner already in the Dominican Republic. As I conjecture in my earlier book on migration to and from the sugar estates, "It is probably a rare man who would accept his wife emigrating on her own to the Dominican Republic, knowing the strong chance that she will take a new man there" (Martínez 1995: 124).

9. My interview with Solange Pierre, 2 July 1999, Santo Domingo, Dominican Republic, my translation.

10. As military officers at the frontier gathered together enough Haitians to fill an order from one of the sugar estates, the immigrants would be held for days or even weeks at army outposts or holding pens. During this time any woman who caught a soldier's eye might stand in danger of being raped. Similarly, those workers who were brought in under the old bilateral guest worker program were transported first to bateyes where they would be held until being assigned to a particular plantation, a step called the "*concentración de braceros*" (bracero round-up). Based on an interview with residents of Batey 9 on the Ingenio Barahona, where the *concentración* took place, I found that it is common knowledge there that company bosses would pick out the most beautiful women to be their own, at times even separating them from husbands with whom they had traveled from Haiti. If her mate dared raise a finger to resist, he would be beaten up and handed over to the police for a couple of weeks of "conditioning." Beaten, jailed, his woman taken who knows where, he would emerge at best an embittered man, at worst gone mad.

11. Interview with Solange Pierre, 2 July 1999.

12. A MUDHA pilot survey in Batey Palmarejo, located on the outskirts of the Dominican capital city, found that almost two-fifths of the women who live there are sex workers (Gallardo 2001: 74).

13. Interview conducted by Ana Jiménez, 15 September 2002.

14. FLACSO 2002: 43; author's interview with staff of the *Movimiento de Mujeres Domínico-Haitianas*, Santo Domingo, 22 May 2002.

6

Places and Flows

> Does it make sense to speak of a "reading" of space? Yes and no....
> That space signifies is incontestable. But what it signifies is dos and
> don'ts—and this brings us back to power. Power's message is invariably confused—deliberately so; dissimulation is necessarily a part of
> any message from power. Thus space indeed "speaks"—but it does not
> tell all. Above all, it prohibits.
>
> —Lefebvre 1991: 142

In the many articles and books that offer "reflections on fieldwork" it is commonly observed that we ethnographers can rarely, if ever, adequately repay the debt we incur to the people whom we study in the field. Our gestures of gratitude are nearly always inadequate to reciprocate what we gain from ethnography—scholarly credentials, reputation, and career. Just as importantly, our attempts to say thanks often as not end up generating lasting lessons for us but only temporary recompense for our hosts. Richard Lee (2000[1969]) brings this point home in his essay, assigned in many undergraduate introductory courses in anthropology, "Eating Christmas in the Kalahari." Lee recounts how, once, as a token of goodwill, he gave a group of !Kung hunter-gatherers with whom he was doing fieldwork an ox to slaughter at Christmas. Expecting gratitude, he was shocked when the !Kung complained about having to make do with such a scrawny "bag of bones." Only later did Lee learn, to his relief, that the !Kung belittle all gifts: ridiculing gifts is their way of diminishing the expected return and of enforcing humility on those who would use gifts to raise their own status in the group. One other point that I draw from "Eating Christmas in the Kalahari" is that, for an ethnographer, *every* human interaction in which he engages in the field has the potential to yield information and insight, even when he is not consciously gathering information. A good deal of the distinctiveness and value of ethnography lies in the field worker's more or less continuous awareness of the goings-on around him and his openness to taking it all in as potentially important information. We ethnographers may even gain knowledge as we think we are "paying back" part of our debt to our hosts in the field.

I learned a similar lesson during my dissertation fieldwork in Monte Coca. From my earliest days there, people there sought to include me within the circuits of reciprocal exchange of gifts and favors—all on a minute scale of pecuniary value—through which they cement friendships and neighborly ties among themselves. I grew to be unsurprised, if not less grateful, each time a plateful of cooked food was delivered to my door, a fresh egg or fruit was given to me during my rounds of the batey, or when I returned in the evening to find that a neighbor had swept the three square meters or so of my porch in my absence. I quickly learned to suppress my very *yanqui* attitude of self-reliance, to make reciprocating these kindnesses a part of my daily routine.

Among the exchanges that linked me with my neighbors in Monte Coca, perhaps the one they valued most was the photographs I took of them. Our explicit understanding was that every one of my neighbors who permitted me to photograph them in their tattered everyday clothes would receive one "pretty" photograph for them to keep. Of course, it was with a measure of selfish calculation that I offered to take these portraits, sensing that these gifts would help ingratiate me with my hosts as well as sweeten the pill of my asking to take candid photographs of them, often at the most unexpected times. Yet most people in Monte Coca probably found my offer generous. Many seemed not only willing but impatient to be photographed. My fame as a photographer soon outstripped everything else I was doing in the field. I knew this for sure when, one hot afternoon, I returned to Monte Coca after an absence of several days and the very first words, not spoken but *shouted* to me by an adolescent boy across an open field, were, "¡Americano, tírame una foto!" I recounted this event to my neighbors and joked that my first name had become "*Americano*," and my surname, "Take me a picture," but most did not seem to find the event either extraordinary or humorous. I kept to myself the thought that my neighbors might really only be interested in me for the goods and favors they might get from me.

Looking back, the only thing I regret is my failure to realize the entire significance and potential of these portrait photos as a source of information at the time of my fieldwork. For, precisely when I felt most certain that I was doing *them* a favor, by taking their portraits, people in Monte Coca were bestowing on me a much rarer gift. Generally, the only instructions I gave them were to look at the camera when it was time to snap the shutter. I left it up to them to decide where and with whom to pose and what things they wanted in the picture. When *they* chose how they would be seen in the picture frame, they enacted a kind of performance before my eyes. Each time they hurriedly gathered people and objects for a portrait and searched for the right spot in which to pose, my neighbors unknowingly offered me a glimpse at an elusive image. They showed me not what they looked like every day but how they would hope to be seen, had fate not consigned them to lives of hard physical labor, and they put on display not their material deprivation but the things of which they were proudest. So it is these portraits, not the candid shots of Monte Coca residents going about their daily business, that say the most to me now. In retrospect, I realize that, instead of begrudging my neighbors' interest in my services as a photographer, I should have taken *more* of these portraits. I should also have been more systematic in eliciting commentary on the photos, by asking my neighbors whether they found their pictures pretty or not, and why.

As it was, I did gradually see through my blind assumption that I was thoroughly in control of the production of field data, to discern by degrees the "coded messages" contained in these portrait photos. For example, the remodeled or added-on rooms, interior decorations and furnishings, and ornamental shrubbery with which my neighbors took delight in posing conveyed the message that I should not only pay attention to the means by which these people were being exploited by the sugar company but take interest in the effort they were expending to make their cramped, dilapidated company barracks into a more decent place to live and raise a family. Unbeknownst to either of us, in the act of posing for a "pretty picture," they were teaching me a lesson in anthropology and in living, putting me even more deeply in their debt.

In this way and through numerous other subtle but insistent gestures and remarks, my neighbors in Monte Coca did not *let* me focus solely on what I had come to study and neglect what were for them equally important issues. Even though I first came to Monte Coca to examine not place or habitation but the flow of migrants between the batey and home places in rural Haiti, I came to feel early on in my fieldwork that I should not—indeed, could not—consign Monte Coca's permanent residents to the status of an immobile backdrop on which to trace the comings and goings of the men and women from Haiti. In saying this, I do not mean to exaggerate the quality or intensity of my relationships with the people there. Anyone who visits Monte Coca can see that the living conditions cry out for improvement, and realize on this basis that it is of importance to study how batey residents modify their living environment to make it conform better to their standards of material and moral decency. Even passing travelers find it impossible to ignore the signs of material deprivation all around. And, once they take a moment to step into a residence and speak to its inhabitants, conversation inevitably turns toward the broken-down state of the workers' barracks and other problems with the batey's infrastructure and services. Yet that I acted on the realization that their way of inhabiting the material world was worthy of systematic study can be credited both to the value that my graduate school teachers had taught me to place on holistic ethnography and to my neighbors' spoken and unspoken signals of encouragement to inquire into this aspect of their lives.

I move from macro- to micro-frames of analysis over the course of this chapter. I begin with a fairly large-scale spatial analysis of the Consuelo estate, to flesh out the context in which Monte Coca's residents strive to make the batey generally more livable and more suitable particularly for raising children. Over the course of the chapter, my attention gradually narrows to ever smaller spaces and more particular concerns.

A Space of Flows

This chapter is largely devoted to a discussion of place but it is appropriate to consider first the economic flows that are Monte Coca's reason for being. Without a detailed look at the functions that the batey was designed to facilitate, my picture of what forces its residents are struggling against as they try to re-shape their material surroundings would be incomplete.

The Ingenio Consuelo, the sugar plantation on which Monte Coca is built, is a quintessential "deterritorialized" environment. Its dynamics "rely on, and are shaped by, activities and forces that are decidedly nonlocal" (Watts 1992: 11). None of its land belongs to the people who inhabit it. And its functioning gives overwhelming emphasis toward commodity production rather than human reproduction. It is what Manuel Castells and Jeffrey Henderson (1987: 7) call a "space of flows." They theorize that a key spatial characteristic of late twentieth-century capitalist restructuring was "the tendency for a *space of flows*" to supersede the *"space of places."* Doubtless this is still a hallmark of the present era of global capitalism. Yet, historically, this may also be another way in which the Caribbean sugar plantation was modern before modernity or, more precisely, went ahead of Europe in the development of modernity. On sugar plantations, the "space of flows" has always superseded the "space of places." The plantation's dynamics have always relied "mainly on the connection of [its] population and activities to activities and decisions that go far beyond [local] boundaries" (ibid.: 7). Plantation space has always been organized not just to grow the sugar industry's raw material, sugarcane, but to facilitate the flow of cane from the fields to and through the mill. Its very reason for being has always been to generate a profitable flow of raw sugar to refiners overseas. And the human needs of its workers have always taken second place to profits.

In Monte Coca, a second dynamic, to which Castells and Henderson give equal emphasis, can also be seen almost literally taking root in reaction to the spatial dominance of flow. "While dominant interests may be losing their sense of place with regard to the development process," they (ibid.: 7) write, "'community' social relations continue to operate, for the most part, according to a local, place-oriented logic." "The new territorial dynamics," they conclude (which, to repeat, may not look so new to Caribbean eyes), "tend to be organized around the contradiction between placeless power and powerless places." If the dominant logic imposes a standardized space of flows, the defense of specific communities' interests "takes the form of irreducible local experience" (ibid.: 7). Living in the interstices of a space of flows confronts the residents of Monte Coca with challenges, which they seek to resolve by superimposing a human-oriented logic of places onto their living space and the surrounding land. The ensuing struggle for space and place is what this chapter is all about.

Mapped onto two dimensions, the ideal location for a sugar mill and refinery would be at or near the center of the fields that provide its raw material, sugarcane. The geographical footprint of the Consuelo estate deviates from this ideal in that the plantation's land has the shape of an elongated triangle, opening from south to north, with the mill situated near its far southern extreme (see figure 6-1). When Consuelo was consolidated into the CEA in 1966, cane that was formerly sent to Consuelo from land to the south was redirected to the Ingenio Porvenir, located on the outskirts of the port city of San Pedro de Macorís. This was done in order to expand production at Porvenir, the country's only refinery capable of making white sugar. Yet, even before this time, the owners of Consuelo had had limited success in acquiring or contracting cane from all of the surrounding property that they wanted, as they expanded the mill's output repeatedly from the 1880s through the 1940s. For example, a sugar mill owned by another private concern owned land and operated within the boundaries of the Consuelo estate for several decades. When this company went bankrupt it was bought by the West Indies Sugar Company, the Consuelo's parent corporation. The highly deteriorated outside shell of that mill still stands in the nearby Batey Las Pajas, its useful contents having long ago been scavenged. From the time when it was a mill town, Las Pajas retains the particularity of being the only rural batey in the Consuelo estate to have a detachment of the National Police quartered there.

Consuelo's less-than-ideal shape on the land heightens the challenge that geographical space poses to all large-scale sugarcane mills and refineries. Because sucrose can be borne out of the cane stalks only in the plant's juice, it is vital to transport the cane from the fields rapidly, so as to lose as little as possible of the water inside the cane stalks through evaporation. Cane from which the water has largely evaporated on route to the mill is just vegetation, usable as fuel or edible by livestock but worth little or nothing as a source of sucrose for the mill. To yield optimal amounts of sucrose, the raw sugarcane should be brought in, from fields as far as 40 kilometers away, within 24 hours of its being harvested, if possible, and at the limit in no more than three or four days. Consuelo's owners responded to this challenge as sugar industrialists have in many parts of the world, by building a network of railroad tracks and all-weather dirt roads with one purpose, to channel sugarcane efficiently from field to mill. Railways and roads finely dissect the company's land, and these transportation arteries are dotted at frequent intervals by the loading stations (*chuchos*) at which

98   *Chapter Six*

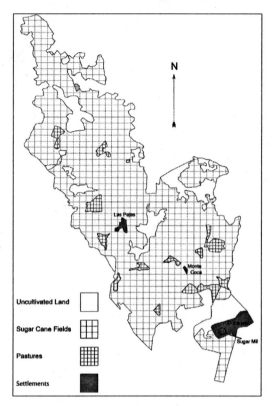

Figure 6-1. Map of the Ingenio Consuelo.

the harvested cane is transferred to trucks and train wagons for hauling to the mill (see figure 6-2).

By contrast, the productivity (and, in a piece-rate pay system, the earnings) of the cane workers seems to matter less to the company. During the harvest, cane cutters and cart drivers often complain that they must walk long distances to get to the fields where they have been assigned to work. The keepers of the company's oxen and horses voice similar complaints during the dead season, about the general lack and far-flung location of the pastures to which they must take their animals after the harvest season, when there are no longer any cane tops left to graze in the fields. Analysis of Consuelo's map provides evidence that the company has invested more in transporting its sugarcane efficiently than in economizing the time its agricultural laborers spend walking to and from the fields (figure 6-2). These disparities have a simple explanation: the productivity per ton of the raw sugarcane has historically been and continues to be of greater concern to the company than the productivity per hour of the workers whom it employs

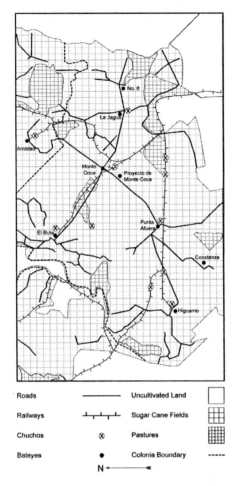

Figure 6-2. Map of the Colonia Esperanza, Ingenio Consuelo.

to cultivate and harvest the cane. Being comprised mostly of immigrants from Haiti, the agricultural labor is cheap and easy to recruit and employ in large numbers, and hence its productivity can be neglected at little cost to the company. Hiring Haitian nationals to do the heaviest agricultural labor, many of whom oscillate seasonally to homes on the other side of the border, has doubtless also enabled the sugarcane growers and sugar producers to escape political accountability for the human welfare and health consequences of low productivity and low pay for the industry's base workers. Without sugarcane arriving in processable quality to the mill, on the other hand, there would be no profit at all for the plantation's owners. This concern makes it economically rational to invest large sums in providing means to transport the cane rapidly while leaving the agricultural workers to trudge often long distances on foot.

I observed in chapter five that the formal organizational structure of the plantation is highly centralized and hierarchical; so, too, is its spatial organization. Monte Coca is "head" batey of the Colonia Esperanza. As such, it is home to the *colonia's* top administrators and is where certain administrative functions particular to the plantation's field operations are carried out, such as keeping track of pay stubs for each cane cutter and cart driver and preparing their pay packets semimonthly. Besides Monte Coca, the Colonia Esperanza has three smaller "satellite" bateyes. Authority radiates outward from the office of the head of agricultural operations in the mill town, to the *superintendente*, the top boss in each *colonia*, and downward from him, through a hierarchy of lower bosses and foremen, to the workers who live in the head batey and its satellites.

Management's power is reflected in the landscape. Unlike the typical Caribbean peasant community, in which huts and modest houses dot the landscape, human settlement on the Consuelo estate is highly nucleated. The company permits no isolated houses or independently owned buildings of any kind to stand in the surrounding cane fields, and it houses all of its agricultural workers in the densely settled bateyes. Monte Coca is located at a narrow gap in the sugarcane fields, largely contained within an elongated parallelogram formed by the intersection of two roads and two railway lines (figure 6-3). Profit seems clearly to have guided the company in deciding where Monte Coca would be built: the batey was built at a site from which little or no cane would be lost from production by housing people there. Both the site's dis-utilities for growing cane and its relative ease of human access make it a particularly suitable place to house workers. Being situated at an intersection in the railway and road network makes it a perfect place for locating a loading station, the point of transfer of the raw cane from the ox-carts that are loaded in the fields, to the trains and trucks in which the cane completes its journey to the mill. The constant coming and going of trucks, tractors and ox-carts to and from the loading station would make sugarcane cultivation difficult within much of the space that is occupied by Monte Coca. The site's transportation links, on the other hand, facilitate the coming and going of humans.

A wide all-weather road links Monte Coca to Consuelo and continues in a northwesterly direction before turning west in a broad arc and then running southwest to the neighboring mill town of Quisqueya. It was originally a paved road, built in 1957, when Dominican strongman, Rafael Trujillo bought Consuelo from its former U.S. corporate owners. Over the ensuing years, the road's surface deteriorated so badly that it was decided at a certain point simply to bulldoze off the pavement. The old road bed protrudes at points, making for a bumpy ride, but the road remains wide and well-drained, passable at all seasons except perhaps

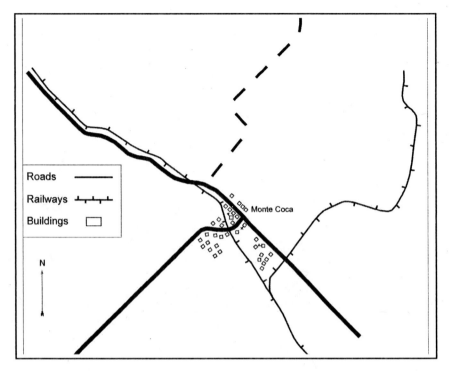

Figure 6-3. Map of the transportation network surrounding the Batey Monte Coca.

after a hurricane or other extraordinary rainfall. The road was probably built to enable Trujillo and his family members to get in and out of his new properties rapidly and hence, in safety (it may be recalled that he would only a few years later be shot dead in his own car on a highway a few miles west of Santo Domingo). Yet no one in Monte Coca can remember their ever having received a visit from "El Jefe." The road did have the immediate effect of facilitating the flow of sugarcane to the mill by truck, a mode of transportation that would ultimately supplant the railway as the plantation's primary means of hauling cane. The residents of Monte Coca refer to this road as "the highway" (*la carretera*) and call the narrower minor roads that branch off from it, "*carriles*," the same name that is given to the cart roads that run between the fields of cane. Heavy rain can turn these side roads into lagoons, at times difficult to traverse even by tractor. The improvements made by Trujillo to the main road also greatly facilitated the coming and going of people. Fee-charging pick-up trucks and sedans used to be the main means of transporting goods and people to Consuelo and to neighboring bateyes but four-wheel vehicles have today been largely replaced by *motoconchos,* motorcycles or scooters that carry passengers more promptly and cheaply. Once you arrive in Consuelo, it is easy to get a bus, taxi or motorbike to the nearest cities, southward to San Pedro de Macorís, or northward to Hato Mayor.

Sugarcane's dominance over the landscape is almost palpable in Monte Coca. The cane surrounds the batey so closely that at points the fully grown plants almost touch certain barracks. Insects, spiders, rats and snakes, which proliferate in the cane, often visit the batey's homes and by-ways. And, because the cane is highly flammable, a fire in any of the adjoining fields would almost certainly endanger lives and property. Little land in the batey's surroundings is left for any other purpose than growing cane. The subsistence gardens that are crammed into just about every unused plot of land in and around the batey stand in constant danger of being destroyed. During my twelve months of continuous residence in 1985–86, I heard only once of the company compensating a garden's "owner" for the value of destroyed crops. This happened when the *superintendente* decided there was a need to clear a fairly large space, in between two rows of barracks, of the two gardens that were planted there. In uncounted cases of accidental damage—e.g., when crops were smashed under the treads of a company tractor or killed by a drift of powerful herbicides from the neighboring cane fields—the *superintendente* claimed the company bore no responsibility for damage done to gardens planted in places where no one should have planted subsistence crops in the first place.

From the view of a plane flying above, the plantation appears to be a rationally planned, hierarchically organized space, a neat checkerboard of fields, veined with roads and railways. The balance of the evidence suggests that this is on aggregate an accurate impression. The evidence indicates equally that the priorities guiding Consuelo's spatial development have been skewed toward maximizing the company's profit by planting as much land as possible in sugarcane, with much less consideration being given to the workers' convenience, incomes, and well-being. It is as if the sugarcane plant were the real sovereign of this space, and had only grudgingly and out of absolute necessity permitted people in, restricting them to small, densely inhabited spaces, like Monte Coca. Other concerns, such as the loss in productivity incurred by the cane workers in the time that they spend walking to their places or work, have been recognized but often compromised in favor of King Cane. The design and lay-out of the plantation tacitly confirm that sugarcane and the profits it brings matter more on the plantation than human convenience and safety.

WALKING IN THE BATEY

Viewed at ground level, Monte Coca does not appear to be nearly so rationally laid out as the plantation network looks in reduced scale. The dilapidated state of its barracks and the profusion of food crops and trees that grow in many spots around the batey make it look like a pastiche of work camp, shantytown and peasant village. Yet it would not be accurate to say that the batey has developed haphazardly, for every building there has been erected with the permission of the local company bosses. The workers' barracks have by and large been built in tightly concentrated sections of the batey and in highly regular architectural style. Where any paint can still be discerned on their termite-eaten walls, it is usually a standard drab yellow, pink or green. All the barracks are elongated rectangles, containing one or two rows of single rooms. Each room has its own single-leaf door opening to the exterior and usually also one small, unscreened window, shut with a door-like hinged shutter. In barracks that contain only one row of rooms, all the doors and windows open only to one side; the back wall is completely closed and the structure is topped with a simple slanted metal roof. Other barracks sandwich together two rows of rooms, back to back, partitioned with a closed interior wall running the length of the barrack's middle.

These regularities in lay-out and construction reflect the fact that the barracks were built under management direction rather than leaving it to the workers to build their accommodations wherever and in whatever style they would prefer. Yet, even though the batey is a place where everything very much resembles everything else, few of the barracks are *exactly* identical. Only among the cement-block barracks built subsequent to Trujillo's acquisition of the estate (in 1957) is any barrack built exactly like the one next to it. Among the older, wooden barracks, the details of construction vary, in some instances significantly. As of January 1986, 19 of 238 (8 percent) of Monte Coca households inhabited dwellings with dirt floors, while 15 (6 percent) had wooden floors, and most (204, or 86 percent) were built up on a cement footing. The height of the barracks and their doorways vary, and in some barracks the doors are divided into upper and lower sections, each of which can be opened separately, while in others, the doors are one undivided leaf. Some barracks are quite long, with as many as 24 rooms, while others have only three or four rooms. Sometimes the barracks stand slightly out of line or at odd angles with their neighboring structures. Older residents explain that the barracks were not all built at the same time but went up in piecemeal fashion over the years. Typically, a new barracks would be built whenever too many rooms had been taken up by permanent residents, making it difficult to accommodate the seasonal migrants. Variations in construction have also been introduced as the company refurbished barracks. No barracks has been refurbished in Monte Coca since the early 1980s, but this was done in the past when a barracks had become too structurally unstable to be inhabited any longer. Recognizing these differences among the barracks does not make it any less remarkable that, over nearly one hundred years of building, the company always built barracks with the same basic design features as it followed in the 1880s, consisting of a row of rooms with doors on only one side, an architectural legacy of slavery in the countries where barracks with this lay-out were first built (see chapter three).

Monte Coca contains three distinct settlement nuclei and its residents have applied terms of their own choosing to communicate practical information about the space they inhabit. Moving from roughly south to north (see figure 6-4), the district of "El Chucho" is named after the loading station located there, "El Batey" is the central and most populated district, and "La Construcción" is the newest addition, a complex of cement barracks built a short distance from the main road in the late 1970s. El Batey is sometimes called "Los Lugos," after the former managers of Monte Coca's main dry-goods store. Some residents speak about these districts as if each was a different batey, while others regard them as parts of one settlement. Even so, there is agreement about the place name(s). Local terms of orientation also point to the existence of a local system of "practical space" (Bourdieu 1977: 2), with axes linked to batey residents' bodies and carried about with them wherever they go. For example, when you walk in the more or less northerly direction just traced, from El Chucho through El Batey to La Construcción, Monte Coca residents will say you are going "down" (*bajas* or *vas p'abajo*) and when you walk in the opposite direction, north to south, they will say you are going "up."

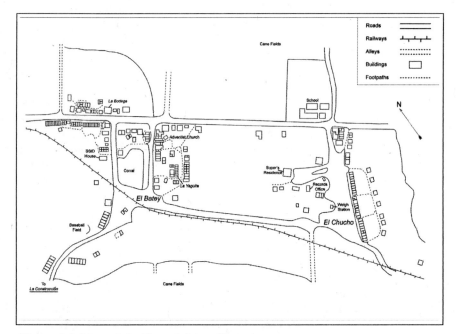

Figure 6-4. Map of the Batey Monte Coca.

Any circuit of Monte Coca should begin with a courtesy call at the house of the *superintendente*, which is located in El Chucho, the first part of the batey you pass by as you enter via the main road from Consuelo. These days, I have no fear of being reported to any plantation authority as I walk about in Monte Coca but, at the time I first did fieldwork there, an unfamiliar outsider would likely be accosted by one of the plantation's private police force and be unceremoniously led off company property if it were suspected that the outsider was up to union organizing or other "trouble-making." The *superintendente*'s house is a modest but well-maintained wooden structure. Its main distinguishing feature is a covered and screened-in porch that wraps around the greater part of two sides of the house. Don Ricardo, the *"super"* when I did my dissertation fieldwork in Monte Coca in 1985–86, liked to lounge in a rocking chair on the veranda on Sunday afternoons. While comfortably ensconced in the shade, he would exchange greetings with passing workers, who would touch the bills of their caps and low a subdued *"mi jeeefe,"* to gain their boss's attention before either going quietly on their way or waiting in respectful silence outside until Don Ricardo asked their business, in a booming voice out of all proportion to his diminutive stature. The *superintendente*'s house is said to be a fraction of the size it was during the era of American ownership, when it had two stories, including an upper balcony from which the *superintendente* could address gatherings on ceremonial occasions. I never dared ask Don Ricardo's permission to climb up on the roof of the house but, considering that the house stands on top of a slight elevation and the space around it is mostly unobstructed, I imagine that the view must have been good from the old second floor. Two important installations are located less than 200 meters from the *super*'s house, the batey's cane weighing station and loading station and the *colonia*'s records office, from which pay is distributed to the agricultural workers every other Saturday.

Doubling back to the main road, you reach Monte Coca's public school. Before it was built in the mid-1970s there was no school in Monte Coca. The school has enough classrooms for all the elementary grades but usually there are only enough teachers to impart the first four years of education. Children must still go to Consuelo to study higher grades. Even though instruction is free of charge, many children attend school only sporadically because their parents cannot afford to buy school uniforms or supplies, or need the children's help earning money.

As you walk down the main road from El Chucho to El Batey, you ascend a slight incline and pass five small free-standing houses at irregular intervals on your left. The first of these is built entirely of cast-off materials and is occupied by its owners. The others are built of wooden planks, in a simple style much like houses in other rural areas of the Dominican Republic. Each has between two and four small rooms, topped with a metal roof, with windows on all sides. The main entry is in the front, sealed with either a single or a double-leaf door, and the roof extends past the front entry to make a covered veranda. Each is painted brightly, in purple, leaf green, or bright yellow, and each is surrounded by a neatly swept dirt yard, planted profusely with vines, food crops, bushes and trees. These are among the few non-barracks residences to be found in Monte Coca, and were built by the Americans for the bosses and administrators below the level of the *superintendente*. They are now occupied by lower-level employees with families.

Continuing along, the main road intersects in a T with a much narrower road on your left. You have arrived at the district of El Batey, which has the greatest concentration of inhabitants in the batey. To your left stands the Adventist church, a small cement block building built on a raised concrete footing, and beyond it lies a tight bunch of barracks linked by narrow footpaths. Amid these barracks is located the batey's bar and brothel, La Yagüita, whose significance in drawing lines between decent and indecent women, and men of Haitian and Dominican nationality has already been noted. La Yagüita's core clientele is made up chiefly of the local area's most notorious drunkards and *"tígueres"* (ne'er-do-wells). On weekends especially, the barroom there is also frequented by company bosses and skilled laborers who come not just from Monte Coca but from the mill town and several nearby bateyes. I have never heard of Monte Coca's *superintendente* being seen passing time there, but any number of other top men and those who aspire to high post can be seen making hours-long displays of lavish spending at La Yagüita. Apparently, it is too much to resist the chance to meet other men who might advance their careers and the opportunity to gain prestige and influence among the plantation's leading men, all while enjoying the attentions of sexually available young women. In spite of the friction with their wives that it surely creates, aspiring company leaders are aware that their presence in the brothel's barroom, engaging in conspicuous displays of alcohol consumption and of generosity in buying drinks for others, can aid their advancement in the company hierarchy.

Leaving this section of the batey behind and continuing perhaps 40 meters farther along the main road, you reach another T intersection, with the road that leads to La Construcción. To your left stands a square, heavy stone house with thick wooden doors and shutters, its walls breached at points by short, narrow vents of the kind through which a rifleman can fire. It was built during the first U.S. military government (1916 to 1924) as a fortified safe house in the event of an attack by the *gavilleros*, guerrilla fighters who waged an armed struggle against the American occupiers. I have no evidence that this building was ever used as a refuge against armed invasion or insurrection. It is now used as living quarters by permanent residents.

Directly across the main road from this house is the main dry-goods store (*bodega*). Before Trujillo purchased Consuelo in 1957, the *bodega* was more than just a store. It was the *company* store and, as such, a symbol of the whole way of life of the plantation. In common with the *superintendente*'s house, the *bodega* was larger in its days of glory, and it is said to have stocked a much wider array of goods, including clothing, cooking pots and other domestic and agricultural implements, making it a veritable shrine to abundance and emblem of modernity in the context of its time and place. More importantly, the *bodega* symbolized oppression. "The Americans" permitted no independent retail vendors on company property, a monopoly which the company reinforced by paying advance wages in scrip usable only at its stores. Price mark-ups and weighing produce on scales calibrated to overcharge the customer speeded the recycling of workers' wages back into company accounts. Unlike ordinary stores in which it is normal to lose some quantity of goods, the *bodega* had to report negative losses: say, for every 100 pounds of flour delivered to the *bodega*, 105 pounds of flour would have to be reported sold. The company even gave this surplus profit the same name that it applied to the analogous short-weighing of the cane at its weigh stations in the fields, the "over." "Over" became the name of a novel published in 1940 by Ramón Marrero Aristy, recounting the story of the fall into poverty and resulting anti-imperialist *prise de conscience* of a young man hired to manage a company store on an American plantation. In the 1950s, Trujillo denounced the evils of the over, payment by scrip and the company store to justify his purchase of the North American sugar estates. Even though personal profit no doubt motivated him more than patriotism, "El Benefactor" stayed true to his promise to divest the company of its stores and open his plantations up to retail competition. Even though it has been privately owned since Trujillo bought Consuelo, the *bodega* has not entirely abandoned usurious practices, such as deducting a percentage of the value of pay vouchers when these are accepted for goods in lieu of cash. It is also still an important batey gathering spot, about which more will be said in subsequent chapters.

Beyond the *bodega*, a few more barracks hug the main road before it leads out of Monte Coca. If you instead follow the branch road toward La Construcción, you pass a number of small structures, including the batey's Evangelical church on your left and the "SSID house" on your right. This breeze block structure was built in 1985 by a Dominican Evangelical service organization, Servicios Sociales de las Iglesias Dominicanas, and served free mid-day meals for about two years to children under five. Even though greeted with considerable optimism, the feeding center almost immediately swirled with rumors that the women who volunteered to cook the meals there were stealing food for their own families. Discouraged, a number of women ceased volunteering their labor, and as a result the provision of meals ceased a few months after I gave up residence in Monte Coca. The house remains, empty and tightly locked. Any conclusions to be drawn from this fiasco about the challenge of collective organization in Monte Coca must take into account that this was apparently an entirely "top-down" initiative: the SSID did not consult with the residents of the batey before setting up the center.

Across the road from the SSID house is a fenced corral, in which oxen are gathered together in a lively scene at the start of each harvest season, to be assigned to the cart drivers who will work with them for the duration of the harvest. Before La Construcción was built, each truckload of newly arrived workers from Haiti would unload its passengers within this corral, too. Farther down the road stand three identical cement barracks, built in 1959 and now in badly deteriorated condition. From the outside, these buildings look much like other barracks, elongated, single-story structures with pairs of doors and windows running their length. Yet they are unusual in having doors in the middle wall that separates the front row of rooms from the back row. The fact that each domicile has two rooms, rather than just one, suggests that they were designed with the possibility of accommodating families as well as groups of single men. This feature seems highly significant to Monte Cocans even though it might easily escape the attention of someone who has never lived in a batey.

Continuing along this side road for a short stretch, and passing in between two cane fields, you reach the settlement called La Construcción. This district is officially a separate batey, called Proyecto de Monte Coca by Dominican census officials, but it is so near to Monte Coca that it is, generally speaking, continuous with the batey. It was built in the mid-1970s, a time of booming world sugar prices, with the aim, some say, of housing the Brazilian or Salvadorean men, or Dominican families, who it was hoped might take the place of the Haitian braceros. Sugar prices plunged in 1978 and have never since recovered more than a small fraction of their mid-1970s prices. With the sugar bubble went any hope of bankrolling the large-scale mechanization of the sugar harvest, which CEA technocrats had dreamt would boost agricultural labor productivity and make sugarcane work more attractive to Dominicans.

The buildings in La Construcción are recognizably barracks but differ in lay-out from all others in Monte Coca. Each building contains one row of small, single rooms, and each room has a single door, all the doors opening to one side. The floor-plan is unusual in that each room has two windows, front and back, and contains a built-in closet divided into four compartments. Each compartment has its own metal door and hasp permitting separate closure. Like the barracks built just up the road, La Construcción is built out of cement blocks, with sturdy metal louvers in the window frames. The most distinctive thing about La Construcción (and other *"proyectos"* built at the same time in other CEA bateyes) is the shape of its buildings. Its barracks are not laid out in single straight lines but are rectangles that have either been folded or cut up in four, so that each group of 12 or 14 rooms makes up a small residential compound in the shape of a square or a cross (figure 6-5). The barracks that are folded in the shape of a square are called "*pabellones*" (pavilions) and those that are cut up to form a cross are called "*casitas*" (little houses). For most of my time in Monte Coca, I lived in one room in a casita. Besides these barracks, there are two stand-alone family houses. At the time of my dissertation fieldwork one of these houses was occupied by the *mayordomo* (the *superintendente*'s deputy) and his family, and the other was held by the children and estranged wife of an independent businessman and former CEA employee, who was a major supplier of firewood to the sugar mill.

The rooms in the pabellones and casitas are absolutely identical, with the exception of the corner rooms in the pabellones, which are somewhat larger than the others. That the storage closets in each room are divided into four separate compartments suggests that the entire complex was designed to be inhabited by groups of single men, one storage compartment for each man. In fact, local bosses generally do house four single men in each room

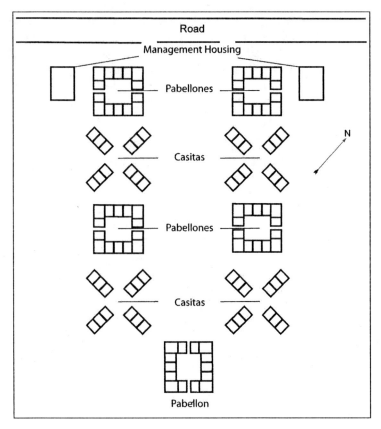

Figure 6-5. Map of "La Construcción."

in the braceros' barracks there. Yet in spite of the uniformity of the rooms, Monte Coca residents favor the casitas and detest the pabellones. The term "casitas" itself suggests a different perception of this kind of barracks, and the casitas were accordingly assigned mainly to families that were already in permanent residence on the estate. Far fewer single men have rooms in the casitas than in the pabellón barracks; none of these are Haitian. By contrast, two of the three pabellones in La Construcción are used exclusively to house braceros. These are the buildings that I have noted are regarded as highly "indecent" places to live.

It is not just the pabellones' association with the braceros but the lay-out of these barracks that residents find irksome. Pabellón residents and others agree that it can be unpleasant to have the door to your room open out onto a small central courtyard. Having to cross this shared space to enter or exit the rooms frequently makes it impossible to avoid seeing your neighbors in various states of emotion, sobriety or (un)dress as well as confronting the sights, sounds and smells of everyone else's laundry and cooking. It seems likely that this design shortcoming was determinant in the decision to house the braceros in the pabellones. The door of each casita, by contrast, gives out to a small open lot. Having no door that gives direct access from their rooms to the space outside the courtyard also makes it difficult for pabellón residents to use the small spaces immediately adjacent to their residences as private yards. As I discuss in the next section of this chapter, staking out, planting and decorating a yard is one means by which batey residents personalize and enhance the comfort of their living environments.

To the discerning eye, this quick walk through Monte Coca reveals a number of ways in which power is inscribed into the design and lay-out of the batey. I have already noted that one reason for constructing densely inhabited, nucleated settlements is to minimize the amount of land that the workers and their human needs subtract from sugarcane cultivation. Dense settlements also facilitate surveillance and control, as does the lay-out of the workers' barracks following more or less regular lines, with enough space between each building to leave sight lines open. The barracks built in La Construcción in the 1970s have essentially the same floor plan as the first barracks built in Monte Coca in the 1880s, and, for that matter, are the same as those built even earlier on sugar plantations in nineteenth-century Cuba, Puerto Rico, Brazil, Guyana and Trinidad. With windows and doors that open to one side only, these barracks were obviously constructed to make it easier to keep an eye on the workers' movements. At points in the past, thought was also clearly given to the possibility of having to contend with open insurrection, such as in the decisions made about where to locate management's surveillance, command and security points. The *superintendente*'s house is located within sight of three sensitive installations, the weighing and loading stations and the local company office, as well as the barracks in El Chucho. The fortified stone house stands directly across from the company store.

Power is also a part of the "silent violence" that the company has inflicted with impunity through its persistent neglect of the needs of the permanent residents and families with children, who have long made up the greater part of Monte Coca's population. The primary purpose of the batey is to house the personnel, livestock and equipment needed to plant, cultivate, and harvest the sugarcane, and then transport the cane from field to mill. True to this purpose, the company barracks are obviously intended for a work force that is male, adult, unaccompanied and temporary. Looking beyond the dwellings themselves, few family oriented public services and amenities are available. Generations of children grew to maturity in Monte Coca before the first school was built there. The batey's infrastructure, services and amenities are still woefully inadequate even for temporary adult residents, let alone the developmental needs of children. The only local health care workers are two stalwart but absurdly underpaid *promotoras de salud* (health extension agents), whose basic level of training enables them to do little more than give nutritional advice, encourage women of child-bearing age to see a doctor during pregnancy and tell about measures to prevent the spread of AIDS and other contagious diseases. The nearest doctor or nurse is in Consuelo. During the 1990s, a government-subsidized pharmaceutical dispensary was set up but remained in operation for only a few years. Perhaps the only lasting improvement in basic services of recent years has been the construction of more pit latrines, with USAID funding. In 1986, I counted 48 pit latrines in the entire batey, some of which were completely unusable and others padlocked for restricted use. Most of the batey's 249 households and over 1,000 inhabitants would defecate in the neighboring cane fields, greatly increasing the hazard of propagating gastrointestinal infections. The present, increased supply of latrines is a great improvement. The potable water supply was and still is precarious. For some years, residents have been used to collecting water from common spigots drawn by two electric pumps and one hand pump—one in each of Monte Coca's three residential districts. All three pumps broke down at various points during my year of continuous residence in 1985–86, and tended to remain broken for a long time with only apathetic repair attempts by company technicians. For one period of several weeks, none of the water pumps worked. During that period, residents had to rely on the meager amounts of water that company trucks would deliver unannounced, nearly always setting off chaotic scenes as I described in the last chapter. If you missed the truck, the only other option was to set off on walks of up to two kilometers to get water at neighboring bateyes or natural springs. Other bateyes have experienced even more shocking neglect than Monte Coca. A recent survey in the province of San Pedro de Macorís found that one-half of the dwellings in rural bateyes lack electricity (FLACSO 2002: 19). Yet the needs most often identified to be important by the respondents to this survey (ibid.: 71)—more employment, better salaries, and more and better housing—are all things that Monte Cocans would be likely to mention, too.

The perspective that I have developed thus far in this chapter is largely an external one, relating to how the batey has been shaped by the plantation's owners and managers. I have looked primarily for evidence of how the company's profit and labor control agenda have translated into a specific organization of space and the built environment. What is missing from this picture is what the residents of Monte Coca think about the space they inhabit and do to change it.

Here, again, there is a contrast between what people say and what they do. Generalized and context-specific verbal assessments of the batey suggest that its inhabitants have almost no feelings of attachment to it. Batey residents voice overwhelmingly negative evaluations of the place where they live. Even people born and raised in Monte Coca at best speak of the batey as a stopping point on the way to a place where they would rather live. Hard though it was for me to imagine at first, Monte Coca seems to be a place *no one* considers their home. I recall overhearing one exception to this generalization. Two *viejos,* seated in conversation on a bench under the *bodega*'s veranda, were warned, "Watch out! You're talking bad about my batey!" by a young Dominican woman, born and bred in Monte Coca. Her expression of place attachment was immediately challenged by one of the *viejos,* who retorted loudly, in heavily accented Spanish, "*Your* batey? Ooooh! None of this belongs to anyone but the company. Even *we* belong to the company!" "Is it not so, *compadre*?" he asked his companion. Her rejoinder, "You can say what you want but I am not a slave and I am from this place!" triggered an explosion of guffaws and shouts of admiration for her having answered "just like a man." Yet, even though she and her interlocutor were ordinarily on friendly terms, this exchange evidently displeased the young woman. After making her purchase she sent a cutting glance at the *viejo* and left the *bodega* without saying another word. Assertions of place attachment are not only rare but, as this anecdote suggests, are subject to rapid, destabilizing rebuttal.[1]

Yet the near unanimity with which life in the batey is disparaged does not prevent Monte Cocans from devoting scarce resources to making their lives better. (Again, what they do stands significantly at variance with what they say.) To reach a more complex understanding of how they relate to the batey environment, you have to enter Monte Coca fully, by getting off the roads and treading one of the many footpaths that crisscross the batey. In doing so, you leave the space laid out by the company and enter "social space," defined by the personal initiatives and unorganized collective actions of its inhabitants. Whereas it may be said that planned space is a "product," which matters to its developers because of its utility toward meeting certain ends, social space is a "work," labored on by its inhabitants (Lefebvre 1991: 73–79) and imbued with meanings as they use it for purposes unforeseen by its planners.

HOME IMPROVEMENT IN HELL

When I think about walking the batey's footpaths, the memory that comes most often to mind is of being pulled up short in mid-stride by a length of barbed wire on my neck or face. Propped up on long sticks, nailed to outhouses or strung up in other improvised ways, the barbed wire is used as clotheslines. Luckily I never got cut but in one of my run-ins I did once suffer the embarrassment of bringing down the line and soiling all of a neighbor's clean laundry, a gaffe that generated considerable amusement at my expense as the story was retold in the days that followed. While there are some very tall men in Monte Coca, most people there are noticeably shorter than my 6'0" and pass easily under the barbed wire-turned-clotheslines. I do not know where all the barbed wire comes from—I assume some of it is diverted from company supplies—but I can say that it is almost as commonplace and multipurpose a substance in Monte Coca as Scotch tape is in the United States. Children even fashion it into toys by hammering out its spikes and shaping it into big hoops that can be rolled along the ground with a stick. It was with some amusement and amazement, therefore, that I once saw an article on Haitians in the Dominican Republic, in *Le Monde diplomatique*, which bore a striking photograph of several sad-eyed black children looking out from behind a barbed wire fence. The article's author, André Corten (1992), delivers a more complex analysis than the "Haitians are enslaved in the Dominican Republic" message that has so often been presented by journalists who briefly visit the bateyes. Yet much of that textual subtlety is undone by the photograph and its caption, which reads, "In a batey: An atmosphere that borders at times on a pogrom" (my translation).[2] As a characterization, "an atmosphere of pogrom" is both bold ("it's a pogrom") and imprecise ("it's an atmosphere"). Even so, I wonder how many people must have seen that photograph, read its caption, and concluded, "They're holding children behind barbed wire fences there!"

Turning barbed wire into an item of household merchandise is an appropriate metaphor, I think, for what people in Monte Coca and so many other CEA plantations do to turn the cramped and shabby living spaces provided to them by the sugar company into something more adequate for their needs. Batey housing is ceded to company workers free of rent but is woefully inadequate in quantity and quality. The typical family inhabits one or two small barracks rooms.[3] Permanent residents have taken over so many barracks in Monte Coca that they take up much more space in company housing than the seasonal migrants. The barracks are unadorned, are supplied unfurnished, and have no space set aside for cooking, bathing or children's play. Rain easily penetrates the rusted sheet metal roofs and wind and pests pass through holes, often big enough to stick an arm through, in the termite-eaten walls.[4]

A stroll through the alleys and back ways of Monte Coca (watching out for that barbed wire!) reveals many ways in which its residents try to adapt the meager resources ceded to them by the company to make the batey a more liveable environment. As you step behind the barracks, certain resident-installed structures jump to your attention. Most residents have demarcated a small portion of the land immediately behind their dwelling as a yard, often constructing living fences by planting cactus or tree stumps bound together with barbed wire. The fences vary in height. Some are punctuated with shade-giving trees but almost none are high enough to block an adult's vision or prohibit entry by a determined intruder. Looking into these yards, you will also see that many have either small stand-alone shelters, typically located near the barracks, or lean-tos built directly onto the back sides of the buildings. The stand-alone structures are cooking shelters, topped with low roofs made of sheet metal, discarded tin, or palm bark, supported by rough-hewn wooden posts. To let the smoke of cooking fires dissipate, these shelters either have no walls at all or are sealed off on one side with corrugated metal or cardboard, to shelter the charcoal-burning stoves and cooking pots from wind, dust and rain. The lean-tos, on the other hand, are usually enclosed structures, with earthen floors, built directly onto the side of the barracks out of cast-off scraps of wood, cardboard and sheet metal. Even though small, these lean-tos can create space for a kitchen or an extra bedroom, or, when added to the front of the barracks, can be used as a family dry-goods shop during waking hours and double as added sleeping space at night (figures 6-6 and 6-7). A handful of residents have strung together as many as five or six rooms by adding one lean-to after another to the front and back of their barracks. When a family moves from one barracks to another, they usually disassemble the lean-tos and reassemble the pieces in their new home.

Sitting down to talk with Monte Cocans and taking time to observe their activities open further insight into the satisfactions made possible by having a yard. The herbs, shrubs and trees in the yards are not just decorative; many have medicinal uses. Traditionally, a child's first possession is the tree under which its placenta is buried by its parents. Planting a coconut tree is also a symbol of permanence, because of the many years it takes to reach maturity.[5] Chickens, or more rarely, ducks or piglets, scatter underfoot as you enter, and a lucky few households have a fat pink sow decorating a muddy corner under the shade of a tree. Living fences also create shade and offer a modicum of privacy. In an enclosed yard a woman feels less exposed to view as she squats down over her wash basin, skirt tucked modestly between her legs, to do the laundry and dishwashing. Some yard fixtures enhance sociality, as when benches are built into cooking shelters to give visitors a place to sit, share company, break the day's monotony and share personal and

Figure 6-6. Lean-tos and clotheslines, behind a cement barracks.

community news as the woman of the house does her chores. A handful of households have built bigger shelters with more seating space, structures whose more obvious social use earn them the florid name of *"enramadas"* (bowers). Resourceful and labor-saving additions to the barracks' exteriors include gutters improvised out of halved bamboo stalks or lengths of PVC

Figure 6-7. A partially built lean-to (lacking roof covering).

tubing, rigged up to channel run-off into storage barrels placed next to the dwelling, obviating the need to haul wash water and creating a reserve supply for days when the batey's wells are out of order. Dishwater is simply thrown out the back door after use, and the residents seem indifferent to where peelings, pits and charcoal ash may fall. Household members can drop trash with seeming indifference because they know that the woman or women of the house are fastidious cleaners and will likely not tarry too long before thoroughly sweeping the entire yard. Cleanliness and pride in one's surroundings are admired qualities. Last but certainly not least, a fenced yard diminishes tension among neighbors in the crowded batey by defining a clear boundary around each household's territory. Accordingly, even people who freely drop trash in their own yards will reprimand a passing child who does so. The ways in which yards enhance their owners' convenience and enjoyment may seem small but I think it safe to say that the yards assume added value for their holders when seen against the bareness of the surrounding common space. In spite of not owning so much as a square inch of it, many Monte Coca householders evince a strong sense of de facto ownership of their houses and yards.

It is not too much to say that part of the value of the yards inheres in these being spaces that residents can call their own. Indeed, it is virtually a precondition that a space be held privately if it is to be planted and built upon, for no one will invest their effort or personal resources in improving a communally held space. There is at least one communally held gathering spot, which consists of a pair of benches, hewn out of a split log, inserted at the base of three low trees on the other side of the main road from the Adventist church. This is a popular spot for residents to sit in the shade while passing the time in conversation or waiting for transportation to Consuelo. To my knowledge, every other gathering spot in El Batey and El Chucho, whether it be a kitchen, an *enramada*, a roofed gallery built onto the front of a family shop, or simply an open yard, is a space that belongs to a particular resident.

In La Construcción, the company built open-sided communal shelters at the center of each pabellón and set of casitas. These structures consist of nothing more than a rough cement floor, topped by a square cement roof supported by four bare metal poles. They are called *"enramadas"* or, diminutively, *"enramaditas,"* in spite of being constructed entirely out of industrially manufactured materials. The architects who designed La Construcción were obviously aware of the social importance of such gathering spaces elsewhere in the Dominican Republic and company administrators laudably supported the idea of devoting some space to community life. Even more apparent to anyone who lives in La Construcción is how dismally this social spatial experiment has failed. The general lesson seems to be that if you want to make a place that *no one* will appropriate for social uses, then do as the company did in La Construcción: keep that place as a common ground rather than permitting people to claim it as their own "property."

In the pabellones, the presence of these common areas at times seems even counterproductive to maintaining cordial relations among the residents. The *enramadas* there do get frequent use but this is not because the pabellón residents like these spaces very much but because these are the only coverings they have within convenient reach of their rooms. In the pabellones, the *enramadas* are used much more frequently for cooking, laundry and other outside chores than for playing dominoes, conversation or other primarily social or recreational purposes. It often seems that bickering is the main social activity taking place there. The tired and frustrated braceros are understandably often on a short fuse as they struggle to get a meal cooked at the end of a hard day's work. Women who live in the pabellones as partners of seasonal migrants easily get into arguments as their children tussle or as two or more women try to pursue conflicting activities under the *enramada*, such as building a smoky fire to bake bread just when another wants to hang up her clean clothes to dry. Permanent residents who have rooms in one of the pabellones seem to get along with fewer squabbles, which suggests that part of the difficulties relating to the use of space under the *enramadas* in the braceros' barracks stems from these quarters being inhabited entirely by newcomers.

The *enramadas* that are located at the central axis of each group of casitas are smaller but seem to have greater potential as a place for friendly social exchange. Cement benches are built onto the side of each building in the common area and, because the doors of the casitas do not open onto the *enramada,* there are fewer tense encounters there. The scene under the casitas'*enramadas* is exactly the opposite as in the pabellones but in a mostly negative sense: these areas are seemingly very rarely used at all other than for hanging up wet laundry on wires suspended between the *enramadas'* support poles. For years, much of the space under one of these *enramadas* was taken up by a pick-up truck owned by a resident.

Regardless of their location, all the *enramadas* in La Construcción remain bare and hence are less inviting for social activities than they could be if they were planted to create more shade and furnished with wooden benches. The only way that residents have found of making the *enramadas* amenable to their intended social function is, in fact, to claim a chunk of the common space as their own private gathering spots. For example, a company accountant who moved into my room in La Construcción, after I gave up residence there, enclosed the area between his room and the two nearest *enramada* support posts with a stout high fence made of halved bamboo stalks. His neighbors were displeased but not so much because this space had been sealed off but at *how* it had been enclosed—with a fence too high to look over. Being too protective of one's privacy arouses suspicion.

In general terms, demarcating yards and modifying the structure of their dwellings seem to be motivated more by territorial and social imperatives than by concerns about security or privacy. Monte Cocans express worry about thieves but few take great precautions against intruders, leaving their doors unlatched if not open altogether when they step out for just a few minutes while their children or a trusted neighbor is around. The low and easily breached fences around their yards are more a means of saying, "This is mine," than of warning, "Keep out!" Privacy is valued but not so much that it will not often be willingly compromised for the sake of encouraging neighborly relations or letting cooling breezes circulate through. Among households that occupy more than one room, the inner doorways are usually partitioned with a light cloth curtain, providing visual but not auditory privacy. In some of the older barracks, the walls between rooms do not reach all the way up to the ceiling, leaving a large gap for sounds and smells to propagate between the dwellings. Only the omnipresent blaring radios cover the sounds emanating from inside neighbors' dwellings. People are therefore not physically shielded from perceiving each others' private activities as much as they are in tacit agreement to pretend not to notice these, at least not if the goings-on at the neighbors' fall within reasonable limits of decorum.[6] Batey residents place great emphasis on maintaining respectful relations with their neighbors, and discretion seems to be the greater part of respect. It is easy to imagine how the everyday practice of life in the batey could inculcate such discretion. Younger children circulate freely among the dwellings and often go in and out of the sleeping quarters of neighbors' dwellings, where an adult would never dare intrude. As they grow older, being in the habit of spending more time outside than inside during the stifling heat of the day habituates people to more or less constantly seeing and hearing their neighbors and being seen and heard by them. Indeed, there are women whose primary leisure activity on sunny days seems to be observing the activities of others, from regular posts at the front entryways or steps of their dwellings.

Of course, batey residents want more than simply creating a place that feels more their own when they take the trouble to modify their living quarters. They also seek to counter the inadequacy of their accommodations for the purposes of raising a family, for holding ceremonial gatherings, and as a frame for "social consumption." Even small changes in the structure of a barracks can improve the living environment for the family that occupies it. Families that occupy two or more contiguous rooms in wooden barracks generally obtain permission from company bosses to open doorways between their rooms, which increases family privacy by allowing people to pass between rooms without stepping outside. Opening an inner passageway can also enhance the comfort and health of recent mothers, who generally avoid exposing themselves or their newborns to cold or damp air for forty days after childbirth, believing that such exposure can cause illness.

For most batey families, one or two small rooms in a company barracks are not enough to permit them to house all the members of the household and their belongings. Not all Monte Coca families confront the problem of limited living space on an equal footing. Men who stand a step above ordinary workers on the job ladder—foremen, cane weighers, clerical workers, steady employees at the mill, and a handful of informal right-hand men of the local bosses—can obtain three or four contiguous rooms, rather than the one or two rooms held by most residents. These families can mimic the square, three-to-five room single-family houses which most batey residents would build if they could afford to move off company property. As I have noted, families who cannot obtain extra rooms through influence or bribery can often gain permission to annex one or more lean-tos to their dwellings.

Having extra rooms does not just enhance comfort. It also makes it possible to draw clear functional and stylistic distinctions between each room, by dividing the domicile into functionally distinct rooms for sleeping, cooking and receiving visitors. The ideal house has at least four rooms. One is an indoor kitchen in which utensils and pots are stored, where food is processed before cooking, and from which the main meal of the day is served out. Households that can set aside one room or build a lean-to to be the kitchen usually locate this in the back, with a door to the outside, to enable the woman of the house to cast an eye on the pots on the boil outside while tending to matters inside the house (figures 6-8 and 6-9). Whatever table there may be in the kitchen is used for meal preparation and presentation. With few exceptions, even among the more prosperous households that possess formal dining tables, Monte Cocans eat their meals holding their plates and utensils in their hands or on their laps. One room in front should ideally be reserved as a parlor (*sala*), for hospitality, leisure, and display. In Monte Coca, it is generally only households with steady, relatively high incomes who have the funds to make their *sala* into a full-fledged ceremonial environment. Two or three bedrooms (*aposentos*), one for the parents and younger children, the other(s) for the older children, complete the ensemble. A very similar tripartite division is described as typifying the houses in a coastal Brazilian town (Robben 1989: 571), in a manner conforming exactly to the rural Dominican ideal:

> The kitchen is the area where the inhabitants reproduce themselves as a household. Household relations are expressed in material and emotional ways by sharing meals, affections, worries, and hardships. The parental bedroom is the area of conception, sexual intercourse, and physical recuperation. Here, in a very literal way, husband and wife shed their clothes and retreat within the intimacy of their bodies. The front room is the space in which the family relates to the outside world, receives guests, and presents itself to the community with the display of its more precious status symbols.

120 Chapter Six

In common with the multi-household residential compounds in Accra, Ghana, observed by Deborah Pellow (1992: 202), batey houses and yards display a "sociospatial continuum of public to private." Within this continuum, yards are transitional, semi-public spaces between the street and the home, bedrooms are the most private, inner circle of the home, and parlors represent an in-between space, reserved for television-viewing in the evening or for receiving particularly honored guests, such as the anthropologist on his first visit. The tripartite spatial division of the dwelling also permits a temporal division of the home into day-time, evening and night-time zones: the yard, parlor, and bedroom, respectively.

Women invest more work and concern than men in household maintenance and in childrearing and domestic tasks, and are more preoccupied than their husbands with improving the family dwelling. Women report spending a higher proportion of their own, independently earned incomes on home improvement and decoration. Even when a man spends his money or when a couple pools incomes to purchase more expensive items—e.g., a bed, dining or living room furniture or a refrigerator—these expenditures seem to be most often made at the woman's behest and are invariably installed in the place of her choice. Women's greater involvement with esthetics of the domestic environment gives rise to farcical scenes whenever a certain vendor of art reproductions comes to Monte Coca on a motor scooter, to collect payments for the pictures he has sold on installment. Every person whom he deals with is a woman, and, if you

Figure 6-8. The kitchen of one of the batey's more prosperous households.

Figure 6-9. The kitchen of one of the batey's poorer households.

move ahead of him discreetly as he makes his rounds, you will notice that it is only women who are scooting through the back doors of their houses to hide from him.

It does not take long to notice that the family dwelling is a female space in Monte Coca. Nowhere in the batey is there a space set aside exclusively for either sex, nor are there rules or tacit understandings which exclude either men or women from gatherings attended by members of the opposite sex. It is quite common to see mixed-sex groups gathered in conversation. Yet, in practice, gender-specific dispositions toward certain activities tend to divide household gatherings into male- versus female-centered groups, which members of the opposite sex may hover around or join fleetingly but do not consistently participate in. To begin with, the gender-based division of occupations keeps most women in their homes and yards for the greater part of the working day, and sends most men away to the cane fields or their subsistence gardens. Dominoes and other competitive games, as well as viewing action movies or baseball and other sports on TV, are male pastimes, in which women say they take little interest. The nightly soaps on TV are more likely to engage women's interest, as do gatherings focusing on personal grooming.

Men are not strangers to the lives of their households, even though women devote longer hours of time to the tasks of keeping house and caring for the children. Elderly, men, too, invest labor, earnings, and emotion in maintaining and improving their families' well-being. Many men especially prize spending time with their children, and successful male wage earners take pride in keeping their children and elderly parents fed, clothed and sheltered. Neglecting to provide her support is the only unquestioned grounds that a woman has to split with her mate, and certainly the produce from men's subsistence gardens enables numerous batey households to avoid starvation late in the dead season, when cane work is least available.

Just as work in these gardens is managed by men but at times involves women's labor, so, too, is the household a female-dominated space in which men even so find approved ways of contributing labor. When a man takes on the construction of a cooking shelter or a lean-to, for example, he invariably speaks of it as something he is "doing for" his wife or mother. Men's construction projects thicken the fabric of reciprocity between the sexes that binds together the household and defines the conjugal and mother-son dyads, adding nuance also to the ways in which gender difference is projected onto space. Parallels may be found in Daniel Miller's (1988) study of how the residents of a state-developed North London housing project have decorated and remodeled their kitchens. These living environments, more standardized than any batey, are personalized through men's self-help home improvement projects, and Miller concludes that the development of "do-it-yourself" as a form of male labor appropriate to the home environment complements women's control over the esthetics of the home, giving spatial-temporal expression to values relating to gender and conjugality.

Home improvement also provides men who belong to the plantation's middle-tier of steady employees a channel for communicating confidence in their own income-generating capacity and for gaining prestige via conspicuous consumption. Adding on an extra room, stocking a parlor with showy ornaments and abundantly varnished, thickly padded furniture, or buying a store-made table or a cookware set for the kitchen are activities permitting even those men who do not have money to burn at the batey's brothel to be ranked by their peers, according to the standard of living of their households. Expanding living space and acquiring material tokens of decency lift these men and their wives a notch in socioeconomic status, above the propertyless braceros and their poorer neighbors in Monte Coca.

A fortunate few are hard pressed to find enough room for all the nice things they have bought over the years. Recall that the room where I ended up living in La Construcción was being used just to store one avid collector's surplus furniture. I am still boggled by the inventory of furnishings that can be found in the nine or ten square meters of some Monte Coca rooms. One, not very extreme, example is the front room in a set of four rooms occupied in a barracks by a family of Haitian ancestry. This household is headed by a cane cutter foreman (a very low management position), who supplements his income by managing Don Ricardo's private gardens. The house is shared by the man's wife, who earns money doing laundry, and seven of their children. In one corner of their parlor stands a dining room table, pinning two of its four matching chairs to the wall, topped with yellowing doilies and plaster figurines. Next to it gleams a small black and white television on a varnished stand. Over the TV is draped a knitted doily and on it perches a plaster figurine of a songbird. A large refrigerator stands in the corner opposite the dining room table. On the walls hang seven vividly colored photo reproductions of humorous or pretty scenes: e.g., kittens gazing at a caged parrot, pale maidens skipping rope in a meadow, a horse-drawn buggy passing under a covered bridge in a New England autumnal landscape. Electrical wires drape down from the parlor's ceiling like bunting, to feed several appliances from a single light bulb socket. Much of the remaining floor space is taken up by a set of four rocking chairs, with knitted backrest covers, and a low wooden table, leaving open a narrow corridor to walk through and just enough leg room for one adult to sit. Rooms such as this remain mostly closed and empty during the day and may pull in a few family members and neighbors to watch TV in the evening. Mostly these rooms wait for major holidays or auspicious ceremonial events such as christenings to come alive with activity.

The number and condition of the pots and furnishings in the kitchen more subtly distinguish haves and have-nots in the batey milieu. In the kitchens of more prosperous households, you may find one or two store-bought tables, and count a dozen or more shiny pots hung on nails from the walls or perched on neat, painted wooden shelves, along with stainless steel eating utensils, enamelized and plastic jugs and mugs, and bowls and plates made of porcelain, glass or plastic. In other households, the kitchen may have a roughly made wooden table, a few pots, plates and utensils, and perhaps a shelf or two propped up off the ground on a stick or suspended from the wall by wire. Most, but not all, households re-use bottles as containers for oil, tomato paste, margarine and other cooking ingredients. Poorer households use cans as cooking vessels.

Whether or not you can spare a room for one specialized purpose is of course an even more obvious point of distinction. Large families with only one or two rooms at their disposal cannot avoid the intrusion of bedding, clothing, and charred and dented cooking utensils into all parts of the dwelling. The clutter can make it difficult to move around in these small spaces. When mattresses and bedding are present in the same front room that opens out to the street it also infringes upon the privacy that should ideally shroud the sleeping quarters. The worn appearance of many of these households' possessions and the jumbling together of objects that are preferably segregated into a separate kitchen, bedroom and parlor are also reasons why the inhabitants deem these domestic environments "ugly." All permanent residents, except perhaps the poorest *viejos*, may set aside money from a lottery winning or a company bonus to buy a saint's image or a couple of second-hand rocking chairs for their front rooms. Yet no amount of patch-ups, add-ons, or decorations can adequately compensate for the overcrowding and dilapidation of most of the barracks. It lies beyond the means of Monte Coca's residents to remedy the overcrowding, decay, and anti-familial design of the barracks or overcome the general poverty and dependence on the company of the community as a whole.

Even the lowest of Monte Coca's permanent residents can find some consolation in not being a *"congó."* In the eyes of batey residents, the bracero stands in many ways lower even than his fellow Haitian national, the *viejo*. Each *viejo* generally has a room of his own in a company barracks, even if he is without a wife or children, while company bosses generally place four to eight braceros together in each room, only nine or twelve square meters large. Braceros with wives and children are housed two families per room, with a rope strung across the middle of the room for the occupants to hang a sheet on for "privacy." In contrast with the near total material deprivation of the bracero, the *viejos* commonly own a few yard fowl, may have use-rights to plant subsistence gardens in one or more tiny plots of unused land, and have some modest household possessions — a small wooden table, a low chair, and a kerosene lamp. When first built, the braceros' barracks in La Construcción were equipped with electrical fixtures and even had showers and sinks in a separate building next door. All these fittings were immediately stripped from the buildings and sold by local men. Only the louvered windows built into the concrete walls of the barracks could not be dislodged. Residents even defecate in these barracks and deface them with graffiti while they stand empty during the dead season. Before the 1986 harvest began, the company paid a few women to clean up but this failed to remove the stench. Nothing has been done to repair the damage caused by theft and prolonged misuse.

THE FUTURE

If I were writing this in 1987, the year when I finished my dissertation fieldwork, I would have said that it was up to the CEA or its owner, the Dominican state, to rebuild Monte Coca and make arrangements for the provision of appropriate services and amenities for its families. Already atrocious living conditions have deteriorated even further in the ensuing years, largely as a result of the financial ruin of the state sugar consortium. Yet, today, I am less certain that the answers to Monte Coca's problems can come from above, or need to. Surely, the state still has a role to play in stimulating, coordinating and implementing measures to improve the overall well-being of batey residents. In fact, the CEA's slide into bankruptcy has brought about conditions which demand an opening of the sugar estates to state-led and non-governmental humanitarian outreach. The virtual disappearance of the CEA from the management of its own plantations has eroded the long-held assumption that the fate of its employees and their families lies in the hands of the company alone, with minimal interference from other agencies of the state. For the first time in Dominican history, the country's president, Hipólito Mejía, identified the sugar plantations as a pole of poverty in need of a major state social welfare investment. The president's proposal that the Dominican government take on the challenge of improving standards of living and promoting "alternative development" in the bateyes (development of what kind, it must be admitted, no one is sure) is a de facto admission that the people who live in sugar-producing areas now have no one to look after their needs.

The break-up of the CEA plantations into private leaseholds has also created opportunities for locally organized initiatives where virtually none existed before. I became aware of this when I accompanied staffers from a Haitian-Dominican human rights organization to a community meeting in Batey 9 of the Ingenio Barahona, another privately leased CEA estate in southwestern Dominican Republic. With encouragement from their priest, the renowned advocate of Haitian immigrants' rights, Father Pierre Ruquoy, the people of this batey collectively determined their community development goals and delegated two community members to take a proposal to the European Union's Fondo Micro-Realizaciones (Micro-Projects Fund). With the support of this agency, they built a new school, a basketball court, and a small public park, and installed sidewalks and curbs on the streets of their batey to help residents move about in the rainy season without getting their clothes and shoes muddy. No community development initiative of this kind has as yet been mooted in Monte Coca. People there seem still mired in the assumption that solutions to local problems have to be petitioned from the company and then patiently waited for. It is even so unlikely that dependency is any more deeply entrenched in Monte Coca than in Batey 9. The difference between the two communities sooner rests in external factors, such as the absence from Consuelo of a strong catalyzer such as the residents of Barahona have, in Father Ruquoy.

Among the less positive changes brought by the loosening of the company's grip on the bateyes must also be mentioned an increase in economic disparities between different bateyes, largely according to how isolated each community is from outside sources of employment. In bateyes with easy access to nearby cities, the availability of free housing has helped retain their residents and may have even attracted low-income workers from elsewhere. In these fortunately situated bateyes, outside wages have converted such consumer durables as color televisions, motorbikes, refrigerators, propane stoves and washing machines into common possessions, and it can be astonishing to see the contrast between the deteriorated exterior of the dwelling and the relative richness of its interior contents.[7] In bateyes, such as Monte Coca, which are more distant from sources of urban employment, few residents have chosen to remain after finding work on the outside, bringing about a population decline and putting a brake on the growth in consumption standards.

The bateyes, at one point in history strictly regimented spaces, may now be reverting in terms of spatial organization to an older pattern of less centralized planning and management. Already in the mid-1980s the level of management control over the buildings and the land had loosened considerably in comparison to the iron grip that was held over Consuelo by its former North American owners. "The Americans" prohibited a range of activities that could diminish the workers' dependence upon company wages or challenge management control. Unattached women were barred from living in company barracks, workers were not permitted to cultivate subsistence gardens, and it was against the law to set up a family store or other independently owned business on company property. A number of signs point to the conclusion that the company no longer places great stock in strictly controlling the workers' movements and living environments. I have already noted that, even before the abolition of the forced relocation of undocumented Haitian nationals to the CEA's sugar estates in 1997, only new recruits were ever kept under strict surveillance and that only for their first days in Monte Coca. Today, the company no longer keeps the barracks under watch at any time. It can nonetheless be said, without undue romanticism, that even residents' small ways of coping continue to constitute an effort to exert control over an environment that was built to control them. For, even if the austere and regimented space of the batey no longer fulfills all the control functions it was designed for, it still has built into it features that are antagonistic to the human needs of its inhabitants.

It is conceivable that Consuelo's private lessees could seek to reinstate certain such controls or try to charge fees for housing and services hitherto provided free of charge. For example, the new management of the Ingenio Consuelo has already announced its intention to charge batey residents a monthly fee for electrical service. Yet, short of doing away with sugar production entirely and thus pulling the community's main source of livelihood from under its feet, it is hard to imagine the new management ejecting families or undoing living arrangements that have in some instances been in place for generations. Certainly, community initiatives such as I observed in action in Batey 9 would have been unthinkable fifteen years ago, suggesting that a new type of relationship may be unfolding between workers and management concerning the governance of space in the bateyes. I can easily foresee management willingly relinquishing certain obligations and prerogatives that cost it money to maintain, and compensating for this institutionalization of neglect by granting residents greater autonomy in resolving their problems. (Is that not the essence of neo-liberalism?) The resulting style of living-space management might harken back to the Caribbean slave plantations before the era of the great *centrales*. The owners would still control the location of the workers' villages and hold the authority to decide who should live in them but otherwise intervene little in how the houses should be laid out and who should occupy each house (Higman 1998: 127). Regardless of the accuracy of this prediction, families in Monte Coca will for some time to come face the challenge of keeping their dwellings from deteriorating further and shaping suitable housing out of barracks built to house and facilitate surveillance over a temporary, male labor force. Though it will be crucial to mobilize their own energies, skills and imaginations, they remain too poor to resolve these problems without outside help.

Notes

1. Based on a perhaps overly literal reading of Setha Low's (1992: 165) definition of the term, Monte Coca's residents *do* have feelings of "place attachment": "the symbolic relationship formed by people giving culturally shared emotional/affective meanings to a particular space or piece of land." Even though their feelings toward the place where they live are thoroughly negative, these feelings are shared and provide a basis for understandings of the environment.

2. *"Dans un batey ... : Une atmosphère qui frise parfois le pogrom."*

3. Of 238 households inhabited by permanent residents in Monte Coca included in my census of January 1986, 183 (77 percent) occupied company barracks, 218 households (92 percent) occupied CEA-owned housing free of rent and 15 (6 percent) owned their domiciles. Of the 176 families in this census (excluding solitary men and women), 17 (10 percent) inhabited one room, 88 (50 percent) had two rooms, and 71 (40 percent) possessed three or more rooms.

4. Of 234 households in my January 1986 census of the households of Monte Coca's permanent residents, 134 (57 percent) have wooden walls, and the interviewees in 105 of these (78 percent) said the walls were in bad condition. 162 (69 percent) of households lived in dwellings with metal roofs, of which 124 (76 percent) were in bad condition.

5. I will never forget the gracious hospitality shown to me the first time I visited Monte Coca by Norbert Richardson, a kind of ritual that would be repeated in my visits to the batey in subsequent years, which always included felling a fresh coconut for me to drink from one of the trees behind his dwelling in El Chucho. He began planting these trees in 1942, after quarreling with his parents and siblings about his decision to remain in the Dominican Republic as they returned to St. Martin, the parents' island of birth. Sadly, this quarrel led to their becoming permanently estranged. In *Peripheral Migrants*, I note also that Haitian President François Duvalier, at the time of a major confrontation with the Dominicans in 1963, was rumored to have said of Haitians in the Dominican Republic, *"Yo mèt plante kokoye"* (Let them plant coconut trees), to suggest that they should give up hope of ever returning home (Martínez 1995: 46). To this day, the mere mention of this phrase can elicit accounts from the men who were marooned in the Dominican Republic at that time of where they were and how they reacted when they heard the news that the border had been closed against their return.

6. Leaving a radio running loudly all night, for example, is tolerated (unless there was a person with an ailment nearby whose sleep might easily be disrupted) but not if accompanied all night by loud talk and carousing. While I suspect that batey residents would willingly accept architectural improvements designed to increase their privacy, especially in the inner circle of their bedrooms, I cannot find a single instance in my field notes where a person complained about lacking privacy (the one exception relating to the living arrangements that the company provides for the braceros).

7. E-mail communication, Dan Kappus, Peace Corps volunteer, Ingenio Angelina, 26 May 2003.

7
High Times in Hard Times

"How can I receive a visitor in this house, if I have no place here for them to sit or sleep, and if, when the rain falls, water pours through the roof like a river?" Whispered with a grimace by a long-time Haitian resident of the old wooden barracks in El Chucho, this question echoes in my mind. It joins with my memories of the anxious apologies offered by my neighbors, on those occasions when, for lack of money, they were unable to receive me into their homes with the small gesture of hospitality considered appropriate for an esteemed visitor. (A glass of cool water, beaded with condensation, and a small, steaming cup of heavily sweetened coffee, carried out on an enamelized, painted metal tray by one of the older children of the family—the proper things, served in the proper style, the stuff of hospitality's nice distinctions.) Expressions of displeasure, at being unable to enact everyday ceremonial in proper style, are far from explosive. They are not the raw material of social revolution. They are acts of protest, even so, striking for what they denounce: not the everyday discomfort or deprivation brought by poverty but the indignity of not being able to receive a visitor in proper style. A social need, not a physical one, goes unmet, and a wound to the pride, not to their chances of survival, is endured. In spite of the general poverty of people in Monte Coca, the meaning of want for them is no more restricted to basic physiological needs than it is in any other place. Rather, the needs that define states of abundance or want include obligations of a social or ceremonial character, as defined culturally to be appropriate for kin, living and dead, neighbors and visiting strangers.

Eric Wolf (1966: 7) refers to just this, quite general, aspect of human life, in this passage from his book, *Peasants*: "Even where men are largely self-sufficient in food and goods, they must entertain social relations with their fellows.... But social relations of any kind are never completely utilitarian and instrumental. Each is always surrounded with symbolic constructions which serve to explain, to justify, and to regulate it.... All social relations are surrounded by such ceremonial, and ceremonial must be paid for in labor, in goods, or in money." In characteristically understated prose, Wolf makes a point about what it means to be free, and hence, to be human, under capitalism. Freedom from want means more than reproducing the means of livelihood (seed, feed, implements) or meeting culturally defined minimal requirements of food, clothing and shelter. In societies marked by significant inequalities of wealth, all people also have material needs of a social character, motivated by culturally shaped desires to establish and maintain social relations with others, to gain their approval and be considered worthy of respect.

Many students of agrarian societies regard peasant villages, of the kind Wolf writes about in *Peasants*, as the antithesis of the plantation. Peasants manage their own small farms, even if they do not own all the land and productive property therein, while the rural proletarians on plantations work for a wage, following instructions issued by overseers. In peasant villages, the very household that cultivates the farm often consumes much of the food that they grow. Plantation workers often consume nothing of what they produce, the entire crop being sold for a profit, and they subsist mainly by buying food that others have grown (Mintz 1974). Yet peasant and rural proletarian livelihoods also overlap, inasmuch as the same individuals may be peasants during one part of the year and rural proletarians at another time, as they migrate back and forth between village and plantation. The contrasts between plantation and peasant village pose a challenge to the peasant migrant. Much though they may have heard about the plantation beforehand, upon first arriving there migrants confront a way of life and a set of choices different from any they have hitherto experienced. While on the plantation, they are likely to handle more money and confront a broader range of consumer choices than they ever had in their village of origin. Temporarily isolated from the judgmental gaze of their fellow villagers, the migrants may feel less restricted by customs and beliefs that tend to restrict individual discretionary spending.

These new experiences can be a source of psychological and social conflict. If the migrant's goal is not just to survive during the time away but to bring money home, to the household of origin, then overspending is not just an individual's life-style choice but a potential source of tension with the family left behind. The goods that tempt the migrant to part with her/his hard-earned wages are direct enemies of the peasant village. Whether the spending consists of seeking momentary relief from drudgery in dance halls and bars or making a statement about wishing to be "in style" and more modern through the latest clothing, accessories or recorded music, every penny the migrant spends is a penny less to bring home. The attitudes of the plantation's permanent residents pull the migrants the opposite way, into new spending habits, which if engaged in too liberally may cause a shortfall of the savings target needed to go home. Though the full-time residents of the plantation may show much the same disdain as peasants do for any individual who "puts on airs," they will also generally exclude migrants socially until they show a willingness to begin entertaining cordial relations with them. This is rarely possible without a monetary outlay, prompted, for example, by neighbors' requests for material aid or by the satisfaction of taking part in socially approved channels of display and sociality, such as improving and decorating the domicile or swapping drinks after work at a local shop.

If we consider also that nearly all the people in Monte Coca either began life in peasant communities or are the children or grandchildren of displaced peasants, then Wolf's concept of the "peasant funds" is a good starting point for broaching questions about consumption among plantation residents, too. How does the peasant's more closed attitude toward innovation in consumer behavior change into the rural proletarian's avid interest in the latest consumer trends? What attitudes toward material culture, on the other hand, remain unchanged as people make the transition from peasant to proletarian or shuttle between the two worlds? Wolf theorizes that peasant households the world over allocate resources toward socially mediated goals of reproduction, rent, and ceremony. He calls the fund that peasants draw upon to reproduce themselves and to replace the equipment they need to earn a livelihood the "replacement fund" (ibid.: 4–6). The segment of peasants' surplus incomes that they pay out to people who hold "some superior claim to [their] labor on the land," he names the "fund of rent" (ibid.: 9–10). (The existence of such a claim to a share of the produce of the peasant's labor by members of a higher social class(es) is virtually the defining sociological feature of a "peasantry.") Lastly, the resources that people set aside for their ceremonial obligations, Wolf calls the "ceremonial fund" (ibid.: 7–8).

Conspicuously absent from the peasant funds is anything that includes or resembles spending on personal consumption. Though Wolf does not pause to analyze it systematically, there is evidence that such spending occurred in the Puerto Rican and Mexican villages where Wolf studied peasant social life at first hand in the 1950s. Examples would have included things like carfare to town and admission to a movie, the purchase of a new hat or dress to impress members of the opposite sex at dances or community fiestas, or buying a set of playing cards or dominoes to enliven leisure moments and provide a focus for male social gatherings. Almost certainly there was already also the sense fifty years ago in these villages that the young aspired to have more than their parents had, more, especially, of the mass-produced consumer goods that were entering from the outside world. What explains the absence of a "consumption fund" from the peasant funds, then, is not that expenditure on personally enhancing goods was non-existent. There was sooner a lack of legitimacy, in the peasant societies Wolf studied at first hand, to the *attitude* of "consumerism." In the peasant world view, there is (or was) no sense that the pursuit of a growing and unlimited personal share of material wants is either economically desirable or socially legitimate.

Cultural anthropologists have repeatedly confirmed that people in agrarian communities in Latin America and the Caribbean frown upon ostentatious displays of wealth by their fellow villagers. In these communities, not only social disapproval but spiritual danger surrounds conspicuous displays of any desirable resource or quality (Foster 1967). Flaunting wealth, beauty, fertility or health can bring ostracism or, worse, attract negative spiritual energy even from people who mean you no wrong but merely look upon your possessions or your children with envy. It appears that peasants have internalized the sanctions against conspicuous consumption so that the wealthier among them hide their wealth and at times spend large sums of it on large community festivals, earning the donors the good will of their neighbors and accruing prestige of an entirely socially legitimate kind. It is unwise, if not necessarily morally wrong, to do things that provoke envy. Envy can give rise to gossip that you are trying to "lord it over" your neighbors, or no longer care what happens to them, or are perhaps even preparing to abandon the village for the city. Villagers can and do combine to bring down people who aspire to status advancement by suspending ties of commerce and of economic reciprocity with those people, by vandalizing their property or even physically attacking them. People on the Caribbean island of Providencia compare their efforts to escape poverty with the antics of crabs in a barrel: any advantage one of them gains by climbing over another's back toward the mouth of the barrel will be promptly erased when that one is dragged down into the heap again by another clambering up onto that individual's back (Wilson 1995[1973]). Envy can generate rumors that your greater prosperity has been gained through evil means, such as acquiring a spirit that sucks the fertility and vitality out of the neighbors' crops and livestock, to multiply and fatten your own. Even worse, other people's envy can make you or your children ill. All these beliefs add up to a tacit ideology of shared poverty. No one community member's opulence can be justified as long as there is another going hungry, who could be fed by sharing some of the wealth, a moral precept that seems reasonable enough when the resource base is obviously too small to provide adequate sustenance to all.

Belief in the wrongness of unrestricted acquisitiveness is certainly not restricted to peasants. Such beliefs are voiced in Monte Coca, along with a host of rumors and tales that link specific instances of personal acquisition or divestment of wealth to malevolent spiritual forces. Where Monte Coca differs strikingly from the peasant villages studied by many cultural anthropologists is that these beliefs seemingly do not dissuade people there from making conspicuous displays of their acquisitive power. One of the cultural features of the plantation is the relaxation of the opprobrium peasants commonly attach to displays of wealth. Whether it be in the home or in leisure-time gatherings, people with greater wealth in Monte Coca flaunt it. Of course, when I say "people," I mean "some people," for

Monte Coca has its frugally minded residents, too, chiefly people sixty years and over, among both Haitians and Dominicans, who inhabit very modestly furnished living quarters, never go on drinking sprees or spend large sums on luxuries but who even so may possess dozens of cattle and goats. Values are mixed on the plantation and no longer offer so clear or uniform prescriptions for proper conduct as they do, or seemingly once did, in peasant villages. The contradiction between beliefs and conduct, pertaining to material acquisition, is salient.

The value conflict is real (or, at least, it *was*: the fear and disapproval shown toward acquisitiveness and display have probably diminished greatly in the Puerto Rican and Mexican villages Wolf studied a half-century ago). Yet the contrast between proletarian consumerism and peasant anti-consumerism is not as stark as anthropologists often would have us think. The "selfishness" of personally enhancing consumption might seem to be the antithesis of the "spirituality" of ceremony. Yet a moment's thought makes it apparent that the two overlap in some of their social effects. If you consider that many religious ceremonies enhance the status of their sponsors, then it may in practice not always be easy to distinguish status-seeking expenditures unambiguously from ceremonial ones. You might try to resolve this ambiguity, in time-honored anthropological fashion, by applying a special, more restricted definition to "ceremony" and "consumption," making each seem quite clearly distinct from the other. It might make sense, for example, to say that the prototypical social act in ceremonial is to *give* things away, through codified and bounded rituals, to living or spiritual beings, while the point of status-seeking is, by contrast, to possess or consume things *oneself*. Yet the theoretical clarity gained via this definitional gambit may be false: for example, a great many of the commodities that people in Monte Coca purchase for their personal enjoyment and status appeal are not used in isolation but are shared or given away by their purchasers. If commodities are given away, then, is the act ceremony or consumption?

My point is neither to blur the line between consumption and ceremony nor to ignore the overlap between them but to look for their common ground—i.e., the ceremonial-like aspects of consumption—and ponder this in terms of *how* consumption or ceremony has meaning, rather than *what* these acts mean. (In the context of chapter nine's discussion of the anthropology of ritual and religion, I will say more about the importance of this shift in analytic focus, from "the what" to "the how" of meaning.) The sharing out of the satisfactions derivable from consumption is, I think, the main reason why so little disapproval is expressed toward personally enhancing spending in Monte Coca. Acquisitive displays can be tolerated, if "socialized" by making these acts venues for valued social exchange, even as people voice distrust of conspicuous spending, for its inherent tendency to bring existing economic inequalities out into the open.

It follows that attaching the label of "status-seeking" to a range of expenditures says less than it may appear to at first, because the behavior and values that go along with consumption in Western Europe or North America cannot be assumed always to accompany personal status-seeking consumption elsewhere. It is important to avoid assuming that the existence of status-enhancing personal expenditures necessarily carries with it a particular "Westernized" attitude toward consumption. It is necessary instead to ask, What *uses* of goods enhance a person's standing in any given society?

I seek, in this chapter, to develop an analysis of Monte Cocans' relationships with commodities that rejects any effort to say where they stand along a continuum between the traditional and the modern but is organized around experience. I ask, How do fear and attraction coexist in people's outlook on personally heightening consumption? How is this conflict conceptually mediated through their understanding and organization of the physical world?

Time, the main organizing topic of this chapter, is one dimension in which these opposed attitudes are braided together. The staples of cultural anthropological research and theory include rituals, festivals, carnivals and other ceremonial events that are clearly delimited in time and internally organized according to activities in sequence that depart from the normal routine. Consumption is less well studied with regard to its temporal rhythms. The briefest reflection on your personal experience can show that conflicting attitudes toward consumption are segregated in time: forms of consumption that are reproached during work hours and on ordinary days may be encouraged at moments of leisure and on holidays. The meanings that people ascribe to consumption behavior also shift in calendrical time. Within the special temporal frame of the weekly day of rest or yearly festival, consumption can have symbolic effects not entirely dissimilar from ceremonial, heightening participants' sense of self-worth, defining boundaries of group membership, and expressing the group's commonly held values.

TIME OUT OF TIME: HOLIDAYS AND LEISURE IN THE BATEY

Perhaps nothing more clearly evinces the emotion that surrounds ceremonial than when circumstances deny people the opportunity to enact it according to their expectations. It must perhaps remain at its core a mystery why working people stoically endure grinding poverty and life-endangering official neglect to provide basic sanitation and health services for 364 days a year, only to cry out in anguish when denied the ability to greet the 365th day with proper ceremony. Yet, when the available labor, goods, or money do *not* suffice to meet culturally defined standards for major ceremonial, the deprivation seems to be felt almost as keenly as physical pain. An example arose in Monte Coca in 1985–86, when a series of events delayed the start of the harvest by two months. For all but a few higher-paid employees and families with livestock, the lack of harvest income made it impossible to show their neighbors hospitality during Christmas and the New Year. Poverty also kept many from buying new clothes or a small toy for their children on Epiphany (*el día de los reyes*, Three-Kings' Day, January 6).

The lack of a usable surplus for holiday celebrations occasioned unmistakable emotional distress. Many Monte Cocans experience hunger commonly during the dead season. Yet, in my time in Monte Coca, material deprivation never brought out more jagged-edged expressions of despair than when people were denied a "decent Christmas." Soon after the holiday, during a taped interview on an unrelated topic, I chanced to record the following exchange between two of my neighbors in La Construcción, a *viejo*, nicknamed Chulo, and Juanita, one of the poorer Dominican women in Monte Coca (her husband's main source of income was cutting cane), in which they discuss this turn of events:

> **Chulo**: ¡*"Rráncale*! (Damn it!) I, here, in all the years I have in Santo Domingo, I've never seen [a year] like this year, no!
> **Juanita**: If '86 is anything like '85, you can bet that they (the company?) have screwed this [place? situation?] up for themselves. (*Si el año '86 entró igual que el '85, dí tú que se le jodió esto*).
> **Chulo**: No, this [year] is the worst.
> **Juanita**: But let's see, maybe things will straighten out, *concho* (darn it)....
> **Chulo** (interjects): My God!
> **Juanita**: Because you can't!
> **Chulo**: My God!
> **Juanita** (in a tone of increasing distress): For me, [this is] the first time in my life that Christmas Eve comes to my house ...
> **Chulo** (interjects): O!
> **Juanita**: that there wasn't dinner at my house.
> **Chulo**: *Muchacho*! (Man!)
> **Juanita**: Listen, I cried, I shed bitter tears (*yo lloré a lágrima viva*), I, the next day. I couldn't ... Shit! I tell you that, no, thinking about that I cried.

At this point, I and the others fell silent for a moment. It seemed to me that the normal frivolous humor in the face of adversity would have been inadequate or inappropriate, perhaps partly because Juanita was not known for making emotional outbursts.

The emotions surrounding Christmas are likely heightened by two local circumstances. The first is its temporal coincidence with the early weeks of the harvest season. The Christmas season marks not only the passage of another year but the end of another hunger season, and this, indeed, is reason to celebrate.

Secondly, but I think more importantly, Christmas on the sugar estates is socially extroverted. Rather than being aimed primarily at confirming human bonds within the family, Christmas celebrations are oriented externally. Their special activities aim as much toward solidifying the family's relationship with the rest of the batey as toward validating social bonds within the domestic unit. Measured in monetary value, the greater part of Christmas exchanges seem not to be contained within the family household but move out, in the form of food and drink, to neighbors and visiting relatives. Holiday hospitality affords batey men and women an opportunity to project an image of themselves as more than anonymous, low-income workers. Those families with the space and disposable income to decorate a front room as a parlor open up space there to share out rum, hot chocolate and platefuls of cooked food with their neighbors on Christmas Eve and New Year's Eve. Others may lay on smaller quantities of food and drink and share these out for only an hour or so, among a smaller circle of nearby neighbors and visitors. But never more so than on these holidays, the permanent residents of Monte Coca, poor as they may be, regard their living quarters not just as shelters but as settings for ceremonial obligations.

The affect expressed by Juana, concerning her inability to prepare and share out a special meal on Christmas Eve, also shows how much emotion surrounds food as a medium of sociability, in the everyday "ceremonies" of hospitality batey residents observe in their homes. The close association between food and the family dwelling is perhaps another reason why Monte Coca residents accord ceremonial consumption activities a privileged place as an index of the state of their lives. Food is more than the most basic human need and primary condition for household viability. Just as food sufficiency is an emblem of a good life, its insufficiency symbolizes deprivation in a wider sense than whether the family is getting enough of the right kinds of food. What defines sufficiency is not just physiological need but culturally specific criteria regarding what constitutes a "decent meal" (*una comida decente*). The social unit in relation to which food sufficiency is defined is not just the household but a wider circle of neighbors with whom cooked food is commonly shared.

Having enough food to share with people outside the household gives tangible evidence of sufficiency and confirms the capacity of income-getters to provide adequately for their households. The sharing of cooked food on ceremonial occasions also cements ties of reciprocity with neighbors, who may someday serve as sources of aid in a time of crisis. Food sharing between households is not limited to special occasions but, when supplies permit, is a daily custom, even among solitary men. Monte Cocans think it proper to offer a plate of food to anyone who drops by their homes at mealtime and they commonly "take out food for the neighbors" if there is enough in their pots to share. Children scurrying from house to house with covered plates are a common sight around the noon hour. I found no evidence that Monte Cocans keep close tabs on what cooked food they give out. The plate of food symbolizes neighborliness sooner than it constitutes a deposit in some unseen fund of credit, to be drawn upon in hard times. This observation is in keeping with my general sense that the main motivation for sharing is that it feels good and proper, true though it may be (and as Monte Cocans say) that a woman who does not share with her neighbors will likely find them less forthcoming with care and assistance at a time when her household runs short of money.

For Monte Coca's devotees of Haitian vodou, acts of feeding also tie them to the spirits of the dead, called *lwa*. No act of devotion to the *lwa* can be carried out without preparing some of the foods known to be favored by the spirit to be honored, and ritually laying these out for the *lwa* to consume. In Monte Coca, believers in vodou employ the same idioms of "service," "remembrance," and "protection" that describe the relationship between living and dead in Haiti. These and other features of the beliefs and practices of vodou devotees have been amply described and analyzed by students of Haitian religion and will only be given an abbreviated summary here.[1] Significantly, vodou ceremonies go by the name of "services for the *lwa*" and among believers the religion is not so often called "vodou" (the label non-Haitians have given it) as "serving the *lwa*." In Haitian Creole, *"M sèvi lwa"* ("I serve the *lwa*") is the normal way of saying, "I believe in vodou" or "Vodou is my religion." Believers call themselves the *lwas*' "servants." Remembering the dead involves not just feeding them but inviting them, through drumming, song, and dance, to manifest their presence, as *lwa*, by coming down among the living and "mounting" and "riding" the heads of their servants in states of trance possession. In return, the servants of the *lwa* ask their blessing, either in the form of protection from illness or misfortune or a remedy of an existing ailment or run of bad luck.

In Monte Coca, women shoulder the greater part of the work in the maintenance of both spiritual bonds with the *lwa* and social bonds with neighbors. Women are the leading organizers and participants in services for the *lwa*. They know the lyrics and songs of the ceremonies as well as the appropriate moments to intone them. They have participated in vodou ceremonies for many years and know all the most important rites. Even when a ritual leader (*houngan* or *gangan*) with an established reputation is invited to lead a ceremony, the women form the core of his essential assistants. They decorate and clean the altar and the *enramada* (roofed resting place) beforehand, procure and prepare the favorite foods of the *lwa* who is to be feted, as well as carrying out punctual services during the ceremony itself, like gathering clothing of the colors favored by each *lwa* who graces the gathering by mounting the head of one of the congregants. The women thus extend outward into the spirit realm the work of remembering and feeding through which they create and maintain ties of reciprocal obligation within their households, extended families and neighborhoods.

It is likely that people's preoccupation with the food quest, in the midst of so much hunger, gives added potency to food as a symbol in everyday speech. An example of this emerged on one of the many evenings when electrical black-outs silence televisions and radios in Monte Coca, and oral literature comes back into bloom. A group sat outside under the *enramada* next to my room in La Construcción, as an elderly neighbor told us the story of the most hunger she had ever felt in her life. She treated us to a pantomime of how her stomach was so empty it jumped up and down in her belly, her tale so hilarious we laughed ourselves sick, literally dropping out of our chairs with aching bellies and tears rolling from our eyes. Her tone of levity was not unusual, inasmuch as the mention of hunger is more likely to elicit laughter in Monte Coca than just about any topic, except perhaps sex. When a Haitian-Dominican man remarked acerbically that the poor in the Dominican Republic lose half of the years of their lives to hunger, it elicited laughter from the people standing around. Similarly, when I returned to Monte Coca after an absence of several months, around the beginning of the 1986–87 harvest season, I commented to a *viejo* that several people looked noticeably thinner. He responded, with laughter, "The dead season is a thing that pulls on people's butts!" (*Tchenpo mwèt se bagay ki rale bounda moun!*). The laughter that greets talk of hunger has a spontaneity and openness that conveys neither anxiety nor callousness but instead expresses the hearers' full identification with the predicament of the narrator. In a far more serious tone, Evangelical pastors easily introduce references to hunger and AIDS in the bateyes amid news of wars and catastrophes around the world, as warnings of the imminent second coming of Christ, citing the New Testament passage (Matthew 24:6), "Ye shall hear wars and rumors of wars.... For nation shall rise against nation ... and there shall be famines and pestilences."

MONTE COCANS IN THE WORLD OF GOODS

Yearly holidays are not the only days of the year on which batey dwellers think it proper to honor obligations beyond their basic responsibilities to feed, clothe and shelter their families. Batey residents also mark each Sunday as a special day with a number of leisure and consumption activities that people either cannot afford to indulge in during the week or reserve especially for their day of rest. Families that can afford to eat meat only once a week save that occasion for the midday meal on Sunday. (A woman passing by my room once called a chicken and rice dish that I had just sat down to eat, "a very Sunday-ish dish" [*un plato muy dominguero*].) The braceros, too, prepare a special midday meal on Sundays if they can afford it, and may try on any "good" clothes that they have bought out of their harvest earnings. Impromptu barbershops spring up to meet men's grooming needs on Sunday mornings under *enramadas* and in the shade of trees and under the eaves of barracks. Women meet at their homes to trade grooming advice and help each other dress. After cooking the midday meal, a woman may dress her children in their best clothes, and take them along to visit friends and relatives in Monte Coca or elsewhere. Their spouses may tag along but more often gather with other men to spend the afternoon playing dominoes, conversing, or watching baseball or freestyle wrestling on television.

Sunday evening brings the weekend's leisure activities to a climax. Those men who have to work on Sundays hurry to bathe and dress before sunset, and join the crowd of people that gathers in the evening in the road in front of the batey's dry-goods store (*bodega*). The *bodega* carries dozens of different kinds of foodstuffs and household supplies but it is the liquor which is most prominently on display, occupying nearly all of the shelves that cover the wall behind the counter. Men and women stroll on the road, in mixed pairs or single-sex groups, making way for passing vehicles or stopping every so often to chat with neighbors who sit on front steps and landings, partially obscured in the shadows cast by the *bodega*'s bright lights. Dance music blares from loudspeakers perched high on shelves behind the counter of the bodega. As a passing pickup truck slowly parts the strollers, a passenger shouts, "¡*Échame agua, Amarilis!*" (Pour water on me, Amarilis!), a refrain from a hit *bachata* (a genre of Dominican popular dance music), raising laughter from bystanders who recognize the lyric's allusion to sexual love. Some people sip soft drinks, eat salty, fried snacks bought from wayside vendors, and stand and talk quietly in the road. At the counter of the *bodega*, men swap drinks, poke fun at each other's unsuccessful romantic pursuits, and try to catch the attention of unmarried young women with flirtatious banter and buffoonery.

Not far away, activity is picking up at La Yagüita, the tavern and brothel in the center of the batey. A Dominican anthropologist, who visited me one Sunday afternoon from the capital city, poked his head inside the door of the barroom, only to emerge an instant later, his eyes wide and mouth shaped into a perfect circle of astonishment, exclaiming with a hearty laugh, "This is the house of the devil!" Ducking your head under the low front door of La Yagüita's barroom during peak hours, you are hit face first by a sauna-like wave of heat, tobacco smoke, and noise. The sway of men and women dancing in sweaty embrace, to commercially recorded *bachata* and *merengue* tunes played at deafening volume from the barroom's jukebox, provides a dynamic counterpoint to the men seated in silent concentration over handfuls of cards at tables around the periphery of the room. A hand of poker finished, the gamblers break their silence with shouts and laughter, some slump into their chairs and others clap their hands and rock back and forth in their seats. Every so often one player rises to buy more beer or go to the toilet. On weekends, there always seems to be one or two solitary drinkers, seated and looking glumly out the door or standing alone, swaying hips to the music, bottle in hand and foolishly grinning. Visually condensing the barroom's licentious ambiance are the murals painted on its low walls, depicting naked men and women on the verge of copulating and, separately, male dancers dressed in the regalia of the Lenten *rara* festival (described and analyzed in chapter nine). Dialogue bubbles are painted next to the mouths of the lovers: in one mural, a mulatta lies on her back, legs spread wide, and exhorts the naked man standing over her, "Hurry up, *papo* (a common name of endearment), before it gets cold on you!" In a fit of prudishness out of keeping with the prurient nature of their business, La Yagüita's owners decided to cover over the huge, erect penises and gaping vulvas of the couples in the murals with white paint. Concealment, for me, has the ironic effect of drawing my gaze more insistently to the images.

The prostitutes in the barroom provide a variety of services, including but not limited to the gratification of men's lust. The women share dances, sit with customers, and make small talk—for all of which they are paid standard fees by their customers—activities that "decent women" only share publicly with their husbands on occasions of festive license, if ever. One of the owners or a hired attendant keeps watch on the activities and passes out bottles of beer and rum from inside the caged bar. La Yagüita's customers revel in a range of affect-intense experiences—liquor-induced euphoria, the attentions of sexually available women, and male camaraderie, shot through with the unspoken ambition to be the most generous in buying and pouring beverages—and overlap these with several simultaneous consumption activities—drinking, smoking, gambling, plugging the jukebox, and dancing with the prostitutes.

Some men celebrate payday by spending all that is left of their pay in a binge of drinking, gambling and whoring at the *bodega* or La Yagüita, generally after giving their wives enough money to buy the biweekly groceries but at times without taking this precaution. These men come in for a lot of criticism from other people in the batey, particularly if in their drunkenness they get into a fight or carry out some other antisocial act. Observing a local man being taken away in handcuffs by the police after going on a drunken rampage, an elderly Dominican man reproachfully intoned a refrain often heard in the batey, "When they get a little money, they drink too much and go crazy."

Some Haitians insisted that most of the braceros who get stuck in the Dominican Republic do so by wasting their earnings in binges of this kind. The contrast between the spending habits of *viejos* and braceros are legendary. "When [the] *kongo* come here," a man who had made several seasonal trips from Haiti informed me, "every ten pesos is ten dollars for them" (this aphorism refers to the practice, discontinued after 1985, of exchanging the contract braceros' earnings at the border at a rate of one dollar per peso, up to $200), "but, once they become *vieho*, a hundred pesos is nothing, they waste it drinking rum and fucking women." "It is the women who eat [i.e., consume] the *viehos'* money," another veteran seasonal migrant told me emphatically. Every batey resident of Haitian ancestry knows a story, which he or she claims to be true, about a *viejo* who solemnly proclaims for years that he will return to Haiti as soon as his number comes up in the lottery, because he has suffered too much in the Dominican Republic. In these stories, the *viejo* finally wins a big prize, but spends it all on women and drink, or takes a mate who leaves him when the money runs out, and he ends up just as poor as before. "Each [time] they have money, they forget Haiti," one returned migrant told me in rural Haiti. "Each [time] they are broke, they cry out to return to Haiti." One particularly colorful story begins with a *viejo* smashing his handheld radio to the ground upon hearing his number announced as the lottery's big prize winner, joyfully shouting "*Kèt ti manman Bondyè!*" (literally, God's little mother's cunt!). After spending all his winnings in a days-long binge, he crawls back to his barracks only to find that a neighbor has gathered together the pieces of his radio, carefully reassembled them, and is sitting outside with the radio listening to the announcement of the day's winning lottery numbers.

Evangelical Christians suggest that the spendthrifts should save the money they normally waste on payday binges. Only thus, they point out, might a poor person accumulate enough to buy a cow or to make some other productive investment that could put food into the mouths of one's children, pay for school expenses and perhaps provide a little extra cash to buy a television set for healthier, home-based amusement. A young Adventist criticized the "bad management" (*mala administración*) of people in the batey, for spending money on luxuries during the harvest, when they know well that they will soon have to go through six months of hardship in the dead season.

While distinct patterns of consumption are discernable among households in Monte Coca, it would be an exaggeration to say that the batey is divided into camps of hedonists and ascetics. Waste and frugality to some degree characterize everyone's spending habits. Nearly every adult in the batey spends money impulsively or frivolously at times, even if it is just to buy sweets for their children. And nearly everyone regularly saves money, too, whether directly, through rotating credit associations of the kind social researchers have described in detail in other parts of the Caribbean and West Africa, or, much more often, indirectly, by regularly betting small sums of money in the local or national lottery. Though I do not have a large enough household income sample to say for sure, I see no evidence that Evangelicals are wealthier on average than non-Evangelicals. To the contrary, a woman especially may find that maintaining moral purity can limit income. One woman in mid-life during my year-long stay in Monte Coca in 1985–86 was widely praised as a "saintly woman" for never having once compromised her virtue to get money from a man. At the same time, she was pitied for living in abject poverty and for earning money primarily through the hard physical labor of gathering stray rocks to shore up the bed of the company's railroad tracks.

Admonitions against wastefulness point to the larger absence of any consensus among Monte Cocans about how money should be spent. Patterns in their consumption habits and assessments of each other's spending are sooner to be found in the common premises of an implicit dialogue about value, in which sharply opposing positions are staked out. The hedonistic and entrepreneurial impulses that the Evangelicals perceive in their neighbors' consumer behavior seem to be more an ideological construct than an accurate description of behavior, aimed at making an implicit case concerning the proper way to spend money. More, the principle of deferred gratification espoused by the Evangelicals is the mirror image of the immediate indulgence that they profess to abhor, forming a unity of opposites. Prodigality and frugality prescribe divergent conduct and opposing values but share some underlying premises, including a lively appreciation for the things that money can buy. Neither frowns upon acquiring wealth but differ regarding where the balance of it should be allocated, whether toward immediate consumption or productive investment.

The virtue of deferred gratification and the vice of immediate indulgence merge also in positing that a person largely is what or how s/he consumes. Spending habits reflect the person's inner purity or corruption, self-restraint or licentiousness, and foresight or improvidence. Any fundamental change in a person's identity, such as conversion to Protestantism or entry into matrimony, ought, in the Evangelicals' eyes, to be expressed through changes in the way a person consumes. Narratives of conversion, for example, routinely highlight the abandonment of habits of drunkenness, frequenting bars and dance halls, and chasing "free women" (*mujeres libres*) or keeping the company of "ne'er-do-wells" (*tígueres*). The testimony of former "sinners" bundles the formation of desirable versus undesirable social bonds (with "decent" or "indecent" people), "quiet" versus "scandalous" uses of leisure time, bodily practices—particularly relating to sexual restraint versus licentiousness—with frugal versus spendthrift ways of handling money. Even as residents' assessments of "good" and "bad" behavior differ, the same domains of experience form the basis of distinctions, drawn in tight parallel, regarding who a person really is and the value of her/his way of being. Space, time, commodities and the body, rather than some remote or abstract realm of thought or the spirit, are the stuff of moral judgment

Note

1. A few of the major works on Haitian vodou are Brown 1991; Cosentino 1995; Desmangles 1992; Métraux 1959.

8

Material Passions

When I made my first round of Monte Coca to explain that I had come to study how people lived in the bateyes, nearly everyone had one response in common: life is hard and getting worse all the time; raises in wages were just not keeping up with the rise of the cost of living. An elderly second-generation *inglés* explained that, even though the company might pay a man 10 pesos more to weed a cane field than the 60 or 70 pesos it paid five years earlier, the money would not buy half of what it bought before. "Dis is slavery heeah," he added in English. "Dey compel us to wuk fo nuttin!" With time, my observations of daily life in Monte Coca would confirm that consumption is perhaps more often a source of frustration than of satisfaction.

That an anti-materialist streak survives in the world view of many Dominican sugar plantation residents is suggested by the impression, unavoidable to anyone who has lived in a batey for any length of time, that most of them fault each other for being too selfish and too envious of others' possessions and good fortune. Taken to its extreme, acquisitiveness gives rise to avarice and can become a source of open conflict. An example of this is the story of the child-feeding center, founded by the Evangelical humanitarian aid organization, Servicios Sociales de las Iglesias Dominicanas (SSID, Dominican Church Social Services). The SSID house provided cooked meals of rice, beans and fresh vegetables, with meat dishes on some days, to children under the age of five. Large numbers of women initially brought their children there. Yet even during its early days there were arguments among the women who volunteered to prepare the meals, about the distribution of tasks among them and about the free-loaders who brought their children without cooking food and washing dishes one day per week or paying the 10 centavos per day requested by the SSID. The crowds were always biggest on the days the center provided meat. Worse, some of the women who helped prepare the meals took it as an opportunity to steal uncooked food. That the local caretaker of the center was reputed to be the one who stole the most was a major source of bad feeling. Having said this, it could be that nothing could have overcome one main underlying problem with the SSID house, the implicit assumption that batey residents needed handouts instead of a "hand-up" toward attaining skills and building organizations that might help them better provide for themselves.[1] Indeed, the two problems—corruption and alienation—were no doubt related: if the women had built the feeding center through their own initiative, then they might not have tolerated theft. Beset with such problems, the center functioned for only a few months' time, leaving many women feeling that some among their neighbors had taken advantage of their credulity and commitment to fairness.

One of the most frequently heard terms of abuse in Monte Coca is *"comparón/a,"* meaning stand-offish, hard, and un-neighborly. Haitians have picked up the term and integrated it into the batey's Creole lexicon (pronouncing it *"konpalonn"*), reserving it chiefly for people (usually Dominicans) who treat them unscrupulously and restrict their favors to a closed circle of people. The force of the term *"comparón"* is evident in that it is almost never said to a person's face, except in jest, but is instead directed at people behind their backs. I overheard an exception when a woman who lived close by in La Construcción chided the spoiled teenage daughter of a company boss for being "too *comparona."* She enunciated so many of the understood negative social characteristics and consequences of being *comparón/a* that her diatribe is worth quoting in its entirety, from the note I immediately made of it: "You are always making enemies with everyone," she told her. "You think that you are never going to die, that you are never going to get old, that you will always live in [your mother's] house. You are never going to fuck anyone. Queens do not need anyone! That is not good. That is bad. Your husband will be an old rag of a man." After a brief pause, she concluded, "You have to need people" (*Tú tienes que necesitar a la gente*). I never found out what in particular provoked this verbal attack. The poor girl was so stunned that she could only whimper that all that was her own business and not anyone else's, before turning her back and walking away without another word. What stands out is that neighborly reciprocity (the opposite of being *comparona*) is both a form of enlightened self-interest (it can get you friends and a good husband) and an important ingredient to living well (at least if being liked and respected are things you value). Part of the warning my neighbor was delivering is that isolation and unhappiness will flow from selfish behavior, especially once a woman loses her youthful bloom of beauty.

Fear of envy-induced malady and the danger of being labeled a devil's familiar take up where shame and the threat of social ostracism leave off, in encouraging people to be generous and participate in local circuits of hospitality, sociality and reciprocal aid. In Monte Coca, it is widely believed that spells, potions and even spirits or monsters acquired through witchcraft or contracts with the devil can help individuals become wealthy. Though I never heard any suspicions voiced about a particular person's having made a contract with the devil, the idea that such a thing is possible is widely believed in the batey. It surely compounds the underlying anxieties, among Dominicans at least, that the sugar plantations are reputed to be places of magic and intrigue, largely because the sugar estates are heavily populated with Haitians, who are feared and respected by Dominicans for their greater knowledge of the world of the spirits. Narratives of an absurdity verging on parody at times enter official knowledge as evidence of Haitians' miraculous powers, as when police in the Cibao Valley mill town of Catarey justified fatally shooting a Haitian man because he purportedly had sent a machete spinning up off the ground and toward them, without even touching the implement.

While often exaggerated, the reputation is not entirely unjustified: Haitian spiritual/herbal knowledge is worthy of admiration. Also, it is hardly surprising, given the considerable uncertainty, danger and difficulty of the trip to the Dominican Republic, that some braceros seek magical assistance for their journeys. In the Gaillard area of southeastern Haiti, where more than half of the men over 35 have taken at least one voyage to the Dominican sugar estates, I visited a *bokò* (spirit healer), who had himself made one voyage to "the Spanish" (*nan panyòl*). I asked him if people ever come looking for supernatural assistance in earning money in the Dominican Republic. He answered that someone had once even offered him a child to sell to the devil but that he had refused to help them because his spiritual gift came from God, not the devil. He showed me a silver-colored ring with a black stone in it that, when put in water with *poud chans* (luck powder) dissolved in it, could enable him to divine the future. He claimed to have given many Dominican-bound men magic for luck in the lottery and strength to work without tiring. A bracero in Monte Coca told me of another magical means of maintaining strength, a liquid sold in pharmacies, called *"Rápido,"* which is applied to the forearms and behind the knees before going to bed at night. Awakened before dawn by the twitching of their leg and arm muscles, the user springs up from bed ready to work immediately. Magic of an entirely defensive sort is practiced by *viejos* in Monte Coca, who put charms or poisoned fruit in their subsistence gardens, to ward off thieves. A man in Monte Coca is said to have died after eating a poisoned squash in 1981. One *viejo* confided with a wry chuckle that he places *fake* charms in his henhouse, confirming that the very knowledge of malevolent magic being practiced tends to keep would-be thieves' hands to themselves.

Other spiritual channels of enrichment offer higher rewards but come with greater moral and physical peril for their users. Sitting in their barracks room in La Construcción with two braceros, whom I would later meet again near Cayes-Jacmel, Haiti, I heard a story about a Haitian man who sold lottery tickets in La Romana. With magic he bought from a *bokò* in Haiti, he had a way of making all the money he paid out in winnings come walking back to him. I also heard about a man who carried a *zonbi* (enslaved spirit, not necessarily a physical being) in a suitcase under his arm. All he had to do was brush up against you and the *zonbi* would pick your pocket.

Across the border, in these men's rural home area in southeastern Haiti, stories make the Dominican Republic out to be a magical free-fire zone. The irony is obvious: Haitians regard the Dominican Republic in much the same way as Dominicans look at Haiti, as a place of magic, madness, murder, and mystery. Fortunes won and lost in the Dominican Republic loom large in the legends of this part of Haiti. I was told, for example, how a woman, who slept in the rough on the riverbank next to a waterfall near Cayes-Jacmel was turned mad by a magical curse from her husband. He kept a substantial sum of money in a big wooden box, stored up in the rafters of their house. One day, when he was away, she took the box down and ran to Santo Domingo with another man. With the help of magic bought from a *bokò*, her husband tracked them down, killed her lover, took back the money, and threw his malevolent spell on her.

In spite of being the ones with the reputation for magical intrigue, Haitians are not the only ones peddling magic in the Ingenio Consuelo. A young Haitian-Dominican man once took me for a consultation with a Dominican spiritist whom he said was working to win spiritual influence over the plantation's top administrator, to regain this young man his job in the mill. Both Dominicans and Haitians tell stories of *bacás*, terrible creatures who labor at night for their human masters, sucking the life force out of neighbors' animals and crops and transferring it to their masters' livestock and fields. The man who makes a contract with the devil to acquire a *bacá* may become fabulously wealthy but gains nothing in the end, because the *bacá* will one day turn on its master and deal him a horrifying, painful death. All the wealth accumulated through this means is sterile, earning nothing if reinvested, and is squandered on luxuries and debauchery.

Envy-induced illness and occult dealings are not just a matter of legend in Monte Coca. In some instances, magic or envy are known to have had dreadful consequences for known people. In a handful of cases, immigrants told me they had to flee their homes in Haiti because their neighbors or family members wanted their land, and would go to any lengths to take it. One woman left the Fond Verette area of Haiti in 1956, with her husband and two children, convinced that neighbors, who wanted land that she had planted in coffee trees, had used magic to make her ill and cause her third pregnancy to be stillborn. She left to escape further danger, abandoned the land, and has never returned home because she is still afraid. Nor are beliefs concerning magical retribution restricted to Haitians.

Once in Monte Coca there occurred a workplace accident, neither the details nor the approximate date of which can be divulged, in the interest of protecting the anonymity of its victim. The accident did not kill him but left him unable to continue pursuing the amorous adventures for which he had something of a reputation. The sad event was interpreted by my neighbors not to have been an accident at all. Rather, everyone seemed convinced that it was the result of either a magical spell or ill will directed at the survivor. It was widely speculated who the perpetrator of the mystical aggression might be: some thought it was his long-suffering wife; others pointed to his envious friends or lovers; others still laid the blame on one of the cuckolded husbands.

I have repeatedly made the point that beliefs in occult wealth accumulation and magical social leveling should not be considered apart from how people act in the world of goods. It is also worth placing these beliefs in the context of popular knowledge concerning all forms of illicit gain. If we judge purely on the basis of prevalence, then it must be concluded that rumors of gain through political corruption of non-magical kinds worry Monte Cocans much more than sorcery. Whereas gossip about envy-induced maladies and magical retribution is common, political corruption has been a virtual obsession.

During the years when the plantation was managed by the state sugar consortium (Consejo Estatal del Azúcar, CEA), the corruption ranged from the petty theft of a share of the braceros' wages by unscrupulous cane weighers through large-scale theft from the cash accounts of the CEA by candidates for public office belonging to the party in power of the moment. During my year-long stay in Monte Coca in 1985–86, residents were particularly quick to draw links between delays in payment of company paychecks and the activities of then leader of the ruling Partido Revolucionario Dominicano, José Francisco Peña Gómez. Peña was a very dark-skinned man with African facial features and was known to have distant Haitian ancestry. Partly because of this he was a highly polarizing figure, commonly referred to by his detractors as "the Haitian" or "the darkie" (*el prieto*). In Monte Coca, his admirers included many but not all Haitian-Dominicans who dubbed him with superlatives like *"el mayimbe"* (Number One) or *"pi gwo bèf towo-a"* (the heftiest bull). After Peña returned from a lengthy trip overseas, one of my neighbors remarked, "Once the darkie arrived in the country, nobody has cashed in [a paycheck]." Just before he left on this trip, it was rumored that another pay delay was caused by CEA funds being spent on a public rally to give Peña a big send-off. Though I do not know if Peña actually benefitted or how much of the money siphoned out of CEA accounts was spent on political campaigns, it is virtually an established fact that official corruption weighed heavily among the reasons for the CEA's financial crisis and ultimate collapse (Tejada Yangüela 2001: 5).

Sound and Light

Located only a little over five kilometers from Consuelo, Monte Coca is connected to the sugar mill's electrical power supply. Electrical power broadens the consumption horizons of its residents beyond what is possible in other, more distant bateyes, which lack this service. It has created new needs and introduced new means of defining domestic space and using leisure time, and has also contributed to placing permanent residents—even those who can afford only a single light bulb—at least one step above the seasonal migrants, whose barracks were stripped of electrical wiring soon after construction of these was completed. Even inexpensive appliances, like fans, blenders and radios, are tokens of decency that, when compared with the spartan material possessions of the braceros, signal their owners' economic superiority.

All these goods have practical as well as display or entertainment functions. Television and radio deliver information as well as entertainment. In a country hit by three major hurricanes in the last quarter of the twentieth century, having rapid, up-to-date and accurate information about approaching storms and evacuation orders can save your life. Similarly, a *viejo* told the story of one evening having screwed in the light bulb he keeps loosely attached in its socket just before putting his daughter down to sleep, to find a huge spider perched on her bed! Everyone who heard the tale agreed the hand of God was at work *and* having electric lighting is important. On another occasion a woman complained that she needed to buy an electric fan to help her sleep, because the air got too stuffy in her cement barracks. Having noted the utility of many electrical appliances, television sets and radios are owned in numbers as great or greater than more practical appliances—such as refrigerators, which can produce income through sales of cold drinks and popsicles—and electric fans—which are far cheaper and enhance comfort in almost any weather (table 8-1). I have no opinion data to say whether most people simply grew up without fans and do not feel they need them or consciously choose to purchase more expensive information and entertainment goods first.

One reason why you might decide *not* to buy a television set in Monte Coca is that you will always find a number of neighbors within easy walking distance who have theirs on in the evening and who will invite you in to watch as soon as you appear on their doorstep. It is the exceptional

Table 8-1. Rates of Ownership of Five Household Appliances, Batey Monte Coca, January 1986

	Number of Households	
	Own	Do not own
Radio	23 (34%)	44 (66%)
Television	16 (24%)	52 (76%)
Stove (electric or gas)	11 (16%)	56 (84%)
Refrigerator	15 (22%)	53 (78%)
Electric fan	16 (24%)	51 (76%)

household that does not attract at least one or two visitors when they turn on the television in the evening. With three or four stations' signals reaching the batey, as a choosy viewer you can probably go from house to house until you find a program that suits your preference. No one is offended if you decline an invitation to sit and watch by saying you are not a baseball fan, or do not follow the *telenovelas* (Spanish-language soap operas) or do not like whatever else is being broadcast.

Whether you choose to stay and watch or prefer simply to exchange greetings and move on can be interpreted in many ways. *Where* you decide to watch from, if you stay, more clearly expresses the social proximity or distance that you, as guest, perceive to exist or wish to establish between yourself and your host. I never once saw a bracero plop down in one of the more comfortable chairs around when invited to come in and make himself at ease. The braceros and even those *viejos* who are most notably uncomfortable in the Spanish language or unfamiliar with citified ways seem loath to enter the dwellings of even the more prosperous Haitian families for social interaction. They will instead stand outside, looking in through the doorway or the window, or, if they cannot see from there, will sit next to the door, on the floor or on a stool or an upside-down bucket. Even if invited in Creole to come in further and view from a more comfortable angle, these men will smile meekly and shake their head or gently wave one hand to signal no.

Reluctance to share space with the host, if accompanied by a different sort of facial expression and gesture, can convey not humility but disdain. One evening, I sat watching the latest *telenovela* with a group of two women and four children in the house of a Haitian-born factory employee. The daughter of a neighboring Dominican family sat on the floor nearest the television, playing with two pairs of shoes, to make a square enclosure open at one end so that she could "drive" the remaining shoe into and out of it like a car. Everyone else, including her mother, sat watching the show "María de Nadie" in rapt attention from different points in the room, using the commercial breaks to share excited comments on the latest plot twist. A woman neighbor showed up at the door, carrying her infant son. I do not know if she considered herself "white," but she was visibly lighter-skinned than the vast majority of Monte Coca residents. It is certain that she was known for her sour disposition. Promptly greeted by name and invited to enter and sit by the woman of the house, she curtly responded, "Hm!" and remained expressionless, even as she pulled up a small wooden bench to watch, placing this right outside the door, as if disdaining to sit with the rest. The host's composure was not visibly altered in the least, outward indifference being considered by Dominicans and Haitians alike to be much better than getting angry at such minor slights.

Not just domestic space but time is organized by electronic media. The radio provides a nearly ubiquitous auditory accompaniment to daily life in Monte Coca's barracks. In households that have a radio, it is usually left playing loudly all day, from morning news through evening news, with musical or talk programming and midday news in between. Generally, music is preferred over talk. As women go about their household chores, they can sometimes be heard singing along with the song playing on the radio nearest them. Quite a few radio stations can be heard in Monte Coca, each having its distinctive specialization in one musical style or blend thereof. As each style of music has particular social connotations, the listener's choice about where to put the dial expresses not just idiosyncrasies of personal taste but something about his/her outlook.[2] There is even so always the chance that a song that fits none of the ordinary categories will unpredictably seize the public's fancy. The worldwide mega-hit, "Zouk-la Se Sèl Medikaman," by the French Caribbean group, Kassav, seemed to be loved by everyone in Monte Coca (and in the rest of the Dominican Republic) during the time of my dissertation fieldwork in the mid-1980s. This, even though its lyrics were surely comprehensible only to Haitians and perhaps those few Dominicans who have some understanding of the Creole language from having grown up from earliest infancy in a batey.

As people gather in the evening or on weekends outside the main dry-goods store (*bodega*) and in the barroom at La Yagüita, the music of preference is always *bachata*, for many decades now the music of the uprooted masses, who live in the Dominican Republic's plantation work camps and urban slums. Adherence to *bachata* has grown only stronger in recent years as recordings in this style have become more easily available and gained greater interest outside the Dominican working classes. *Bachata*'s appeal is something like that of country music in the United States, in that the artists generally sing with the same "bad" diction as their working-class devotees and craft lyrics suggesting they have experienced the same vicissitudes ("Ay! Por qué, Dios mío dime, tanto problema en esta vida? Ay!" [Why, God tell me, so many problems in this life?]). I have already mentioned how the refrain from one *bachata* needed only to be shouted on the spur of the moment to garner mock squeals and laughter. Deriving humor from electronic entertainment media is another constant, there being always a bit of lyric from one or two hit songs circulating as a stock item of humor, only to fall from use as people tire of it and another song comes into fashion. The incorporation of popular song lyrics into everyday conversation is but one way in which television and radio have added to expressive culture in the batey and opened new avenues for its residents to define who they are by opposition with the world outside.

Richard Wilk refers to media products and spectator events, such as soap operas, pop songs, beauty pageants and cultural festivals as "structures of common difference." Wilk (1995: 129–30) defines these as activity domains that provide "a common channel and a point of focus for the debate and expression of differences [and thus] take the full universe of possible contrasts between nations, groups, locales, factions, families, political parties and economic classes, and ... systematically narrow our gaze to *particular kinds* of difference." In a structure of common difference, the frame is pretty much the same, the world around—i.e., people know what to expect when they see a beauty pageant—but the "self-portraits" of society being drawn within the frame may differ considerably from country to country. Values, social distinctions and political concerns particular to a given place and time place find expression through venues—soap operas, pop music, soccer matches, cultural festivals, and much more—that follow pretty much the same sequence and have largely similar format the world around.

Sports contests are one such global structure of common difference. One of the few points of local pride for the residents of Consuelo and other sugar plantations around San Pedro de Macorís is how many young men from this area have entered the major leagues. In an exhibition baseball game held in a converted pasture in Monte Coca in September 1985, the company provided a microphone and amplifier so that the name of each batter could be announced, just like at the big stadium in San Pedro de Macorís. A young Dominican man from Monte Coca took over the mike for a while, adding commentary on the action and even imitating advertisements for national cigarette companies and local businesses, as heard on broadcasts of North American major league games on television and the radio. Garnishing the game with play-by-play, commentary and mock advertisements not only brought a bit of the major leagues home to Monte Coca, it conveyed batey residents' implicit sense of being more cosmopolitan and in tune with trends in global popular culture than the people of other, less highly proletarianized rural areas. At that moment, Monte Coca's standing as an exporter of its most talented athletes to the major league training system produced an audible echo of the major league's excitement, incongruously situated in a pasture-turned-playing-field.

Another bit of media-referential humor made batey residents' sense of their standing in a national and global social hierarchy even more explicit, this time by opposition with the peasants who cling to small plots on the plantation's outskirts. During the national electoral campaign of 1986, a fictional peasant, named Don Chencho, was featured on television commercials delivering praise for the opposition candidate, Joaquín Balaguer, in a chewy vernacular Spanish. Though it is likely Don Chencho's creators expected him to raise a smile, I think they did not foresee or approve of the hoots and squeals of derision that greeted his appearance on television each evening in Monte Coca. Don Chencho came to life in Monte Coca, not as a campy *campesino*, evoking the nation's agrarian roots, but as the butt of rude jokes, witticisms, and ridicule. One day, I observed an old man ride through Monte Coca toward Consuelo on a mule with a wooden saddle and heavily laden woven saddle bags, being chased by little boys with whoops and cries of "Here comes Don Chencho!" and "Bye-bye, Don Chencho!"

Impoverished and rural though they are, batey residents look down upon the peasant for being "countrified" in ways they are not.

Yet if the denizens of some other rural areas in the Dominican Republic are looked down upon as more backward, Haiti is the true locus of primitivism for Dominicans and even second- and third-generation Haitians in Monte Coca. For evidence, they need look no further than the braceros' dark, hot barracks. Not only the braceros' standard of living but the entertainments they indulge in their hours of respite from work confirm their backwardness. In the days leading up to the Easter weekend street processions of the *rara* festival, the braceros somehow find the energy to make music, to sing and to dance. Converting cast-off PVC tubing, plastic containers and bottle caps into horns, drums and scrapers, they venture out in a small group on one or two evenings in the run-up to Easter. Trailed by gleeful neighborhood children, these impromptu ensembles circulate around La Construcción, tipping their hats to ask for a few coins. They do not limit themselves to Haitian folk songs but may throw in one or two pop tunes for good measure. Integrating hit songs into their repertory ingratiates their neighbors but falls flat as an effort to put their cosmopolitanism on display. Some of the batey's permanent residents show no hesitation to voice derisive comments at the sight. My sense is that when the braceros generate their own musical swing from scratch, using instruments improvised out of cast-off materials, it is entertaining only in a humorously quaint way in their neighbors' eyes. For people who generally prefer to obtain musical entertainment passively, by tapping into the ceaseless electronically generated flow of sounds and images that emanate from the radio and television, such displays evoke both pity and admiration. At such moments of spontaneous festivity, the braceros embody both the backwardness and the rich culture that Dominicans commonly associate with Haiti. Even as batey residents feel a certain attraction for Haitians' famous aptitude for communicating with the spirits, through music, dance and trance, I have no doubt they identify, and would always wish to be identified, with the modern side of the binary of primitiveness and modernity (Martínez 2003).

***

Amid all this ambiguity, the larger point concerns where the balance of the evidence rests and how seeming contradictions are managed and mediated. There is an important amount of information supporting the notion that disapproval of status-striving behavior (expressed, for example, using the term *"comparón/a"*) as well as beliefs linking wealth, envy and sorcery have important social referents. Gossip, legends and supernatural beliefs link conspicuous consumption and intra-community socioeconomic inequality to evil and occult dealings, and thus implicitly denounce untrammeled acquisitiveness. It is widely said or implied that ostentatious displays of consumer goods can provoke envy and with it bring illness. Yet I see no evidence that these beliefs actually constrain anyone's discretionary spending on prestige-enhancing goods. When I think of the near-absolute deprivation experienced by many in Monte Coca and compare this with the payday binges indulged in by some men and the unapologetic pride that some women take in possessing the trappings of a "decent household (*un hogar decente*)—e.g., plush furniture, electrical appliances, wall hangings, art reproductions, and porcelain figurines—the contrasts are so jarring that I find myself asking, Have they no shame? Have they no fear? With the conversion of growing numbers of people in Monte Coca to Evangelical Christianity, it may well be that the strict, family centered Evangelical codes of ethics are doing more today to rein in displays of prodigality than fear of shunning, envy or rumored association with occult. Yet it is, perhaps more than anything else, sharing that diminishes ill will against the people in Monte Coca's middle and upper social tiers. Even the payday binger differs from Western consumers in that the reference group of his consumption activities is always the people who sit with him at the same table sharing drinks rather than an imagined community of distant, unknown fellow consumers. Solitary consumers of any kind are rare in Monte Coca.

In general terms, modeling your consumer ambitions on the niceties possessed by wealthier people is one thing; modeling your social behavior around pretensions of higher status is quite another (and quite unforgivable). Much of Monte Cocans' consumer behavior conveys an inexplicit sense that it is OK to want nice things, as long as you do not start withholding favors, keeping to yourself or otherwise acting as if you think you are better than your neighbors. Other than nice clothing (and even that is borrowed at times by young women who wear the same size), few prestige goods are used in isolation by their purchasers. Alcoholic beverages, television viewing, special holiday meals are all liberally shared. Even a man or woman who buys a single cigarette will typically ask his/her companions if they want a tug.

Batey residents' concerns that some of their neighbors might be enriching themselves through illicit supernatural means pale before their outraged knowledge that some in government have enriched themselves, and directly harmed the sugar workers' interests, through corrupt mismanagement of the CEA. Their anxieties about shunning, envy and supernatural aggression are nothing compared to their anguish about the drastic decline in the general quality of life in Monte Coca over the past two decades and how this has made it more difficult than ever to realize their social needs of ceremony and distinctive consumption. These concerns may be most often voiced through complaining about food shortages but revolve also around the corrosive effect that increased poverty is having on the social fabric. No one in Monte Coca would deny that nutrition, education, and health care are the most important things and have all declined in quality and availability over the past two decades of neo-liberal reform. Yet it is a measure of their humanity, in the face of adversity, that they desire more.

When they cannot receive a visitor in proper style, batey residents also feel themselves diminished in the eyes of their fellows, and, when customs of sharing are curtailed or verge on disappearing entirely, they sense a threat to the network of customary reciprocity that has stood them well in the past as a source of support in times of extraordinary need.

Mediatized structures of common difference frame batey residents' place in the wider world. The importance of radio and television as sources of knowledge about the outside world is magnified by the absence of any competing media except the geography and history books and lessons studied by the children at Monte Coca's elementary school. No books, magazines, or newspapers of any kind are sold in the batey. There is no mail, telephone service, or movie house. Radio and television are therefore virtually the only sources of news. As one might expect among people who get their information solely through these media, there are important gaps in Monte Cocans' knowledge of the world. I think it probable that most could not find their own country on a world map. Even fewer seem to have more than the vaguest notion of world geography, and would not know, for example, that New York is a city and not a country or that Israel is a small country, very far away from the Dominican Republic, while Colombia is a big country, much closer by.

While they might not be able to situate Israel or Colombia on the globe and may be perplexed by the news they see and hear about these places, some people in Monte Coca are aware of the conflicts going on there. During a visit in 2002, I sat a borrowed boom box down on the veranda of the *bodega* to play a world music tape I had brought from the United States, and was surprised to find that the by-standers recognized a *cumbia* as a style of music from Colombia. This same song's reference to Donald Duck shaking his tail prompted chuckles, and the listeners could explain to me that "El Pato Donal" is a cartoon character on television. Those whose memory of the news extends back more than a decade could also tell me in 2002 that the United States seemed poised to intervene as muscularly in Colombia as it had before in Nicaragua, Grenada, and Panama. In nearly every visit to Monte Coca, I have confronted some version of the question one man asked me in 1985, in relation to Nicaragua: Why is it that the United States is always beating up on some small country? Where facts are lacking, rumor moves fast to embroider over the gaps in what is known. From a telephone conversation I had with a former Monte Coca resident in 2003, I learned that an outbreak of a flu-like ailment had been attributed to gases emitted by U.S. munitions exploding in Iraq. Incompletely informed they may be but isolated from the currents of world events they are not.

Not only is everyday talk in Monte Coca rich with references to national and global culture. Through acts of subversive appropriation, such as mockingly shouting, "Adiós, Don Chencho!" to a passing peasant, batey residents also give evidence that they are not passively imbibing from the national and global cultural streams but giving distinctive, local meanings to the images and ideas imported from these sources. The global is inextricably a part of the local in Monte Coca also in that the people there conceive of their own way of life largely in terms of the differences they perceive between it and the ways of life of people elsewhere in the country and the world. They look down on other rural folk, such as the few, forlorn peasants who live in their vicinity, as being hopelessly out of touch with and closed to the entertainment and fashion trends in the outside world. Yet they are at the same time painfully aware that city dwellers look down on them and regard the very term "batey" as synonymous with poverty, backwardness and tedium. This knowledge surely adds to the desire of the most informed residents to escape the batey.[3]

Notes

1. It seems that the center was established with little or no prior consultation with Monte Coca's residents. One woman's complaint, that her pride was wounded because the directors chose to give food, is telling: "They think that, because you are poor, what you need is food, as if you did not eat in your own house."

2. *Bachata* is regarded as the earthiest and most soulful, and attracts mainly working-class devotees. *Merengue* is musically more propulsive and sunnier, and is seen as expressing a more cosmopolitan outlook, its recordings generally having higher "production values" than *bachata*. *Merengue* has greater respectability also because it is known to have acceptance among Dominican elites and to be the most popular style of Dominican music in the wider world. Listening to *salsa* and *balada* music from overseas connotes broader views and a greater curiosity about the world outside the Dominican Republic.

3. I was impressed with the negative image of the bateyes even during my first visit to the Dominican Republic, before I had decided to study the sugar industry. I will never forget how a young man, the friend of a friend, explained his burning desire to emigrate, as we sat conversing on the capital city's *malecón*. Looking out across the wide, busy boulevard toward the Caribbean Sea, he flicked his wrist at the city and the nation behind him and said, contemptuously, "This is a batey."

9
The Hot and the Cold

> [This] distinguishes humans from all other forms [of life]: their capacity to conceive beyond reality, to desire beyond adequacy, to create beyond need.
>
> —Deren 1953: 138

When an object grows overly familiar through repeated exposure, its sudden disappearance may make you more aware of it than you were all the while it was there, before your eyes. Even more, when it is something of *value* but is taken for granted, we become aware of that item's meaning to us only when it suddenly disappears or becomes unavailable.

In just this way, sudden deprivation of needs conditioned by the availability of electrical power cast new light on the meaning of distinctive consumption activities in Monte Coca. The sudden cut-off of electrical supply was not a cause for fear. It garnered no news headlines, and posed no threat to the survival of the people involved. It may even so be looked back upon as marking the definitive beginning of this community's decline.

THE "THEFT OF THE LIGHT"

The suddenness, lack of warning and inexplicability of the first lengthy suspension of electrical power transmission added an element of surprise to the cognitive dislocation caused by the sudden cut-off of light and electronic media. After I gave up residence in Monte Coca in August 1986, a new government brought new administrators to the plantation. These men promptly cut off electrical power to Monte Coca, and in the middle of the night took down the several kilometers of electrical cable that connected the batey to the mill. In my next visit to the batey after the loss of the electricity, I found my former neighbors sunk in an unfamiliar mood of lethargy and sadness. They described their darkened and strangely quiet batey as "cold," "sad," and "ugly," terms with which they had previously described more isolated bateyes further inside plantation grounds.

The loss of electrical power seemed to have had a much greater impact on Monte Cocans' consciousness than the months-long interruptions in water supply that plagued them throughout the previous year. When the water pumps broke down, people spoke about it as simply the latest instance of the neglect that they had always received at the hands of the company, and did nothing about it other than complain to one another. The interruptions in potable water supply were a major nuisance and a health threat: people had to walk far to fetch water when all the pumps were broken and some made recourse to drinking bacterially contaminated river water. Yet the broken water pumps did not shake Monte Cocans' view of where they stood in the world. The suspension of the batey's electrical service did.

One practical reason was that the supply of electricity could not be replaced as easily. Unlike the water, which could be delivered by truck or procured elsewhere with some effort, few other alternative sources of electricity were available, batteries being expensive and electrical generators installed only in the *superintendente*'s house and the *bodega*. Residents also spoke of the electrical hookup as having been "stolen"—giving a moral dimension to their grievance—and, perhaps for the first time in decades, a few residents organized to appeal to the government for redress. Local organizers of the recently victorious Reformist Party informed the national press about what had happened, and petitioned newly elected President Balaguer to reinstall the electrical connection. In less than a year, the electrical supply was restored.

Power would be cut off again, when the lines were knocked down by Hurricane Georges in 1998, and this time the cut-off would last three years. The second suspension of electrical service triggered despondency but not the same outrage or activism as before, perhaps because it occurred as a result of a natural disaster, rather than a human act. Also, everyone focused their energies in the storm's wake on reassembling what they could of the pieces of their homes. Yet I also wonder whether their passivity the second time around might have reflected a deepening pessimism. Perhaps Monte Cocans no longer expected anything but entropy, so deflated had their hopes already been by the decline in the state sugar consortium's fortunes during the intervening decade.

In other parts of Latin America it has been observed that rural electrification is an emblem of social progress. Given electrification's status as an emblem of modernity, it is perhaps not surprising that some Monte Cocans saw the withdrawal of electrical power as an ominous sign that the Ingenio Consuelo had no future in its existing form as a sugar plantation. The "theft of the light" ("light" being the metonym through which electricity is most commonly referred to in the Dominican Republic) was more than just one big step backward in convenience and entertainment. Being well aware of Dominican sugar's redundancy in world markets, Monte Cocans were quick to interpret their being unhooked from the electrical grid as a possible first step toward closing the plantation or converting it to another, probably less labor-intensive crop. For the people from Guinea-Bissau in Flora Gomes's film *The Blue Eyes of Yonta*, power blackouts symbolize the failure of the post-colonial state.[1] Like them, my former neighbors in Monte Coca took the suspension of electrical supply for a sign and an index of a larger decline.

The intrinsic value of the forms of consumption made possible by electricity—recorded music, popular soap operas, radio and television news programs, and so forth—was discussed in the last chapter and certainly cannot be left out from the factors that made losing electrical power so hard to accept. Water is needed to cook food, to wash and to imbibe; electricity is needed to gain access to forms of entertainment that excite the mind and to provide information, permitting people to think and feel at a higher level than mundane reality.

Yet it also could not have been more evident that the cut-off produced an emotional letdown, verging on depressive lethargy. It was as if the people had suddenly been denied a mood-enhancing drug, to which all had acquired a habit. Paired with the sensuous, tactile quality of the symbol—"heat"—with which Monte Cocans characterized the noise and commercial activity powered by electricity, this observation leads me to suspect that electrical power was missed for more than the information and amusement it brought to people's lives. The depressive effect triggered by the sudden withdrawal of neurologically stimulating electronic chatter and glare must, I think, be included among the likely causes of Monte Cocans' almost palpable slump. As I noted in chapter six, though the sound of loud voices in the middle of the night may easily bother them, few people in Monte Coca would express discomfort with the sound of a neighbor's radio playing all night. Deep silence seems to be more troubling than the noise of electronic media, perhaps because that noise provides reassurance that other humans are near.

ILLUSIONS OF ABUNDANCE

Questions regarding possible psychological dependency aside, the electronic media peddle illusions of endless abundance. Television and radio offer more than just senseless chatter and glare but deliver programming that constantly promises "more." A superfluity of sensation has become second nature to television programming, conditioning the viewer to need more stimulation. Television and other entertainment media must steadily offer novel and increasingly sensationalistic products to attract the attention of a public already saturated with electronically generated sounds and images. It must be borne in mind that, even if batey residents would find simpler and slower-paced programs appealing, they get the same sophisticated, shocking and fast-moving productions that are considered necessary to find an audience among other "demographics" in the Dominican Republic and elsewhere around the world. It is not that Monte Cocans would find satisfaction or vicarious release from peering at a test pattern or snow on their TV screens. They are not *that* naïve. My point is that the programming conditions them to expect more and want it faster. The flood of sounds and images itself habituates its consumers to excess stimulation. Television producers, seeking to appeal to jaded urban viewers, put forward ever more shocking reality shows, more scantily clad young women, more frenetic action and fast-paced editing, ever louder and more attention-grabbing commercials, ever less information and more jolting sounds, images and motion.

Television is not just a boob tube: it is not bereft of ideas, images and narrative that help its viewers make sense of their world. Yet one key to television's appeal is its immoderation, the never-ending-ness of the sounds and images that it delivers. Some people in Monte Coca express a preference for more sedate programs over more sensationalistic ones. Yet, even for these viewers, television's attraction derives in part from its restless flow, its ever-changing-ness, and its seemingly never-ending promise of novelty. Is it a coincidence that so much television programming, in Latin America even more than in North America, is about the lives of the rich? Beyond whatever intrinsic fascination there may be to seeing the rich suffer ("Aha! They are human, too!"), television's message about itself as a medium is that never-ending abundance is not just desirable but possible. Television advertising insistently and repeatedly reminds the viewer that, after this scene, or commercial, or program, there is more. Plots revolving around people leading lives of limitless abundance nest perfectly inside television's meta-message (expect more, want more, ask for more). If the medium is the message, then perhaps its most important message is "there is more to come." After all, commercial success in television depends on persuading advertisers that the viewer will not want to turn off the set. Even if there is nothing good on, s/he must be enticed to keep on viewing, by the eternal promise that more—something different and perhaps better—is on its way. Between ceaseless flow and ever-stronger stimulation, much of the appeal of television depends, in a word, on *excess*.

Toward an Anthropology of Excess

"Poverty has never had a strong enough hold on societies to cause the concern for conservation ... to dominate the concern for unproductive expenditure" (Bataille 1985: 120). The universality of Bataille's claim is questionable. (What of the "Zen road to affluence" that Marshall Sahlins [1972] famously attributes to hunter-gatherers? What of communities that have sought a higher moral plane by eschewing gratuitous gratification of their consumption desires?) Questions regarding universality aside, Bataille's dictum fits Monte Coca hand in glove. In spite of the community's general poverty, expenditure to excess, not just of money but of energy spent in play and in religious devotion, runs like a thread through personal status-enhancing consumption, ceremonial events and leisure activities in Monte Coca. Batey dwellers are in no way extraordinary, cross-culturally, in marking the passage of socially significant time units with distinctive forms of consumption. Even so, the contrast between the weekday routine, on the one hand, and holiday ceremonial and Sunday evening entertainments, on the other hand, is remarkable. Excess is a measure of success in any holiday feast: enough food and drink must be laid on for all visitors to have their fill, preferably enough even to send guests home with bags of food at the end of the party. Indulgence, waste, and impulsiveness characterize Sunday spending almost as strongly as deprivation, frugality, and caution typify weekday consumption. Walking around the *bodega* or La Yagüita on a Saturday or Sunday night after payday, you get the feeling that men experience a burning urge to spend, brought on by the unfamiliar sensation of having money in their pockets.

Public drinking is a case in point. Drinking in public is essentially a male pastime—when women drink it is done at home—and is usually done in groups of two or more. Drinking alone is looked down upon as pitiful and if done habitually is regarded as a pathological character defect. Drinking is a social activity but to suggest that men drink mainly to form valued social bonds would be to "sociologize" drinking to the point of absurdity. It may be impossible to say with certainty whether men drink because they like the feeling of being drunk, because they seek escape from boredom, because they are medicating themselves against the emotional and physical injuries of lives of poverty, heavy labor and the scorn of higher-ups, or because they seek the thrill of feeling powerful by spending money in a patently and publicly useless way. But men drink because they find satisfaction of some sort in drinking, and not because drinking fulfils a social function.

Several other observations indicate that drinking is its own reward. When men in Monte Coca drink, they are intensely aware of drinking. Stationed on the long rough bench in front of the dry-goods store or at easily visible tables along one side wall of the store, drinkers are more or less constantly attracting their own awareness, and seeking the attention of passers-by, to the fact that they are on a drinking spree. Drinking and buying more liquor are the two most common topics of talk during drinking bouts. When men meet to drink, it is almost always with steady drinking partners. Newcomers are welcome to join but drinking is too serious a form of frivolity to be done without the support of a key group of reliable buddies. Custom requires each man to buy a bottle for the group to match each round of bottles his partners buy, but it is clear that part of the satisfaction of drinking derives from the very act of buying bottles of liquor, opening them up and sharing out their contents with friends. The tone of conversation brightens every time someone in the group cracks open a new bottle. Particularly avid drinkers make busy topping off drinks and urging their companions to drink more. Some men find amusement in trying to press liquor on female passers-by. If the women are friends with the men, they will sometimes stop, exchange greetings and a few words, generally including an admonition not to drink too much, and perhaps take a sip of beer, before moving on.

The drinkers consider a "good man" to be one who drinks his fill and pays for his quota of the liquor without showing concern for expense. Mooching drinks off of others without reciprocating the favor is the behavior of a man beneath contempt, a skinflint, a drunkard and a rascal. Conversely, drinking too slowly or in gulps too small is regarded as effeminate: I had to be taught to *drink*, not sip, my beer. It is generally the case that, when men drink, they drink themselves into numbness, well beyond the point of simple drunkenness. This is true even of men who do not regularly engage in public drinking. Some men go months without drinking, then go on an absolute binge. Therefore, what is being discussed here is not necessarily a manifestation of addiction. Quite the contrary, men who drink in public prefer not to drink at all unless they have enough money to continue drinking indefinitely, to get staggering drunk, get sick or lose consciousness. Evidence of alcoholism is found among the more dedicated of Monte Coca's drinkers, who will, for example, induce themselves to vomit, in the belief that eliminating alcohol from their bodies through this means will permit them to drink longer. Yet whether it be among devotees or occasional indulgers, the aim of drinking is not just the brute sensations of drunkenness and diminished inhibition but seems to include prolonging the display of purchasing liquor for shared consumption for as many hours as possible.

At La Yagüita, a range of affect-intensified experiences adds extra spice to drinking sessions: male camaraderie, a liquor-induced relaxation of inhibitions, and the attentions of sexually available women. Customers of La Yagüita overlap these heady states of being with a thick ensemble of enhanced consumption choices—smoking, gambling, plugging the jukebox, sharing dances with the prostitutes. In this way, too, the patrons of the barroom in Monte Coca's brothel seem to be trying to stretch out their visits as long as possible, making a conspicuous public display of enjoying the moment.

Much the same can be said about commercial sex in Monte Coca: the lead-up to the sex act and its surrounding plethora of indulgence are so protracted and public that satisfaction of the sex drive seems almost secondary. As they wallow in multiple, overlapping sensations, enticements and sources of excitement, the experience of the clients at La Yagüita goes so far beyond sexual release that it would be absurd to reduce their reasons for going there to sexual desire. There is much more to "going whoring" there than a perfunctory drink before picking out a woman to accompany to her room. Far from being a furtive, hurried exchange of sex for money, the patron of La Yagüita seems more often to want to delay the moment of the sexual encounter and sustain the pleasurable tension of commoditized "courtship" in time, by prolonging the lead-up to intercourse with an ornate array of forms of indulgence. All of these are valuable enough to the patrons to spend not just their time but their money on, the women in La Yagüita being paid for their social as well as their sexual services. That so much more besides access to a woman's genitalia is being transacted for cash at La Yagüita throws doubt on the frequently expressed assumption that men's sex drive is what creates a demand for prostitution in the batey.

Neither this biological explanation ("men need sex, and they need it badly") nor any variety of social functionalism ("where there are men, there must be women") fits with the evidence about prostitution in Monte Coca. Luise White's (1990) study of sex work in colonial Nairobi presents instructive parallels and contrasts with prostitution in Monte Coca. Writing in a social functionalist—more specifically, Marxist—theoretical vein, White assimilates prostitution into the category of "domestic labor," regarding both sex work and things like laundry and cooking as services that workers need to be fit to work the next day. She defines domestic labor, in Marxist theoretical terms, as the labor needed for the daily reproduction of the work force. This functional fit, between men's wage labor and women's sex work—prostitutes providing all the services needed to reproduce the capacity for labor of male producers—just does not exist in Monte Coca, in spite of there being a primarily solitary male work force there. The men from whom the sex workers get most of their income do not live alone or in same-sex groups but have wives and children at home, and are not sojourners but permanent residents of the area. The women's prized customers are not the lower-level workers whose capacity for labor must, in functionalist perspective, be renewed on a daily basis but higher-paid supervisory employees, factory workers and bosses. Braceros and *viejos* do visit the women at the brothel but they never join the big spenders who dominate the barroom during peak weekend hours, on whom the prostitutes lavish attention. The spending habits of the batey's solitary men are generally limited by poverty and by their goal to take money home to Haiti at harvest's end.

Where White's picture of prostitution in colonial Nairobi resembles what I observe in Monte Coca is the multiplicity of the services and satisfactions with which commercial sex is associated. The oral histories White elicited from former prostitutes and their clients draw a portrait of a multi-stranded relationship, in which the women provided solitary men with not just sexual pleasure but all "the comforts of home," including a cooked meal, clean sheets, and laundry service. The finding that prostitutes in colonial Nairobi catered to multiple, partly culturally defined needs is in keeping with my observations in La Yagüita's barroom, inasmuch as it suggests that sex is not dissociated in the client's mind from a range of other satisfactions to be had from women's company. It bears noting that much the same suite of services as White describes was provided by prostitutes in Monte Coca as late as the 1940s. A sign of how much better it was than today, I was told by one man who had lived his entire life in Monte Coca, was that a man could procure a complete wife-for-a-night in those times for just one peso. Just as happened in Nairobi during the later part of the period studied by White, this style of wage labor was supplanted by the piecemeal provision of sexual and domestic services.

It is of questionable accuracy to draw links between prostitution and the needs of society or of capitalism, or to reduce sexual profligacy to a strategy to optimize the inclusive reproductive fitness of individual men. But, more importantly, such functionalist explanations distract us from what is most remarkable about La Yagüita on a payday Saturday night: sheer excess. Every man about the place is pursuing more—more drink, more spending, more thrills, more laughs, more attention from the girls. The prodigious spending, frenetic gambling, and erotic overtones of the dancing and conversation between the women and their customers all hold intrinsic fascination for the men who pay to engage in them. All add to the "heat" for which La Yagüita is famous even outside of Monte Coca.

Let me clarify the logic of my point. It is not that analyzing sexuality in functional or instrumentalist terms is invalid. It is that such an analysis is incomplete. At least insofar as we are interested in explaining why men feel drawn to participate in such a display of frenetic expenditure, we must account for what they actually do at La Yagüita. The vast preponderance of what they do is only incidentally related to satisfying their urges for sexual release.

Therefore, *sexuality* is almost beside the point, for what we are talking about here is not sexuality so much as *eroticism*: the complex, ramifying and redundant forms of pleasure to which the sex drive gives rise (Bataille 1991: 27). A defining feature of the erotic is that it is more than is necessary to ensure biological reproduction. To attempt to explain eroticism's many variations by saying these serve one function—social, economic or biological—is to conceal and hence distort the fundamental appeal of the erotic: that it resists containment within the bounds of necessity or convention.

This point holds true for other domains in which cultural anthropologists have tried to come to terms with excess. Whether it take the form of personal indulgence beyond satiety or an act of devotion and sacrifice to the gods, expenditure beyond utility may be a source of satisfaction in itself, alongside the other gains social research commonly attributes to conspicuous waste, such as accruing prestige, gaining the community's goodwill or diminishing inequalities in wealth. This is not an either/or problem. The challenge I pose to cultural anthropology is not whether excess can be validly explained as a rational means to defined external ends but whether it can be explained *solely* in terms of means-ends calculations. Functionalist or instrumental interpretations are not erroneous so much as woefully incomplete ways of accounting for the appeal of expenditure to excess.

This said, functionalism has cultural-political implications that I find troubling. Part of what functionalism does is *contain* forces that seem dangerous—the use of mood-altering drugs, eroticism and the unpredictable quirks of spiritual beings—into neat conceptual boxes, by reducing these forces to one rational cause. Seeking conceptual containment of potentially threatening things is perhaps a universal human activity (Douglas 1966). Yet it is consistent with a particularly bourgeois, Judeo-Christian prudishness that so much social research diverts its readers' gaze away from the wild excesses into which the human mind may roam through drugs, eroticism, and ritual. In the social research literature, drunkenness becomes automedication, sex acts become a means to optimize reproductive fitness, and ritual becomes a way of attaining a non-spiritual goal, typically, the enhancement of community harmony or social cooperation. Functionalism of any stripe desiccates inebriation, eroticism, and ritual of all but their rational ingredients, with the residual implication that profligacy, impulsiveness and sensuality are wrong, sinful, irrational, and to be apologized for. Anxiety—whether internal or censoring their writing from the outside—may be sensed in anthropologists' haste to reduce even the most conspicuously excessive acts to their rational or functional attributes.

It is in the study of ritual where cultural anthropology has given the most attention to excess but even in this field we anthropologists have too often painted in a sad monochrome, explanatorily reducing profligate expenditures of resources or energy to one or another function or instrumental goal. Recent anthropological interpretations of the Northwest Coast potlatch are an example. The potlatch was a type of social gathering, practiced by many native groups along the northwestern coast of North America, where holders of hereditary, ranked and named positions of honor validated their higher status by making gifts of great value to their trading partners. Potlatches were held on the occasion of important rites of passage—initiations, marriages and funerals. The guests were residents of villages that had hosted the potlatch holder in potlatches of their own, so that the privilege and burden of organizing potlatches went around any given tribal group in a circle. The system was notoriously competitive, in that the object of the potlatch was to give away notably more wealth than you had received from your rivals, when you were last a guest at their potlatches. Many other features also elevated the potlatch above mundane exchange. Ostentatious displays and ritualized speech and performances were a conspicuous part of the event. On the day of the potlatch, guests ate huge amounts of food, while dancers impersonating animal gods and spirits entertained them. The host and his followers arranged the piles of goods to be given away to the guests in ceremonial display. The host boasted about his ability to amass such abundance and ridiculed the guests for their "poverty." High-flown speeches of gratitude by guests and the host's use of the guests' formal titles heightened the honorific effect. The potlatch giver might attempt to shame his rivals and awe all in attendance by destroying food, clothing, and even irreplaceable prestige goods. To avoid humiliation, the trading partners would at some future point in time have to reciprocate with an even larger display and ritualized gift.

In light of the wild destruction of wealth that took place at the potlatch and the highly competitive character of the system, it is understandable that some early anthropologists "explained" the potlatch as a collective psychosis (Benedict 1959[1934]). Partly in compensation for such romanticization, a succession of functionalist, ecological, psychological and structuralist theorists have since tried to "make sense" of the potlatch (Kan 1986: 191). Helen Codere's (1950) influential study conceived of the potlatch as more a political than an economic event, a substitute for warfare as a means of making claims to superior power. Other interpretations have emphasized social function rather than conflict, by theorizing that the potlatch tied groups together by promoting orderly visiting patterns and validated hosts' claims of higher status (Suttles 1960; Drucker and Heizer 1967). In Stuart Piddocke's (1965) view, the potlatch actually saved some people from starvation by requiring the redistribution of food from areas of seasonal surplus to areas of seasonal dearth. The accuracy of Piddocke's more extreme emphasis upon the economic rationality and ecological adaptiveness of the potlatch is directly contested by Drucker and Heizer (1967). Some of these interpretations are more believable than others. All of them distract us from what made the potlatch spectacular. All functionalist and instrumentalist readings drain the ritual of the awe that wildly profligate consumption, gift-giving and perhaps especially the destruction of valuables can occasion in the psyche. These recent anthropological interpretations rationalize the potlatch so much that they conceal the excesses that were a major source of the ritual's fascination to its practitioners.[2]

The interpretation given the potlatch by social theorist, Georges Bataille, comes closest in general terms to the kind of analysis that I am suggesting can be done of the wonderment provoked by pointless expenditure. Basing his interpretation of "primitive" or "archaic" exchange systems on information he took from Marcel Mauss's essay, *The Gift*, Bataille suggests that the point of the potlatch is loss, not acquisition. Conceived in Bataillean terms, the question we should ask is not, What is the object of the potlatch? but *How* does the potlatch achieve its object? How does making a highly public spectacle of expenditure bring about the effect of heightening the potlatch host's nobility, honor and rank?

The potlatch is an archetype of the activities that Bataille (1985: 118) calls "expenditure": loss, in the form of valuables given away and destroyed at the potlatch "must be as great as possible for that activity to take on its true meaning." *Acquiring* goods is an undesired outcome of the potlatch, its waste product. These goods are not just unwanted by the recipients but quite obnoxious to them, symbolizing the debt into which they have fallen and the deeper shame into which they may be plunged if they cannot reciprocate on an expanded scale of profligacy. "The ideal," indicates Mauss, "would be to give a potlatch and not have it returned." To gain a victory is to disrupt the cycle of reciprocity, not perpetuate it, by giving a gift so large that it throws one's rival into disarray. "This ideal," Bataille (1985:122) adds, "is realized in certain forms of destruction to which custom allows no possible response." "Doubtless potlatch is not reducible to the desire to lose, but what it brings to the giver is not the inevitable increase of return gifts; it is the *rank* which it confers on the one who has the last word" (Bataille 1988: 71). Only Western political economy and its many variants, including Marxism and Darwinian theory, could be so obstinately focused on marginal utility that it could insist that material gain is the object of this ritual, which so obviously revolves around grandiose expenditure, waste, and even destruction of material wealth.

In *The Accursed Share,* Bataille (1988 and 1991) defines a theory of "general economy," in which "expenditure"—the using up of wealth, energy, power, matter, time—rather than the acquisition of resources through production and exchange, is the primary object of human action and measure of value. In Bataille's view, it is neither necessity nor scarcity which confront humankind with its most fundamental problems but the super-abundance of energy on the face of the Earth and in the body of each human being (Bataille 1988: 12, 28). The object of general economy is to describe and analyze the forms in which the human organism's surplus energy is expended. The assumption of surplus and the primacy of expenditure in Bataille's general economy turns upside down formal economists' assumptions that exchange is, and always has been, oriented primarily toward acquiring scarce goods and hence is guided by calculations of utility.

General economy also encompasses a wider range of activities than is normally considered subject matter for economics and, more importantly, focuses upon activities that present a challenge to utilitarian analysis precisely because their aim is loss, not gain (Bataille 1985: 118). Among these Bataille includes "luxury, mourning, war, cults, the construction of sumptuary monuments, games, spectacles, arts, perverse sexual activity (i.e., deflected from genital finality)—all [of which] ... have no end beyond themselves." The term, "general economy," must therefore not be understood as a theory that competes with formal economics. It is instead a theory that rejects formal economics, for the part this academic discipline plays in supporting the tyranny of the necessary and the ideology that all branches of human endeavor can be understood in terms of individual means-ends rationality, enforced by markets or market-like competition.

Chapter Nine

Bataille's concept of "expenditure" brings us closer to the spirit of Monte Coca's most intense ritual, the Lenten festival known as "*Rara*" to speakers of Haitian Creole (called *"gagá"* by Spanish speakers). It is not that *Rara* serves none of the functions conventionally attributed to ritual, such as the creation of a sense of community, harmony and trust. It is, for example, almost too obvious that *Rara* binds vodou believers more closely to each other, through the shared experience of states of heightened spiritual consciousness and the collective enactment of belief. Yet the functionalist interpretation distances us from the experience of the participant. The person who joins the *Rara* celebration may be drawn to take part in it not at all out of her/his belief in the spiritual realm or for the sense this ritual helps her/him make of the world. Many doubtless join in for the sensations to which the ritual gives rise, or for the awe, the fun, the elation, or any of a wide range of emotional or physical states experienced by the doing of it. Others still may take up the great spiritual work of *Rara*—indeed, it can without exaggeration be called an ordeal — for a combination of the reasons above. A Bataillean approach, while not negating the possible existence of multiple determining factors, turns the anthropological gaze toward the thrill and wonderment occasioned by wildly excessive ritualized expenditure itself.

It would verge on mystification to claim to represent the "inside view" of *Rara*, premised as this would be on my claiming to know what people in Monte Coca think and feel about their own ritual (Turner 1977: 11). Even so, any analysis of ritual based solely on an objective description of the behavior you observe would be judged sadly deficient by the anthropological profession. An example, to which many cultural anthropologists can relate, is an article assigned widely in introductory-level anthropology courses, Horace Miner's "Nacirema." It amazes me that when my students discover the truth behind "Nacirema"—that it is a fictionalized spoof of American hygienic practices (i.e., spell "Nacirema" backwards)—no one ever says, "Hey! This is truly a *bad* description of our society!" or asks, "Does ethnography always distort the perspective of the people that badly?" The only reason Miner can describe tooth-brushing in terms that cast it as an exotic ritual is that his "ethnography" is bereft of exegetical material, statements from the people that offer their explanation of what they are doing. Part of what makes an analysis of ritual an *ethnography* is what is missing from "Nacirema": translation and etymological analysis of the terms and symbols used by the people of the group under study, as well as analysis of the interpretations of the ritual elicited from the participants.

Even as we may never know the inside perspective with any certainty, I also think we anthropologists should try to avoid being *untrue* to the insiders' view. Ethnographers court ethnocentrism of the worst sort when we impute reasons or meanings to ritual that relate to things not referenced in the participants' own explanations. Unfortunately, this practice, of imputing larger functions or meanings to ritual, is common in the anthropology of religion. Most ethnographic studies of religion at one point or another reach for larger, external explanations of what a particular ritual does or the studies even pretend to say what ritual in general exists for. Ethnographers of all theoretical stripes and methodological persuasions assert that reasons and meanings that are not obvious to the participants "stand behind" or are expressed by ritual. Some say that ritual conveys veiled political protest. Others think it draws society or some segment of society into closer solidarity, or—to the contrary—that it legitimizes the domination of one group over another. Others still speculate that ritual creates incentives to cooperation that pay off in enhanced individual reproductive fitness or group ecological adaptation. I think this whole tendency is suspect, regardless of what theoretical agenda it advances. Saying what ritual is for, or what it means, beyond whatever the people who do the ritual say it does, invites ethnocentric distortion. This, because all efforts to explain ritual as serving one or more function(s) are premised on what David Hufford (1982) calls, the "tradition of disbelief." The unspoken assumption is that whatever a particular ritual is for, it cannot exist for the reasons the participants offer for it, because those reasons are premised on supernatural beliefs that are (from the Western scientific viewpoint) objectively incorrect.

For me, avoiding the ethnocentrism that stems from disbelieving the participants' point of view depends on rejecting this established tradition of disbelief in the anthropology of religion. We cultural anthropologists must first actively and consciously resist the habit of employing terms that would seem alien to the people who enact rituals, to say what those rituals are for. The best way to avoid those terms is to drop the functionalist and rationalist questions, What is ritual for? and What does it mean? There are the wrong questions to ask, at least insofar as such questions lead anthropologists into a tacit agenda to provide social, biological or other secular/rational reasons for why the people of some other tradition would believe in spiritual matters that seem unbelievable to our eyes. Secondly, I think we should seek firmer ground for interpretation, by asking, *How* does ritual mean? instead of, *What* does ritual mean? Bataille's concept of expenditure offers one, admittedly incomplete, path of entry into the matter of how ritual produces its effects. With Bataille, we stand on the ground of the how of meaning, more firmly than we would with Durkheim, Darwin, Marx or any other functionalist theorist.

My analysis of *Rara* centers on three phases and aspects of the ritual: (1) the symbolism of the preparatory rites which take place before the main Easter-weekend *Rara* processions; (2) the activities that take place during the processions, among both the core group of musicians and dancers and the crowd of peripheral on-lookers and co-celebrants; and (3) the texts of the songs sung during the processions. Symbolism, action and text alike express a positive valuation of expenditure, which elevates life to the level of life worth living, and not just dull survival. These valued dimensions of experience include:

- a strong flow of human energy generally
- rhythmic, rocking movement and agitation, expressed in the polysemic Haitian Creole verb, *balanse*
- lightness, energy, heightened states of emotion
- and communion with the spirits, all encapsulated in the feeling that the performance should be "hot" more generally, desire beyond necessity.

These various aspects of the celebration of *Rara* point to central concerns and dominant attitudes among its celebrants: the ritual takes work and discipline; but, more than just adherence to tradition, an added spark of physical and spiritual energy is required for the ritual to be done well.

In Search of Spiritual Heat

Rara, in general terms, focuses on death, fertility and the regeneration of life, and aims more specifically to propitiate and please the *lwa*, the spirits of Haitian vodou. The *lwa* inhabit many sacred points in the surrounding environment and are ritually saluted and served by the *Rara* procession as it moves across the landscape. Believed by their devotees to control every aspect of life, the *lwa* may bestow or suddenly and even capriciously withdraw health, luck, wealth, and love. Many, but not all of the central celebrants of *Rara* in the Dominican bateyes are people of Haitian nationality or ancestry, who believe that one or more *lwa* have claimed them for "service" in the form of offerings and ceremonies. In fewer numbers, ethnic Dominicans dance in the *Rara* cortege but they never enter into trance states by being "mounted" by a *lwa*, and hence cannot rise to be one of the festival's central organizers.

Elizabeth McAlister (2002: 3), the leading anthropological authority on *Rara*, writes:

> *Rara* is the yearly festival in Haiti that, even more than Carnival, belongs to the so-called peasant classes and the urban poor. Beginning the moment Carnival ends, on the eve of Lent, and building for six weeks until Easter Week, *Rara* processions walk for miles through local territory, attracting fans and singing new and old songs. Bands stop traffic for hours to play music and perform rituals for Afro-Haitian deities at crossroads, bridges, and cemeteries. They are conducting the spiritual work that becomes necessary when the angels and saints, along with Jesus, disappear into the underworld on Good Friday.

McAlister (2002: 139) observes that offices in *Rara* bands in Haiti "may correspond with, or be distinct from, a sponsoring Vodou, Chanpwèl, or work society." At times, the sponsors are secret organizations, like the feared *bizango* or *bann shanpwèl*, who walk by night, but much more often *Rara* bands are sponsored by peasant groups whose existence simply goes unobserved by city dwellers and whose importance has been insufficiently unacknowledged, even by cultural anthropologists (one notable exception being J. Smith 2001). Often these are farmers' or petty traders' groups that provide mutual assistance, hold yearly feasts, and in recent years increasingly often organize self-help community development projects.

I do not know of *Rara* bands being organized by *sosyete* in the Dominican Republic nor have I found mention of this in the literature on *"el gagá."* Instead, *Rara* bands are affiliated with particular bateyes. Some of these may be allied with occult societies led by residents of those bateyes. Considering the rabid anti-Haitian prejudice and fear of vodou that exists among the Dominican Republic's officialdom, it would be understandable if these secret societies would not wish to make their existence known outside of the Haitian community. Yet in the Dominican Republic, too, *Rara* may be said to make the "people power" of the rural masses tacitly manifest, because *Rara* depends for its successful realization on the labor of the large, unappreciated mass of workers from Haiti.

In common with Carnival, *Rara* is a ritual of reversal involving the suspension of certain everyday norms of propriety. The everyday social order is reversed also, in the sense that the ritual brings the people who stand lowest in the plantation's social hierarchy up high, to occupy the center of public attention by acting out roles with floridly honorific titles (e.g., president, minister of war, colonel, majors, queens). (These are the same kinds of titles as are given to officers in the traditional peasant organizations, or "societies" [*sosyete*], that commonly organize *Rara* bands in rural Haiti.) *Rara* brings a large gathering of workers and their family members, Haitian and Dominican, to take over the throughways within the batey and the roads that link it to other bateyes, each person inching forward with undulating hips, driven by the incessant syncopated rhythm of the band's musicians. Thus the everyday order of social and physical space is inverted. The lowly issue commands, organize a great collective project, and occupy the center of attention, the community at large taking over roads normally dominated by the company's trucks and tractors and using these for the non-material ends of festive release and spiritual devotion.

The path for the procession is opened by one man who goes ahead of the group, loudly cracking a long whip made of rope, to clear the way of malevolent spirits but also to keep bystanders out of the way (figure 9-1). The main body of the procession follows at a safe distance, led by the queens. These young women wear their best dresses, sometimes topped with bridal veils. Each carries one banner of solid color. In Monte Coca's *Rara,* one banner is red and one is white. The banners have more than a decorative and symbolic function. With their movements, the queens signal friendly or hostile intentions when, in their peregrinations, their band crosses paths with another batey's band. When this happens, the presidents of the two bands go ahead to negotiate which way each group will pass. If there is enmity between the two, the bands may fight. On the president's signal, the queens wave their flags from side to side as a sign of peace or move them up and down as a signal of a fight.

172   Chapter Nine

Figure 9-1. Opening the way for the *Rara* band, one man cracks a long whip.

Directly behind the queens march the musicians, playing drums, one-note cornets, and *"vaksin" "banbou"* horns made of hollow lengths of bamboo or PVC tubing. The *banbou* are generally played in groups of three or four, and they are the instruments whose tenor and style give *Rara* its highly distinctive musical signature. McAlister (2002: 46) explains:

> The musicians play the *banbou* using a method called hocketing. Each player takes the instrument and blows a single tone (or a tone plus an octave above it). By blowing rhythmically, the group of *banbou* players improvise until they find a pleasing, catchy *ostinato* (short repeated melody). It surprises many listeners who listen to *Rara* music on recordings, without seeing it, that the melodies are created by players who blow only one note each. To help with their timing, the *banbou* players beat a *kata* part on the bamboo with a long stick, making the instrument both melodic and percussive. Playing the *banbou* while walking takes a great deal of coordination, rhythm, and lung capacity.

As the band moves forward, the *banbou* players march in a tight bunch, often with heads bent close together, as if to hear each other better, their eyes cast toward the ground (figure 9-2).

The most glamorous and sought-after positions in the band are the *majò* (majors), whose colorful regalia and highly stylized dance steps symbolize *Rara* perhaps more than any other aspect of the festival. At any time, there are usually four to six men playing the role of majors. In Monte Coca, the total number accorded this honor is greater, permitting men to circulate in

Figure 9-2. *Banbou* players advance.

and out of the ranks of the majors over the course of Easter weekend. Though most are Haitian, in Monte Coca, as in other bateyes, it is common for ethnic Dominican men to be named majors, too (Rosenberg 1979: 68). When the band is marching, the majors are often obscured from sight, occupying positions at the very center of the procession. When the band stops to salute a family member, friend or prominent member of the community, the majors take center stage in their colorful costumes, forming a circle a few meters in diameter, toward the center of which they face each other and dance, displaying their dexterity, footwork and stamina. The circle rotates slowly as the majors do a shuffling step, undulating their hips in a motion amplified by colorful fabric skirts worn about their waists (figure 9-3). As they dance in this way, each major twirls a wooden baton, sheathed in shiny aluminum, above his head on his fingertips, and shrilly blows the whistle he carries around his neck on a lanyard. Each end of the majors' batons is capped by a cone-shaped extension containing pebbles that rattle as the baton rotates (figure 9-4). At

Figure 9-3. The *majò* in a display of footwork and dexterity.

an unspoken signal, the majors rush as a group toward the individual or the door of the household whom they are honoring with this display. The first man to reach the person or threshold is rewarded by the honoree with a monetary gift, or else the group of majors is sent back to dance again, if the honoree is not yet satisfied with their performance.

When I accompanied Monte Coca's *Rara* band on its processions in 1986, the proceedings dissolved into loud discussions among the band members on a few such occasions. At these moments, the band's *sanba* (song leader) may beckon men in regalia who are resting at the inside edge of the crowd to come in and replace some of the majors. Then the *sanba* exhorts the new group of majors to make a greater effort. On these occasions and other times when the procession stops to regroup, ten or fifteen minutes can pass while the band and any number of on-lookers loudly discuss what to do or where to go next. These conferences are punctuated with impatient questions whether they are there to dance *Rara* or just stand and talk. At any moment bickering breaks out, the argument is quickly settled or silenced, it being considered essential to maintain discipline and unity within the band. The *sanba* plays a conspicuous part in organizing the activities of this, at times, unruly group. He intervenes to resolve arguments, at times becomes irate and chides the majors for lacking unity and spirit, or else jumps up and down and thrusts both hands into the air in mid-performance, to exhort the majors to dance with more energy. With metal rattle (*tchatcha*) in hand,

Figure 9-4. A *majò*, dancing *gagá*.

he leads the songs, improvising lyrics at times, or delegates another man or woman to do so by passing them the *tchatcha*.

The queens bearing the flags at the front of the procession are the only female members of the *Rara* band. Even so, there would be no *Rara* without the singing provided by the men, women and children who walk, dance and sing with the band on its processions. The people who walk with the *Rara* band on its perimeter circulate in and out freely. They do not go through any of the rehearsals that the band members are required to participate in nor are their movements during the festivity bound by the same code of strict discipline as governs the band. To the contrary, a bacchanalian party atmosphere reigns at the band's perimeter, as the people in the crowd freely partake in as much drinking, shouting and playfully eroticized dancing as they please. Yet though its composition changes from moment to moment, the crowd is linked so closely to the band through call-and-response singing and chanting, that it would be impossible for me to imagine the ritual without them. If the crowd may be said to provide a spatial "frame" for the ritual, it is a highly active frame. As McAlister (2002: 5) writes,

> There is no *Rara* audience per se, since the parades' movements through local territory—often at night—can take the bands miles away from their starting point. The people passing by on the roads, or the households that line the roads to view the procession, become momentary audiences who stop and watch or join in and *pran yon roulib* (take a ride) in the *Rara*. In this way the distinction between audience and performer is erased as soon as it is constructed. *Rara* is a popular performance that invites its audience to become a part of the group and move away with it.

Without the crowd to echo the song lines thrown by the *sanba*, *Rara* would be like an engine without wheels. The group of people who tag along on the band's perimeter is an essential part of the proceedings. The crowd might be more accurately described as "casual accompanists" than as "bystanders" or "on-lookers." At times, a man or a woman in the crowd takes the lead in the singing, throwing the tune and lyrics for the others to follow. Thus, women, even though they have no central role in the *Rara* band itself, make the festival their own, by enthusiastically participating from the crowd.

Through their participation among the band's backers, even the braceros contribute to *Rara*. They renew the repertory of songs with new tunes and lyrics brought from Haiti. They add youthful, masculine energy and numbers to the crowd of celebrants. And they are able to carry songs with more difficult Creole lyrics than the Dominican-born can handle. All these augment the "heat" that is the hallmark of a good *Rara*. Even if the members of the band are all permanent residents of the Dominican Republic, as seems generally to be the case (Rosenberg 1979: 67), the braceros play a part that is recognized and respected. Perhaps it is fitting that their role in the festival should be to bring added energy, for it is their energy upon which the entire sugarcane harvest depends.

WHAT IS *RARA*? SOCIAL RESEARCH AND THE CONTAINMENT OF THE UNRULY

Exactly what *Rara is*—street carnival or religious ritual—has been a contentious topic. The confusion about how to define it is understandable, if one considers the dual nature of the festivity, part carnivalesque street procession and part religious pilgrimage. It could not possibly be more clear that *Rara* has spiritual and religious content. Many of the songs sung in *Rara* processions are, for example, the same as songs sung in vodou ceremonies or are adaptations of these sacred songs. The participants' own explanations of *Rara* tend to highlight the spiritual work accomplished through it. Yet I think there is also a large grain of truth in Harold Courlander's (1960: 108–09) observation that, even though *Rara* has links to the rites of vodou, "the general tone of *Rara* is non-religious." In support of this opinion, he points to the dancing and songs of *Rara*, which give freer expression to erotic play than is generally the case in vodou ceremonies. I think he misidentifies what distinguishes *Rara* from other vodou-related rituals, even so Courlander may yet be on to something.

But what? What is it that distinguishes *Rara* from the other rites of vodou? It is hard to understand what Courlander means when he says the "tone" of *Rara* is "non-religious." What are we to make, for example, of the fact that both *Rara* and vodou ceremonies may be spoken of by their participants as "parties" (as well as "work") for the gods? And that, in both types of events, many people take part as if these were nothing but parties? Play is no doubt a salient aspect of *Rara* but I would sooner say this is one thing *Rara* has in common with vodou ceremonies, rather than something that sets it apart, as non-religious. In vodou and its related rituals, the playful cannot be dissociated from the spiritual. If the Gods like to party, then why should their believers not throw a good party for them? More precisely, Karen McCarthy Brown (1995: 218) notes, "*Vodou* puts more emphasis on freeing the body and energizing it than it does on disciplining it, a balance that often shifts in the other direction in religions of the book and the law." Citing the example of one *Rara* member who joined in order to sing, dance, drink and socialize with the opposite sex, McAlister (2002: 32) writes that *Rara* "is considered *vakabondaj* (vagabondage), *dezòd* (unruly, or, literally, disorder), and even *danje* (danger)." *Rara* and the vodou religion of which it is a part permit and more or less smoothly accommodate various individual attitudes and modes of participation, a characteristic it probably shares with many another African-derived religion in the Americas. Freeing of the body and other overtly playful behaviors unite *Rara* and vodou sooner than setting them apart.

Having noted this, I do think the "permissiveness" you see in *Rara* is of a different kind than is seen in ceremonies for the *lwa* (the ancestral spirits of vodou). A specific example may help illustrate how *Rara* differs. A young, deaf man in Monte Coca was able to participate in his way and gain kudos in the *Rara* festival of 1986 by making a large puppet out of cardboard and mounting this on a roughly two-meter-long wooden pole (figure 9-5). The puppet was rigged up with articulated arms and legs that the young man danced to the music of the *Rara* band, via a rope pulley attached to its limbs. Written on the puppet's chest, was the motto, "Gagá Batey Monte Coca Ingenio Consuelo." Nothing of this kind would be imaginable as a sideshow to a vodou ceremony, not because it would be disapproved of or be excluded but because it would simply not make *sense*. Mounting a display of this sort would seem so incongruous at a service for the *lwa* that it would probably raise doubts about the sanity of the puppeteer, simply because a vodou ceremony is not a spectacle in the same sense as *Rara* is. Many vodou ceremonies are public events and welcome on-lookers with a variety of attitudes: serious, playful, in-between, or just curious. Yet a vodou ceremony is not mounted in order to be a show, as *Rara* clearly and emphatically is. Rather than along the lines of sacred versus profane, it is at least in this one way that *Rara* differs from other kinds of service for the *lwa*: *Rara* is quite literally, and consciously so for its participants, a performance.

The ambiguity of *Rara* surely has something to do with why it has remained an understudied aspect of the very heavily studied phenomenon

Figure 9-5. The deaf-mute puppeteer.

of Haitian vodou.³ Fortunately, there are two outstanding book-length studies of *Rara*, each of which makes reference to the confusion about what *Rara* is. Given that each of these provides an authoritative ethnographic account of the symbolism and social organization of *Rara* in the places where their authors studied, I can limit my consideration of Monte Coca's *Rara* to a few selected aspects, referring the reader who wishes to know more to these books. My debt to the authors of these two books is great, in particular with regard to my understanding of the symbolism and social organization of the ritual. Without their studies, I would never have been so bold as to highlight *Rara*'s relevance to the theme of expenditure to excess, having observed only one *Rara* cycle at first hand.

The first book was written and published in the Dominican Republic by the North American cultural anthropologist and Haitianophile, June Rosenberg (1979). Over a span of almost forty years, Rosenberg devoted her life to the development of both cultural anthropology and the study of the African heritage in the Dominican Republic. She had the opportunity to observe *Rara* over a span of eight years starting in the late 1960s, often traveling to bateyes in the company of her students from the Universidad Autónoma de Santo Domingo.

Referring to *Rara* by the name Dominicans have given it, *"gagá,"* Rosenberg gives two answers to the question, What is *Rara*? Her first answer is that it is a religious festival, not a carnival. I will touch upon this point again later, asking, Why are "religious" and "carnivalesque" assumed to be mutually exclusive terms?

Rosenberg's second answer to "What is *Rara*?" is more surprising: she asserts that *Rara*, as it is practiced in the bateyes, is a distinctively *Dominican* religious complex. She points to elements of Haitian practice that have been dropped or simplified as well as citing features that seem to have been introduced in the Dominican Republic as her basis for arguing that *Rara* has undergone or is undergoing a secondary "syncretization," involving the grafting of Dominican festival customs onto Haitian *Rara*'s already hybrid, Euro-African stock. Whether *Rara/gagá* is Haitian or Dominican or has truly changed enough in the Dominican context to merit being labeled doubly syncretic are not questions that I will pause to consider against the evidence. The label, "Dominican" or "Dominicanized" should nonetheless be appreciated for what it is or was, in the context of its time: a *political* gesture. Asserting that *"el gagá"* is Dominican was tantamount to saying that *Rara* should be accorded official tolerance and a measure of respect. Sustaining the opposite—that *Rara* is really a Haitian custom—would have confirmed the sense in the Dominican Republic that *Rara* is worthy only of suspicion, "Haitian" being equated with "bad" by many Dominicans. The full political significance of calling *Rara* a Dominican ritual can only be appreciated by comparing today's attitudes with those that prevailed uncontested before the time of Rosenberg's study. In the 1970s Rosenberg was among a small handful of scholars and artists who felt that *el gagá* was worthy of serious study. Few outside the bateyes knew or cared much about the festival. Today, by contrast, there are Dominicans in New York City who dance *gagá* in the streets as a means of staying in touch with their Dominican roots. Seen in this light, Rosenberg's assertion of the Dominican-ness of *Rara* seems more prophetic than cranky or quaint. That she and a small group of folklorists and musicians could have set in motion this revaluation of what customs deserve inclusion in the Dominican cultural heritage is an achievement that deserves close study.

Nearly another quarter-century would pass before the appearance of the first major English-language study of *Rara*, McAlister's (2002) book, *Rara!* The book is based on fieldwork both in Haiti and among Haitians in New York City. She, like Rosenberg, asserts repeatedly that *Rara* is at base neither carnivalesque nor merely folkloric but a major religious phenomenon. Therefore, even as she compares it with other Afro-Atlantic performance traditions, like Carnival, *Jonkonnu*, and *capoiera*, in its orality, performative competition, and masculinity, she correctly insists that "unlike many Afro-Creole masculinist forms, ... *Rara* is explicitly religious" (ibid.: 7). McAlister likens the festival's carnivalesque character to a mask behind which serious spiritual work can be done. She writes, "What I learned by walking and dancing with the *Rara* bands is that at its deepest level, *Rara* is concerned with performing religious work in the unseen Afro-Creole spirit world. Under the patronage of Vodou spirits, *Rara* bands fulfill mystical contracts, salute sacred places, and pay tribute to the recently dead.... But *Rara*'s religious work is largely secret and is purposely kept hidden. Surrounding and hiding *Rara*'s religious core is an outer layer of carnivalesque play" (ibid.: 7).

McAlister also offers a second answer to the question, What is *Rara*? Beyond the, in itself political, assertion that *Rara* is religion, not frivolous play, McAlister finds considerable evidence that *Rara* is a medium through which peasants convey political messages. Whether through sly double entendres or with the surprising openness sometimes accorded to the oppressed during moments of festive license, *Rara* lyrics articulate subaltern perspectives on both gender and economic inequality as well as critiques of both military dictatorship and foreign intervention (ibid.: chapter 6).

All these assertions regarding "what *Rara* is" constitute—unintentionally, I am sure—efforts to contain *Rara*'s unruliness within categories—the national, the religious, and the political—deemed serious and respectable by ethnography's bourgeois readers. When Rosenberg, for example, asserts—no matter how correctly or incorrectly—that *Rara* became "Dominican," when it turned into *"el gagá,"* she is saying in effect, "Don't be afraid! *El gagá* is a cultural hybrid and hence ought not be rejected" (as it might if understood to be a Haitian intrusion onto the Dominican cultural scene). Similarly, McAlister's position that *Rara* does serious religious and political work—indubitably true though this is—explicitly positions *Rara's* playful, disorderly and erotically charged goings-on as things to be taken less seriously. To her credit, she does not divert our gaze from *Rara's* playful and scatological aspects but devotes an entire chapter to examining the frequent vulgarity of *Rara* songs. That her findings are themselves more "unruly" than the theoretical interpretations she places on them is testament to both the power of ethnography and McAlister's considerable talent as an ethnographic researcher.

My main misgiving about any such containment of *Rara* by conceptual reduction of its meaning to pre-formed Western categories—such as religion or politics—is this: any effort to determine what is the point of *Rara* misses something that I find quite striking about it. Namely, one of the ritual's key points is that its point is hard to grasp. Its meaning evades capture within Western social and philosophical dichotomies. Therefore, it does not interest me at all to ascertain on which side of the religious versus secular divide *Rara* sits best. What fascinates me is that it is impossible—well nigh irrelevant—to determine this. *Rara* resists being pinned down on one side or another of this, or any other, Western philosophical dichotomy. What fires my interest, more generally, is the many binaries of Western thought that *Rara* mixes and blurs: it is carnivalesque *and* ceremonious, work *and* play, serious *and* playful, sacred *and* profane. For me, then, it is pointless to search for the meaning, ontological status or nationality of *Rara*. What matters more to me is to look for the sources of the ritual's power (*how* it means, not *what* it means).

My interpretation gives emphasis to two things, *Rara's* pendular synergism and its fixation on expenditure and transgression. Part of *Rara's* power comes from the ways its participants consistently bring opposing states and attitudes into close juxtaposition. *Rara* requires strict discipline from the band members while freeing those who jump in with the procession to escape into formless pure being. It is structured around a dialectic of containment and mastery of energy, at the core of the procession, and freeform expenditure of energy at its edges. I take no exception to McAlister's conclusions that serious religious work is being done and that this is done under the disguise of the playful letting go of inhibitions along the band's perimeter. Yet I am not convinced that this perimeter play bears no meaning vis-à-vis the more recognizably "religious" goings-on at the procession's spatial core, and works as nothing more than a disguise for that work. The participants' own formulations and evaluations of experience, for example, point to the *Rara* band's disorderly periphery as a source of the "heat" upon which the success of their spiritual mission depends. I therefore choose to give greater emphasis here to *Rara's* blurring of the conceptual dichotomies that structure McAlister's analysis of what *Rara* is (i.e., deep/superficial, core/periphery, sacred/profane). The core and the periphery of the *Rara* procession energize each other, precisely because they are contrastive yet bound together.

Rara also interests me as a form of structured, public and expressive excess. In it, excess takes the form of both prodigious expenditure (primarily of human energy) and the suspension and transgression of everyday social restraints. Rara exaggerates and even glorifies shared dimensions of experience that are central to what defines us as human and makes human life worth living. In addition to the service it renders to the *lwa*, Rara is about expenditure beyond utility, in the form of our capacity to dream beyond perceptible reality and to desire beyond physiological and reproductive necessity. The transgressive character of *Rara* inheres not just in its bawdy song lyrics and the bodily release indulged in by the people who walk with the bands. There is transgression, too, in the festival's rejection of the Western moral epistemology that first separates work from play, discipline from release, the secular from the profane, and then prioritizes the first item in these pairs as a higher state of being than the second. The enormous release of human energy, the transgression of bounds of ordinary propriety and blurring of Western moral dichotomies join to make *Rara* a celebration of excess as well as a great sacred work and an arena for covert or coded political expression. My aim, to repeat, is not to judge what is most central to the meaning of *Rara* as a religious and social phenomenon. It is to add to our theories of how ritual produces its effects on the human being.

RARA IN MONTE COCA

Preparations for *Rara* take up much of the Lenten season. Monte Coca's *Rara* band is organized by an individual, referred to as the *Rara*'s "owner" (*mèt Rara*). The owner of the *Rara* must be a fervent and experienced servant of the *lwa*, with extensive ritual knowledge and an intimate relationship with the world of the spirits (Rosenberg 1979: 70). The *Rara*'s owner is responsible for selecting new members of the band, in consultation with standing members, and procures the costumes, paraphernalia, food, and drink, including the food, rum and candles offered to the *lwa* in the preparatory ceremonies before Good Friday. Each member of the *Rara* band also contributes what she or he can toward the provision of their personal regalia. Much of the organizational work of the owner revolves around gathering the band a handful of times before Easter for "exercises," music and dance rehearsals aimed at sharpening the ensemble before the main event.

Ownership of Monte Coca's *Rara* has been inherited within one single Haitian family for decades. Once held by a Haitian-born man named Ti Boyòt, ownership passed to his widow upon his death. When she passed away, their eldest son, born in the Dominican Republic, became the *Rara*'s owner. The widow of Ti Boyòt was the owner when I resided in Monte

Coca. Though she was surely referred to as "Madame Ti Boyòt" during her partner's lifetime, she was at the time of my dissertation fieldwork referred to solely by her husband's name (so natural did this seem that it was months before I learned that Ti Boyòt was not in fact her own name).

Ti Boyòt was also owner of the *enramada* under which most of Monte Coca's vodou ceremonies took place, as well as a small house that had been built next to the *enramada* to house an altar and the vodou drums and paraphernalia. This structure has been in place for decades, judging by the half-meter or so the ground underneath its roof has been elevated about the surrounding ground by the erosive action of run-off from its roof. It is constructed much like any other such shelter in Monte Coca—a metal roof on four wooden posts over a packed earth floor. It is higher (about nine feet high) and more spacious than any other *enramada* in the batey, has a peaked roof and differs in other significant details. For example, it has one wooden post at the center of the structure, a common architectural feature of vodou temples, to conduct the spirits of the *lwa* into the presence of the living. Sturdy wooden benches run along its two longest sides, worn smooth from years of use. The *enramada* always has several rows of blue and red paper bunting hanging just under its roof. The bunting is replaced once or twice a year, for *Rara* and the Day of the Dead ceremonies, and then left up, gradually turning pink and a ghostly pale blue.

Ti Boyòt's ownership of *Rara* and her centrality to the vodou ceremonies in Monte Coca made her a local eminence. Her quiet manner seemed to deepen her neighbors' respect for her. She never had many words for me or for most other Monte Coca residents but she could often be seen under her *enramada*, bending to listen to the words being spoken to her by one of her sons or by another ardent servant of the *lwa*, or just leaning back in a wooden chair or against one of the *enramada*'s posts to watch people go by. At midday, she seemed always to be serving out a meal to at least one or two of the batey's solitary *viejos*. Other than when mounted by a *lwa*, I never saw Ti Boyòt lose her outward composure and aura of self-assurance. One sensed that her calmness was not just on the surface but reached to her very core, and I think I was not alone in wishing I could taste whatever spiritual sources she imbibed from.

At the time when I lived in Monte Coca, Ti Boyòt's material burden was lightened somewhat by a subsidy given by the CEA. On Good Thursday, the sugar company delivered a long, heavy log to the *enramada*, to fuel the fire that must be kept burning for the duration of the holiday. Monte Coca's *superintendente* also provided copious quantities of rum to enliven the festivities.

More than supplies, the company contributes time and space. The mill closes for the Easter weekend, even though it normally runs twenty-four hours a day, seven days a week during the harvest, except for mechanical breakdowns and scheduled maintenance. Some cane has to be cut on

Saturday and Sunday for the mill to grind when it resumes operation the Monday after Easter but the company otherwise suspends normal work activities for the duration of *Rara*. This suspension of work activities is regarded as an informal right, and it is likely that company managers would have trouble on their hands if they did not respect the custom. The tacit understanding between management and workers seems to be that the company will give its workers this free time and the free run of its property to "dance *el gagá*" between Good Friday and Easter Sunday, so long as the workers do not let the festivity disrupt production in the days and weeks before. When and how observance of *Rara* was established as a customary right has to my knowledge not been researched and remains an unwritten chapter in the story of Haitian immigrants' struggle for cultural survival in the Dominican Republic. At a certain point in time the Haitian workers must have somehow let it be known to their bosses that obligating them to work or banning the celebration of *Rara* during Easter weekend would bring greater trouble than it was worth.

It is fitting that the majors, whose footwork, dexterity, and endurance provide the central spectacle of the procession, wear the most elaborate costumes. Pieced together entirely out of store-bought materials, the majors' costumes aptly exemplify Eric Wolf's observation that ceremonial must be paid for. The colorful skirt is fashioned by knotting the ends of artificial silk scarves of various colors to a man's belt, in large enough numbers—three or four dozen or more—to obscure the belt entirely and form a fairly dense canopy of cloth from the dancer's waist to below his knees. A heavily sequined, fringed red cape, dotted with circular mirrors about two or three inches in diameter, is loosely knotted below neck and covers much of the major's back. The mirrors deflect envy or ill will back upon the source of these negative spiritual energies. Under the cape and skirt, the majors typically wear tight-fitting pants, often the elastic kind that baseball players wear, long athletic socks and sneakers, and a clean button shirt or T-shirt, in good condition. A baseball cap tops the ensemble, covered with ribbons of many colors pinned into tight, undulating curls. Many of the majors wear dark sunglasses.

Significant as the cash outlays are for people living near the edge of subsistence, the main resource that *Rara* demands from its participants is not money or time but physical energy. The processions are preceded by a vodou ceremony the evening of Good Thursday, in which the gods are invited to join in the party and protect and energize the band. In the hours before sunrise on Good Friday, *Rara* bands in bateyes across much of the Dominican Republic begin to play music, dance and march. From the night before Good Friday, the festivity continues uninterrupted for three whole days and nights, until Easter Sunday evening.

In the early hours of the festival, each band visits the homes of the band's sponsors and the band members' relatives, saluting each house with a dance by the majors. At each stop the surrounding crowd grows. When I witnessed *Rara* there in 1986, it took all day and into the night for the band to make its way along each of the paths that wind through Monte Coca's three districts, feet shuffling and hips swaying to the rhythm of the drums, horns and *banbou*. Frequent stops are made for the majors to display their steps not just for neighbors but for the several visitors who come to the batey, as many do each year, to share the first day of the festival with friends. Monte Coca's *Rara* has some renown in the area and the batey's proximity to Consuelo permits visitors to come and go with relative ease. At midmorning of Good Friday, a particularly long performance was held in front of the *superintendente*'s house. Judging by some large-denomination bills that I later saw among the small ones in the hands of the band's treasurer, the *super* was apparently generous to the dancers.

On Saturday and Sunday, the band ventures out to visit other bateyes, making certain to pay respects to the families of any present or former band members who live outside Monte Coca. In this way, the procession covers an impressive mileage on foot, singing and making music all the time they are on the move or when the majors are dancing. Even when the processions return to the home base to rest in the late hours of the night, the celebration continues with drumming and singing around the *enramada*, lit by the log fire kept burning outside the owner's domicile for the entire long weekend. In this all-out effort, the band members may catch a few hours' rest here and there but others take their place and the procession goes on. The festival is a total effort also in the sense that almost all, except the batey's Evangelicals, join the crowd and sing along as best they can with the Creole language lyrics. Dominicans' enthusiastic participation alongside Haitians is perhaps the clearest evidence that *Rara* is, as Rosenberg insists, a Dominican as well as a Haitian popular religious event.

For the majors, *Rara* is not just a test of endurance but a moment to put good-natured male competitiveness on stylized display. As the majors form a ring to begin their quasi-theatrical dance, one among them may issue an unspoken challenge to another major by staring into his eyes from across the ring at a distance of three or four meters. He then poses completely still, poised to dance on the balls of his feet, legs held apart in a slight crouch and the baton held on the fingertips of one hand, cocked behind his head. At times, the dancer will make the challenge emphatic by pawing at the earth with his feet and his free hand before issuing the challenge just described. The challenger begins the dance by twirling his baton and putting the circle of dancers in motion, swinging his hips and moving slowly sideways in a shuffling step, all the while twirling the baton and holding his opponent's gaze in an unblinking stare. After a few minutes, the challenger suddenly stops dancing, grips his baton in one fist, and briefly chases the other majors in a circle until he suddenly stops and begins dancing again. This time, the majors will approach each other, dancing toward the center of the circle as

186   *Chapter Nine*

a group, and then withdraw to the perimeter, and repeat this approach and withdrawal in the same way a number of times, before breaking into a free run at an undetermined moment to claim their monetary reward from the person whom the band is saluting with this performance.

The celebration of *Rara* embodies expenditure to excess not just in energy but in the carnivalesque transgression of normal bounds of social propriety that has been so strikingly evident to its observers. Erotic play features prominently in both the dancing that goes on in the crowd following the procession and in the lyrics of the songs sung while the procession is in motion. Many of the women in the crowd grind their hips in a circular motion, hands held above their heads, in the style called "whining" in Trinidad. This motion is called *"gouyad"* (verb, *gouye*) in Haitian Creole (figure 9-6). At times, a man will sneak up from behind and grind with a woman who is dancing thus, rotating his own crotch against her buttocks in synchrony with her movements. Sometimes the woman rebuffs this mock coupling but if not done entirely too rudely she may let even a man who is not her boyfriend or conjugal partner dance with her in this style for some time. On one occasion, a *viejo* of diminutive stature and slight build got up behind a woman and started to grind but she pushed him away. Alone, he kept grinding his hips, holding a bottle of rum against his crotch to imitate

Figure 9-6. A young woman dances in the style known as *"gouye."*

Figure 9-7. Eroticized dancing on the perimeter of the *Rara* procession. Face obscured to hide identity.

an erect penis (figure 9-7). Moments later, he tried to sneak up on the same woman and she rebuffed him again. This time, the woman's companion, a burly man, grabbed the *viejo* around his waist and ground against *his* buttocks, with increasingly forceful movements. This continued until the larger man was thrusting his hips simulating copulation, sometimes lifting the much smaller viejo up off the ground, sending the smaller man's feet flying upward comically with each thrust. The suspension of normal restraints on behavior does not prevent some men from getting angry at the sight of their wives engaging in eroticized dancing with other men. Upon seeing one woman being pinned by neighbors to the ground, holding a knife in her hand, after an altercation with her husband, one young Dominican man remarked that there are always violent incidents during *gagá* and that people would not think the ceremony was hot enough without at least one good dust-up.

Transgression of normal bounds of decorum is also evident in the lyrics of the many songs sung during *Rara* that make more frank reference to sexuality than is considered proper in any non-ritualized public event. One of the two or three most frequently sung songs in the *Rara* that I walked with in Monte Coca had the following refrain:

Woy, woy, woy! Woy, woy, woy!	Woy, woy, woy! Woy, woy, woy!
Se sa! Se sa!	It's so! It's so!
Yon fanm pa konn gouye	If a woman doesn't know how to *gouye*
rale pwèl-li pa deye.	pull a hair off her butt.

In other versions of this lyric, the advice was changed to "rub her clitoris," making the undertone of sexual trespass more explicit. As McAlister (2002: 60) notes, "The humor of innuendo not only is found in *Rara* lyrics but is firmly established as a form of Kreyòl speech called *betiz*." The greater part of *Rara betiz* songs, like this one, express a male perspective, often conveying "an implicit misogyny, with adultery and prostitution the most common subjects" (ibid.: 64). The implicit reference to women's sexual pleasure, made in the alternate strophe that advises stroking the woman's genitalia to get her to *gouye*, is less common but the clitoris is frequently referred to in *Rara*'s *betiz* songs (ibid.: 74).

Together with other *Rara* songs that refer to women being unfaithful to their partners or possessing sexual appetites too voracious for one man to satisfy, these lyrics encapsulate a double transgression of norms of propriety. As well as breaking the more generalized norm against making explicit public reference to sex acts, these lyrics flout a more particular reticence about *women* taking pleasure in sex. Ira Lowenthal (1984) explains that rural Haitians' ordinary reticence concerning women's erotic pleasure shows neither prudishness nor ignorance but is a product of rural Haitians' implicit view of conjugality as a multi-dimensional contract between men and women. In this implicit contract, a man's material support is generally traded in return for a woman's sexual fidelity. Lowenthal concludes that if a woman were to admit to gaining the non-material benefit of pleasure from the sex act, it would then diminish her bargaining power vis-à-vis any would-be spouse in negotiating the conjugal contract. Women's pleasure in sex, then, is a kind of open secret in rural Haiti, that everyone knows about but no woman publicly admits to enjoying. The lid on this topic comes off completely in *Rara*. The transgression of this taboo on open reference to women's sexual pleasure is never more explicit than in those relatively few *Rara* song lyrics that voice a woman's perspective. One such song that I heard sung in Monte Coca expresses the lament of a woman who has lost her partner to another woman. Even though she feels sexual desire, she cannot replace him with another man because his way of screwing her felt just right.

A more subtle but omnipresent dimension of excess in *Rara* is the repeated expression, in any number of forms and contexts—songs, symbols, rituals, verbal formulations of experience—of a strong positive evaluation of the expenditure of kinetic energy. Especially sought-after states are heat and brisk, rhythmic movement. One song in Monte Coca called for the *lwa* Azaka to "rock" (*balanse*) the celebrants, which it was explained to me meant "dance in people's heads and put everyone in motion." *Balanse* is at times not pleasant but disturbing. Brown (1991: 374) provides a brilliant exegesis on the concept of *balanse* and its centrality to the vodou ethos: "In *Vodou*," she writes, "the term ... *balanse* means to swing ritual objects from side to side or to hold them as you turn yourself around and around. Such balancing 'heats up', or enlivens, the object." When a *lwa* rocks its servants thus it creates agitations that border on perturbation and even loss of control. Brown (1995: 223) gives the following example to illustrate that, when understood in a spiritual context by the believer, the experience of *balanse* can enrich and bring spiritual growth to the people so challenged: "André Pierre, a well-known Haitian painter and a Vodou priest, once used the word *'balanse'* when describing the death of a friend.... 'Death came to our friend's door,' André Pierre said, and then he laughed: *'Gede te balanse kay-sa!* [*Gede* balanced that house!]' Death shook everything up. And from the clash and commotion, more life emerged." Brown (1995: 223) concludes, "Balancing—sometimes a gentle teasing friction, sometimes a shocking but unavoidable look in the face of death, and sometimes a deliberate mixing of mutually intolerant ingredients—raises life energy. It keeps things from becoming static and going dead. Behind the religions of the book there is a fear that human appetites and energies will get out of control; behind the religions of the mindful body there is a fear that those same appetites will atrophy and die."

Heating, uplifting and energetic rocking are key symbolic actions in the "ritual of the seat," celebrated on Good Thursday evening to bring the spiritual blessing and protection of the *lwa* to the *Rara* band. Rosenberg's detailed description adds much to my observations of this ritual. As at other vodou ceremonies, drumming, dancing and call-and-response chanting and singing bring down the *lwa* to join the party and partake of the offerings—cassava bread, wheat bread, bananas, candies, coffee grounds, tobacco, water, candles, and rum—set out for the spirits at the central post of the *enramada*. The majors' batons, the musicians' instruments and the band's other paraphernalia are ritually "baptized" and spend this night "heating up" (gaining mystical energy) in the altar house (Rosenberg 1979: 114; also McAlister 2002: 54). At the climactic moment of the ritual, each member of the *Rara* band takes a turn being heaved up to the ceiling of the *enramada* on a chair by the majors and swung about in the chair above the heads of the gathered crowd in a rapid, rocking motion. The lifting up and swinging about of each band member and the coordinated group effort these require all have symbolic significance, according to Rosenberg (1979: 111). The ritual of the chair symbolizes the social and spiritual uplifting each band member experiences through her/his participation in *Rara*. For the duration of the festival, the members of the band experience a hiatus in their lives, during which they cease to be downtrodden workers and rise to the center of everyone's attention as the main actors in a dramatic work of the spirit. The rocking back and forth of each uplifted band member also anticipates the rhythmic energy of the procession and the dancing to come, as well as underscoring the dependence of each band member upon the others for safely completing the processions.

Brown generalizes that, in the context of vodou ceremonies, "heat" is a metaphor for a state of animation and excitement conducive for the *lwa* to make their presence felt among the assembly. A knowledgeable vodou practitioner knows how to "work with the energies of the people" to achieve this state: "Like a drummer 'pushing the beat,'" Brown (1995: 222) writes, "the *Vodou* priest or priestess raises the energy in the group until the situation is *byen chofe*, well heated up. That is when the spirits arrive and apply their not always gentle healing energy."

In the preparatory ceremony, the heating action of flames is a symbol for the abundant flow and expenditure of energy held to be crucial for the satisfactory execution of the festival. At the end of the preparatory ceremony, in the early hours of Good Friday, the majors emerge from a period of ritual isolation inside the altar house. Their appearance in full regalia for the first time elicits excited shouts among the people gathered around and the drumming and singing gain heightened intensity. As each member of the band appears, the band's "magician" leads each man or woman by the hand to where the log fire burns a few steps from the *enramada* and then guides each person in stepping around and then over the sacred flame. When I witnessed the band's debut in Monte Coca's *Rara* in 1986, one of the queens hesitated for an instant when pulled toward the flame but was dragged forward by the magician and avoided being pulled into the fire only by deftly jumping over the flames at the last instant. In Monte Coca, the magician was a tiny but muscular *viejo*, named Alexandre. During *Rara*, he wore one red sash and one black sash over a khaki CEA uniform, each sash tied under one arm and slung over its opposite shoulder, overlapping to form crosses high on his back and on his chest. Over his shaven head, he wore a tattered light brown hat, its brim tied up over his forehead with rope knotted in front and back. The magician's role is to ensure the safety of the procession by warding off magic that might be thrown at them by a rival *Rara* band. During the ritual of the fire, Alexandre gave the majors particular attention. Working silently, he excitedly motioned each man in turn to lower his socks down around his shoes, then thrust his own hands into the flames and meticulously rubbed their exposed calves with his hands. The magician repeated the heating and rubbing treatment with each calf and forearm until each major had been thus blessed. The heat of the flames, it was explained, purifies the band members of any negative spiritual energies, gives them added strength and makes their step lighter.

After the last member of the band is brought through the flames, the musicians begin to play their instruments. The procession gathers, makes one more circuit counter-clockwise around the sacred fire, and moves on immediately to begin gathering together any devotees who are not yet with the group. At this point I saw Alexandre go rigid, careen backward on his heels through the fire—scattering embers, smoke and wood—and fall flat on his back onto the ground, where he began convulsing. Some of the band members looked down at him but none of the participants betrayed any sign of worry. The procession stopped and the music ceased as the fire was reassembled. Alexandre then lifted himself up onto his knees in front of the fire and began singing in a shaky falsetto. Concerned looks passed over the faces of people in the band as they tried to understand what he was singing, and a passing Dominican man loudly exclaimed, *Coñazo!* ("God damn!" literally, "great cunt!"). The *sanba* quickly began another song, and as the band moved on, a couple of men helped Alexandre up by the elbows and led him gently into the altar house to recover from his trance.

This was not the only episode of ritualized trance possession I was to see that day. Less than an hour later, the procession reached the barracks dwelling of one of Ti Boyòt's daughters, Sil. In front of the door of her house, the majors performed their competitive dance in honor of the dwellings' inhabitants. Sil's husband was a major and her teenaged daughter, a queen, but neither was present for the band's ceremonial coming out from Ti Boyòt's altar house. Before the two left the house, an abbreviated ceremony was conducted to integrate them into the procession. Standing on her doorstep, Sil's daughter fumbled with a lighter for a long moment, trying to light a small wax candle that she held in her left hand. As the candle lit, a deep frown marked her face, the muscles on her forearms tensed, and she seemed to be struggling to contain herself emotionally. Holding the lit candle, she poured water from a cup onto the front steps of the house. Suddenly, the dancers rushed to the door and one by one passed their batons from right hand to left behind Sil's daughter's head, enclosing her in the briefest and lightest embrace. This done, Sil's husband, Grenn, emerged from under a white sheet inside the house and, dressed in his major's regalia, rushed out the door to engage in an energetic display of dancing. Grenn ran out with such force that he accidentally pushed Sil's daughter from his path. The next instant, she was in trance, and danced for a moment with the majors, her face expressionless and her eyes half-closed. After running in a circle with the majors in their ritualized chase, she collapsed motionless in the dirt. Again, the bystanders' reaction was blasé. The girl was carried back in her house, and she reappeared in less than an hour's time, carrying one of the flags at the head of the procession.

The band members reacted differently to another instance of trance possession, on Good Friday afternoon. A woman for whom the majors were dancing broke into trance soon after the procession arrived at her house. She spun wildly from foot to foot among the majors, who were dancing in a circle around a wood fire burning in her yard. Her portly body raised clouds of gray dust as she careened through the fire, scattering burning embers and people in all directions (figure 9-8). Bystanders quickly calmed her, though she remained in trance. Then the woman's teenaged daughter became possessed. Staggering about the yard as if drunk, she mooched a bottle of rum from the *sanba* and poured it all into her bottle of *mamajuana* (spiced rum) herbs. She then turned to shake hands and greet the assembly, in the manner of the *lwa Gede,* grabbing each person first by the right hand and pulling it downward with an elbow-splitting sharp thrust, and then repeating this action with the left hand. One man she slapped hard on the forehead several times, until he leaned back to avoid the blows. Another man she almost knocked clean over, sending his hat flying. All this time, the music continued uninterrupted. Yet a moment later, as if thrown off balance by the violence of the trance states they were witnessing, several of the band members were becoming possessed or struggling to remain lucid, including the *sanba* and one of the majors (figure 9-9). One of the musicians fell to the ground, then picked himself up and stumbled about, finally climbing

Figure 9-8. Woman, in trance.

Figure 9-9. The *sanba* (metallic rattle in hand) and a *majò*.

half-way up a tree and hanging from a branch by the crook of his elbow. He was helped down and taken to one side to cool down.

The arrival of the *lwa*, possessing their believers' heads in trance and helping them dance with renewed energy, underscores the sacred character of *Rara*, contrasting with the playful and transgressive characteristics to which I have accorded perhaps exaggerated importance. As my field assistant, Francis Charles, explained, "If there is a person who serves the *lwa Ezili*, the *lwa* can mount his head in the middle of *Rara*. After the *lwa* start mounting people's heads in *Rara*, you know, the *Rara* changes. You would be there and see guys falling down (in trance). And the *Rara* gets hotter, too." The multiplex, boundary-blurring character of *Rara* is reflected also in its song repertory, in which a *chante betiz* might be followed by a Carnival song, then by a song from the *brizango* secret societies, and then by a song that could be sung, perhaps with modified verses, at a vodou ceremony. The playful, the erotic and the sacred are juxtaposed synergistically at all points.

Hence, it would, I think, be closer to the devotees' perspective to say that all of these things, which may seem mutually contradictory in Western eyes, are and should be bound together in service to the *lwa*. Interpreted in the light of its participants' experience, *Rara* not only demands a huge expenditure of surplus energy. It is a celebration of excess and, more particularly, of humanity's unique capacity for desiring beyond utility and imagining beyond the reality of our senses. *Rara* does not relate antagonistically to the body or to the material domain, generally. Far from constituting either a critique of modernity or an elevation of the sacred above and apart from the profane, batey dwellers' exegeses of *Rara* are shot through with metaphors—e.g., "heat" and the life-giving rocking motion they call "*balanse*—that echo with their positive evaluations of the stimulation and dynamism characteristic of electronic media and eroticism. While never reducible solely to a fascination with excess, a large part of the attraction of ritual, consumption, and Eros is how far these take the human mind beyond "the dreary, reiterative demands of necessity" (Deren 1953: 138). The material poverty and alienation of lives spent producing primary commodities, for the consumption of people at the far poles of the capitalist world order, seem hardly to have blunted Monte Cocans' aspirations for higher states of being. I am left wondering if the opposite is true, whether material deprivation and living in a place no one calls "home" might only increase humans' thirst for those experiences, of pleasure, beauty, and the spirit, that elevate our existence above survival and biological reproduction and are part of what makes us human and our lives worth living.

Notes

1. I thank Monica van Beusekom for drawing my attention to this film.

2. The "intrinsic" appeal of consumption beyond utility, I should hasten to add, suggests neither a universal nor a natural predisposition toward excess. The history of European and Euro-American expansion is full of examples of tribal people who were so unimpressed by the lure of material surplus that they had to be cajoled, coaxed, taxed, addicted to drugs, or if necessary, tied up and beaten before they would consent to working for colonial entrepreneurs. The anthropological record also contradicts any supposition that a desire for surplus is a human universal. It was notably absent among the nomadic foragers whom anthropologists had the chance to study before the disappearance of this way of life in the twentieth century. When confronted with a windfall, these "hunter-gatherers" would simply give their surpluses away to as many of their group as they could (Sahlins 1972: chapter 1).

3. It has not helped either that a certain stigma attaches to *Rara* in the eyes of city dwellers and social elites in Haiti. This stigma is related to the official disapproval that long hung over vodou, within which *Rara* has garnered particular scorn, as the largest-scale *public* manifestation of faith in the *lwa*. When its celebrants spill out by the thousands over the Easter weekend, they are despised three times over by Haitian elites, as *vaudouisants*, as "unwashed peasants," and for clogging vehicular traffic with their slow-moving processions. Even worse, the carnivalesque liberties indulged in by the *Rara* bands contravene the Catholic Church's injunction of temperance during Lent. *Rara* band members give voice to their de facto opposition to this aspect of Catholic orthodoxy through the adage, "You are a Jew once you join *Rara*" (*Ou al nan rara, se Jwif ou ye*), in implicit reference to the Jews who "killed Christ."

10

Conclusions

Bay kou, bliye; pote mak, sonje (Strike the blow, and forget; bear the wound, and remember)
—Haitian proverb

In few places could the gap between the promise of modernity and capitalism's failure to fulfill that promise on the global economic periphery be more evident. As a consequence, the case at hand shows how difficult it may be, in empirically studying the sources of social meaning in things, to detach differing styles of consumption from inequalities in people's capacity to consume (Miller 1988: 370). The meaning of consumer goods inheres not just in the ways people elect to define themselves and others through the medium of things. Meaning derives also from the social and economic limits to consumption—of which scarcity of means is only one—that place boundaries around consumers' freedom of maneuver.

In a community wanting in many basic needs, it is perhaps not surprising to find that Monte Coca residents draw social meanings—implicit and explicit judgments of likeness and difference among people—as often from relative want and deprivation as from the kinds of material things possessed and pursued by individuals. Deprivation may be felt all the more strongly because an important level of intra-community inequality exists in Monte Coca, where higher-paid and more steadily employed management personnel, supervisors and skilled laborers live alongside agricultural workers, who are themselves divided into seasonal and permanent populations. In the batey's poverty-stricken environment, consumption and other distinctive uses of time and space symbolically distance the plantation's permanent residents from the proletarian baseline condition of propertylessness, exemplified by the braceros who stand at the bottom of the plantation social hierarchy. Consumer products and images in the advertising and programs broadcast on national electronic media enter from the outside and are avidly appropriated by batey residents. Embracing these commodities is one way batey residents constitute their identities by opposition with others who stand in close social structural and geographical proximity to them but with whom they do not wish to be confused. These others include not just the braceros but Dominican peasants, whom plantation dwellers look down upon as less-sophisticated, true "country" people.

As batey residents turn their vision thus to the world outside the batey, it becomes apparent that consumption, in common with other global structures of common difference—e.g., sports competitions, beauty pageants, soap operas or talk about television (Wilk 1993)—is hierarchical. The value of different practices is ranked on a scale, and this scale of value has global dimensions: "It moves upwards towards standards that are defined at the centre, not the periphery" (Wilk 1995: 129). The urbane sophistication against which batey residents are comparing themselves and other sorts of people in their midst is a standard set by consumers in Western Europe and North America. Seen in this light, thinking about local/global interactions becomes not simply a question of how exogenous products and values are assimilated or resisted in places on the global economic periphery but of how people make sense of their social and geographical situations in terms of a hierarchy of difference with global reach. An example is the reception Monte Cocans gave the character of Don Chencho, the earthy peasant featured in television commercials for Joaquín Balaguer's presidential campaign in 1986. It is likely that TV viewers in the city of Santo Domingo considered Don Chencho to embody "Dominican-ness," in the form of a romanticized stereotype of "the *campesino*" (peasant), or at least this is probably what Don Chencho's creators were striving for. Part of what defines Don Chencho as an archetypal peasant and an icon for the Dominican nation is that his appearance did not conform to high standards of fashion (he wore the tattered clothes of a farmer) and he spoke in a non-standard dialect of the Spanish language (with the distinctive accent of people from the Cibao Valley). By reference to these same standards, people in Monte Coca ridiculed Don Chencho but also reckoned their own lifestyle to be inferior to that enjoyed by many in the Dominican capital. Deriding Don Chencho's appearance and speech could be interpreted as an act of resistance to the dominant fraction of the Dominican political and commercial elite, led by the late Dr. Balaguer. Or it could be understood as an act of conformity to hegemonic, European and North American metropolitan standards of opulence and taste (i.e., the Chencho figure was ridiculed simply because people thought it was ridiculous). Or both interpretations may be correct; or both, incorrect. The uncertainty suggests that we should not rush to judgment, by using such loaded terms as resistance or acquiescence to hegemony, in assessing Monte Cocans' appropriation of global material and linguistic standards to negate the sign value of Don Chencho. It is just as important, I think, to ponder how media images accrue meaning as it is to decipher what these mean. Global hierarchies are entering into local understandings and judgments about difference within the Dominican nation, yet people's interpretations of these are apt to vary across the Dominican social and geographical landscape.

The braceros differ in turn from the peasants who live on the margins of the sugar plantations. They are understood by Monte Coca's permanent residents to embody not only primitivism but indecency. Here, by contrast, I find it hard to withhold negative judgments. Indecency is a condition attributed to the braceros in a manner akin to "blaming the victim." The degradations imposed on the seasonal migrants are understood to be problems they have brought upon themselves, simply because they enter the batey each year of their own volition. They are reasoned to be less human, because they accept unacceptable treatment: brutally arduous work, humiliating subordination, and inhumanely overcrowded accommodations. Their extreme frugality during the time they live on the sugar estates is perceived not as a temporary strategy, of deferring gratification in order to repatriate the maximum savings they can to Haiti, but as a reflection of an innate, animal-like ability and willingness to do without the socially defined needs that are a part of living decently.

One irony is that both Dominicans and Haitians evaluate the quality of their lives in essentially the same terms but tend to blame each other—the people of the other ethnic group—for the indignities imposed upon the braceros, rather than inculpating the company, the government, the international sugar market, neo-liberal reform or any of a number of other actors and forces that could be said to have created or worsened their predicament. The people of both groups see freedom from want, respect for each other and for norms of social propriety, and acknowledgment of their right to dispose of their own labor as they see fit to be key conditions for a decent life. Both groups agree that the braceros live an indecent life according to these criteria but identify the root problem that underlies this to be a sense of decency lacking in the people of the other group. Dominicans say life in Haiti must be terrible beyond belief if the braceros choose to leave their country to live in the subhuman conditions of the bateyes. Haitians say that Dominicans lack the moral and physical fortitude to do the tough jobs Haitians do and accuse them of having no shame for treating the braceros "worse than dogs." It is through such appeals to group pride that oppressed groups assert their deeply felt claims to equality. Group pride goes wrong, however, when it leads people to blame each other for inequities that result from policies and institutions beyond their control. It is not that Haitians and Dominicans blame each other for everything wrong in their lives. People of both groups say the company and the government are bad. Yet, when it comes to assigning blame for tensions and injustices that flow from the industry's ethnic division of labor, they more readily downgrade their fellow batey dwellers and assert their own group's superiority than question the morality of the corporate managers and national leaders who approve company policies.

Consumption-induced sensations of decency, novelty, stimulation and reassurance may therefore form a part of what W. E. B. Du Bois calls a "psychological wage," the satisfaction that may be derived by members of an ethnic in-group, by being made to feel that they stand apart from and above the members of a despised out-group. Concerning the white workers' experience of racism in the United States, Du Bois (1935: 700) writes,

> [T]he white group of laborers, while they received a low wage, were compensated in part by a sort of public and psychological wage. They were given public deference and titles of courtesy because they were white. They were admitted freely with all classes of white people to public functions, public parks, and the best schools. The police were drawn from their ranks, and the courts, dependent upon their votes, treated them with such leniency as to encourage lawlessness. Their vote selected public officials, and while this had small effect upon the economic situation, it had great effect upon their personal treatment.

David Roediger (1991: 13) emphasizes in his exegesis of this passage that, beyond the incitation to violence against blacks to which Du Bois alludes, racism's tragedy lay in the white workers' rejection of class solidarity across color lines, in favor of the spurious benefit of a feeling of superiority over the black:

> [T]he pleasures of whiteness could function as a "wage" for white workers. That is, the status and privileges conferred by race could be used to make up for alienating and exploitative class relationships, North and South. White workers could, and did, define and accept their class positions by fashioning identities as "not slaves" and as "not Blacks".... Race feeling and the benefits conferred by whiteness made white Southern workers forget their "practically identical interests" with the Black poor and accept stunted lives for themselves and for those more oppressed than themselves.

It gives pause to see a social-distancing mechanism of this kind at work among people as poor and downtrodden as those who live in Monte Coca. Yet the parallel is so exact that it seems hard to avoid concluding that Du Bois's concept of a psychological wage for in-group membership is applicable also to ethnically divided working populations outside the United States. Inequalities in acquisitive power and in command over time and living space may acquire exaggerated symbolic value in the creation of a capitalist pecking order when joined to existing supremacist ideologies.

That the search for enhanced dignity, in the form of material comforts and personally enhancing consumption experiences, may play into management's divide-and-rule strategies does not diminish the role of violence, alluded to in Du Bois's words above, as a segregator of decent and indecent folk in the batey. Violence is inflicted with impunity, in a range of physical and symbolic forms, against the men and women who have arrived most recently from Haiti. In differing ways, permanent residents of all ethnic groups and socioeconomic levels cooperate with and participate in hurting and humiliating the seasonal migrants. Ranging from the Haitian nationals who recruit cane cutters and prostitutes in Haiti, to the company bosses who sponsor and subsidize both types of traffic, the low and the high are accomplices in egregious infringements of basic rights and violations of human dignity. Being targeted for symbolic and physical violence with impunity adds to the indignities that mark the seasonal migrants' existence as "indecent" in batey residents' eyes.

That the *viejos*, Haitian nationals who maintain year-round residence in the batey, are not treated as badly, but are generally accorded the minimal courtesy and consideration due a neighbor, demonstrates the complexity of so-called ethnic divisions of labor. Clearly, ethnicity is of primordial importance. Conceits of group superiority are made more convincing to Dominicans on the sugar estates by spurious nationalist ideology, which holds that the two nations are racially distinct—Haitians being understood to be the descendants of enslaved Africans; Dominicans, a mixture of Spaniard, African and Taíno Indian. Without this racial ideology, it is unlikely that the Dominican residents of Monte Coca would so readily see evidence of innate inferiority in the braceros' behavior and life circumstances. It exceeds the scope of this book to examine the genesis of this "racialized" concept of the Dominican nationality. Suffice it that this story, too, doubtless has its global dimension: would Dominicans despise Haitians so if they had not learned early in their country's history that nearly all of the rest of the world scorned Haiti, too? A primal scene of the Dominican anti-Haitian complex was reenacted before my eyes in Monte Coca, by the Air Force sergeant who asked, "There aren't any Haitians around here, are there?" and my neighbor who answered, "Oh, no! We're all Dominicans here!" (even though her own husband was Haitian-Dominican). In thousands upon thousands of encounters, gaining outsiders' approval has hinged, as it did in this case, upon negating the Haitian within the Dominican community (Torres-Saillant 1998). The desire to be perceived to be "less black" and "more civilized" in the eyes of the world outside the shared island of Hispaniola seems indissociable from whatever internal wellsprings of animosity may fuel anti-Haitian sentiment and ideology.

Yet ethnicity alone does not account neatly or completely for where lines are drawn among the plantation work force. The relative respect accorded the *viejos,* in spite of their being Haitian, suggests that the lines between ethnic groups, occupational statuses and socially honored and dishonored people do not coincide perfectly with each other. Hence, ethnic identity may have less autonomous determinacy than has been accorded to it by theorists of divided labor markets. Clearly, the worst mistreatment is reserved for the seasonal migrants because they are *strangers* as well as

Haitians. They can be subjected to physical coercion and other indignities with impunity in part because, unlike the *viejos,* they are not considered to be "neighbors" (*vecinos*) at all by the batey's permanent residents.

The *viejos* are also perceived to be more human in their neighbors' eyes to the extent that the *viejos* join them in reciprocal exchanges and at leisure. The more prosperous *viejos* even undertake domestic improvements, as their Dominican neighbors do, involving decorating and structurally modifying their barracks domiciles. Yet even those *viejos* who are very poor, live alone in unimproved rooms, and do the degrading jobs involving "struggling with cane" (*bregar con caña*)—physically handling sugar cane—are viewed as less degraded than the braceros, who largely eschew sharing leisure with the batey's permanent residents out of lack of confidence in Spanish and in order to repatriate more money to Haiti. In these ways, consumption habits and the uses people give to space and time also form part of the line between seasonal and permanent residents, and thus become another determinant of the Dominican sugar industry's division of labor. Thus, not only a person's ethnic identity but also perceptions of his larger situation in the material world enter into batey residents' reckonings of the sugar industry's labor hierarchy.

Conspicuously absent from batey discourse is the opinion that the goal of acquiring the minimal material conditions of a decent life justifies changing the larger social order. If calls for large-scale political transformation are scarce in Monte Coca, it is not because people there have no sense of the larger social whole or of their own place within it. In their own concrete terms, they express their views of Dominican society, always locating themselves at the bottom. Batey dwellers are quick, for example, to connect their own deprivation with there being "too many millionaires in the country." Yet these opinions more readily elicit nostalgia for the past than new visions for the future. Monte Cocans, old and young, eulogize the reign of the fierce dictator, Rafael Leonidas Trujillo, and speak glowingly of "the time of the Americans," when a U.S. corporation owned the plantation. They portray this to have been an era of simpler pleasures, with less moral and political corruption, when "the canes were taller and weighed more [than now]," "children did not go hungry," and a day laborer could "drop a peso on the road on payday evening and not bother to go back to pick it up: it did not matter to him, because the money he had left in his pocket sufficed [for his needs]." Given the harsh realities of conflict and deprivation that are known to have characterized "the American times," it seems likely nostalgia for past, failed political systems reflects recent decline, not past comfort, and evinces a lack of viable alternatives in the present. Monte Cocans are aware that a Cuban-style socialist solution is simply not possible politically for their country. Whether this perception be justified in terms of the "failures of socialism" or the implacable hostility of the United States government to any political platform centered on distributive justice, their knowledge of Cuba and of events in other Latin American countries stand as another example of how local consciousness in Monte Coca is influenced by an awareness of international events and processes.

Much of the evidence from Monte Coca is in keeping with Douglas and Isherwood's (1979: 12) insight that goods may be used socially either "as fences or bridges." On the one hand, the things on which batey residents spend most—food, drink, furniture, TVs, radios—can be and generally are enjoyed socially. By sharing these, the owners not only display their acquisitive power but provide a minimal dignity to others as co-participants in novel and stimulating consumption experiences. On the other hand, Monte Coca's inhabitants construe their neighbors' differing relationships to commodities, the built environment, and time, as expressions of enduring occupational, ethnic, and gender differences. As has already been mentioned, this tendency to objectify identity is clearest vis-à-vis the braceros who come to Monte Coca each harvest season from Haiti. Yet the line between decent and indecent women is marked just as clearly in terms of spatial practice, between those who keep mostly to their homes versus the women who are seen openly engaging in sex work in the barroom at the batey's brothel. The link between domesticity and decency also sustains the aspirations of many women to spend scarce funds on expanding and beautifying their families' living space in the company barracks. In the poverty and housing shortage of Monte Coca, the brilliance of certain families' domestic environments throws others' less-improved barracks accommodations into deeper shadow. Even as heavily decorated and over-furnished family parlors put the householders' buying power and esthetic sense on display, as well as providing settings for holiday largesse, these rooms increase the visibility of economic inequalities between the batey's higher-paid steady employees and those who are given mainly low-paid seasonal work. Such distinctions have only grown more pronounced as the effects of neo-liberal reforms and especially the quasi-privatization of the government-owned sugar estates have pushed many into deeper poverty.

Considerable support is also found for Daniel Miller's (1995a: 141) opinion that the study of material culture will assume steadily greater importance, perhaps becoming for the ethnology of the twenty-first century what the study of kinship, myth and ritual were for twentieth-century ethnology: principle loci of sense-making and socializing practices in places around the world. "Commodities, as other material forms, prove able to act as mythic structures, as taxonomic systems creating homologies between different models of sociality, as expressions of the inalienable, and as the objectification of moral and cosmological values" (Miller 1995b: 289). "Traditional kinship studies," Miller (1995a: 156) adds, "excelled in repudiating what might have been thought of as the homogenizing effect of any assumed biological foundation to kin relations." In similar contrast with what many believe are the inevitable homogenizing effects of global economic integration, "actual consumption practices may suggest ... that consumption, like kinship, is simply a domain through which diverse projects of value are objectified."

I think it is safe to say my ethnography brings forward evidence of cultural resilience as well as disturbing social conflict set in motion by commoditization. For example, beliefs about the power of supernaturally endowed persons endure and gain new relevance in this highly proletarianized social environment. There is also little doubt that Monte Cocans feel motivated to share many of their personal status-enhancing consumption activities with their neighbors in part because they are aware at some level that individualized status-seeking is widely disapproved of. Yet I have repeatedly touched upon the point that the question of cultural survival seems harder to define in a community such as Monte Coca, where the ethnographer will not find a clear conceptual line between "Westerners" and "non-Westerners," in the form of enduring autochthonous traditions, under attack from economic globalization. Monte Coca came into existence more or less ex nihilo from the projection of Western power into the tropics. It is a place where culture has had to be pieced together out of the broken fragments of traditions brought there by its settlers. Anthropology's conventional emphasis upon the exotic and anti-modernist does not fit into such communities' maps of meaning very easily, in part because so much of the material culture you will find in places like Monte Coca resembles what you might also find in much of Western Europe and North America.

Let me amplify upon this through an anecdote. At a workshop on visual anthropology I put forward the idea that the portrait photographs that I took of my batey neighbors, to which I have made repeated reference in this book, were a richer source of insight than the candid photos that I took of them in their everyday surroundings and attire. The preceptor of this workshop told me it was not valid to read any meaning into portrait photos, even if my interpretation were aided by residents' commentary, because portrait photography is not an indigenous visual medium and hence is alien to the underlying culture. My only response at the time was to think, "That's too bad, because the closest thing I can think of to an indigenous visual medium in the batey are the 'collages' of newspaper and magazine clippings that line the walls of many people's homes." Looking back, this particular visual anthropologist's rejection of using portrait photos as a tool of investigation points to one of the key interpretive and theoretical challenges I have faced in writing this book. There is no doubt that I and the people with whom I did my fieldwork in this plantation community differ culturally but it is just as certain that our structures of meaning overlap because we both participate in the same international social and economic system. Portrait photos may not be indigenous but they are an "indigenized" medium, familiar to batey residents long before I arrived on their doorsteps. More importantly, portrait photos coexist in the local culture with such exotic phenomena as rumored dealings with the devil. Both expressions of culture convey meaning in and about the world of goods. Any treatment of the meanings of the commodity form among rural proletarians and semi-proletarians would be incomplete without more generally considering both myth and ritual *and* consumption behavior. Considering both leads us away from radically "other-ing" the people with whom we do fieldwork and makes possible a fuller and more accurate picture of how their aspirations and ways of relating to the material world are like and unlike our own.

At the same time, if we give exclusive attention to whether autochthonous customs and meanings survive or disappear under the rising tide of commoditization and other northern-dominated market institutions, anthropologists may also err in attaching too little importance to more subtly corrosive effects. Rituals and supernatural beliefs may endure even as increased dependence upon wage labor erodes customs of sharing and encourages repudiation of egalitarian ideologies. Many of my observations point to the conclusion that the commoditized lifestyle and hierarchical organization of the plantation drive a wedge into the social fabric. Consumption may provide ordinary people with a means of living with the contradiction between the greater material abundance made possible by industry and the tendency of industrial societies to reduce the individual to an anonymous producer of goods (Miller 1987: 14). Yet, even more urgently, my findings warn that, when images from global late-capitalist media enter into a community as poor as Monte Coca is, consumption also creates frustration and worsens existing social divisions. Therefore, the study of material culture gains added importance in today's rapidly globalizing economy. It trains a particularly bright and focused light on the economic dislocations set in motion by free-market reform and the attendant growth in social inequality among primary commodity producers and others on the global economic periphery whose labor is becoming increasingly redundant as a result of neo-liberal reform.

Social distinctions can never completely explain why people struggle so tenaciously to comply with the material requirements of ceremony and of socially approved display, in spite of chronic poverty. To pretend that the mean satisfaction of feeling superior to others accounts satisfactorily for the appeal of commodity consumption, frenetic leisure activities and ostentatious domestic displays is, I think, to "sociologize" material culture too much. Any explanation of the global consumption boom must also take account of the stimulation and satisfactions to be derived from non-utilitarian consumption. No doubt people do at times take the admiration or disapproval of others quite seriously when they ponder how to use their money, time or effort. Foreseeable social consequences can act as motivations for behavior. Yet people's motivations for consumption are rarely reducible to its social effects. Narrowing these effects even further, to attribute determinacy mainly to an interest in setting up invidious distinctions between the self and the other, is impoverishing our understanding of consumption's appeal.

Another, more specific, problem with focusing exclusively on the social meanings of material practice is that this privileges effects and sense over affect and sensation, and hence gives an overly one-sided, rationalist perspective on why people desire to consume beyond utility and mark time and space in distinctive ways. Difficult though this dimension is to get at empirically as an ethnographer, I have made the effort to integrate some consideration of non-rational feeling into my understanding of the appeal of consumer goods to low-income workers ("non-rational" meaning neither "incoherent" nor "illogical" but simply "beyond reason"). There is great relevance in Georges Bataille's (1985: 120) maxim, "human poverty has never had a strong enough hold on societies to cause the concern for conservation—which gives production the appearance of an end—to dominate the concern for unproductive expenditure." I suspect that expenditure on display and entertainment among low-income populations is under-described and under-theorized only in part because of social researchers' rationalist bias. This scholarly neglect can perhaps also be attributed to an inexplicit sense that the poor, in particular, are morally diminished by profligacy. Following Bataille's lead and wishing to develop a less judgmental understanding of seemingly wasteful material practices, I have sought clues concerning the appeal of expenditure beyond utility to the batey consumer.

Decency and excess are conventionally regarded as opposites, by people in Monte Coca as in Western Europe and North America. Yet, even as the payday-weekend hedonist and the evangelical moralizer spend money on different things, they both indulge to a significant extent in expenditure beyond utility. Spending on living room furniture, household adornments and television sets, by the batey's more affluent residents, gains an added layer of meaning when one considers that the money spent on these domestic environments is money not spent on dissolute or scandalous leisure activities. Yet non-utilitarian consumption it still is. Seeking consumer satisfactions beyond adequacy therefore sooner unites than distinguishes those who live decently and those who live scandalously. Indulging in certain approved forms of excess expenditure is a condition for fully realizing batey residents' visions of living decently. In this light, then, the disbursement of scarce funds on material tokens of decency is yet another manifestation of the larger fascination that excess holds in Monte Coca.

Monte Cocans are hardly alone among low-income proletarians in choosing to allocate scarce space, time and money to entertainment, display and ceremonial. The payday-weekend revelry at La Yagüita may, for example, be likened to the varied entertainments hosted by taverns, brothels and other public gathering places, in early industrial Europe and

North America (Brennan 1988). The custom of furnishing a "parlor" with prized possessions and reserving this room largely for special gatherings is also documented among the working people of late nineteenth- and early twentieth-century Britain (Roberts 1973, in Miller 1987: 197) and the United States (Cohen 1985), as well as contemporary rural Greece (Hoffman, Cowan and Aratow 1973).

Nor are Monte Cocans alone in feeling themselves acutely diminished when deprived of the opportunity to mark holidays and moments of leisure via distinctive consumption activities. In the eyes of the Swedish itinerant farm workers of Nexö's (1930: 86–87) *Pelle the Conqueror,* a resented feature of working on modern, commercial agricultural estates was the owners' repudiation of customary obligations to subsidize holiday feasting. I am reminded also of the much more recent testimony of a heroin-addicted prostitute, physically abused by her partner, who begins to realize that she has had enough degradation when denied a proper Christmas celebration: "[W]e arrived at Christmas of that year with no money. Our Christmas dinner consisted of a half pound of ham and three scrambled eggs.... I was in such denial that I remember wishing for Santa Claus to magically appear before morning with a tree and train. He didn't, of course, and I never felt so stuck in my life" (Wardlaw 1988: 112). Even in accounts of famine, frustrated expectations regarding ceremonial consumption crystallize the emotional experience of deprivation. The television documentary, "A State of Mind," provides a rare look at the daily lives of two Pyongyang families. During the period known to North Koreans as the Arduous March, severe food shortages and massive starvation followed from the loss of trading partners, due to the collapse of communism in Eastern Europe and the Soviet Union, compounded by natural disasters, failed harvests and a lack of raw materials. Considering the magnitude of the hardship and loss of life, which was worse in the countryside but could not be escaped from even in Pyongyang, it is perhaps surprising that the mother of the children in one family says the following, when asked about her experience of this period: "The Arduous March.... To let you know how frustrated we felt back then, I only need tell you about our oldest daughter's birthday at the time. On Sun-Yi's birthday, we had nothing but corn. So I ground up a whole ear of corn and made porridge with it. We celebrated our oldest daughter's birthday by giving half a bowl each to the other children, and a whole bowl to the birthday girl. I can't say we live in abundance now but it's much better than during the Arduous March" (PBS 2003).

As the North Korean example implies, appropriate comparisons are not limited to capitalist versions of modernity but may also be drawn from socialist societies. Katherine Verdery (1996: 28–29) remarks, "The black markets in Western goods that sprang up everywhere enabled alienated consumers to express their contempt for their governments through the kinds of things they chose to buy.... Acquiring objects became a way of constituting your selfhood against a deeply unpopular regime." Evidence of this kind from the present and former socialist world (Chow 1993; Humphrey 1995) does not imply detaching consumption from a critique of capitalism so much as it recommends rethinking consumption "as a domain whose alienatory potential might remain just as evident under socialism or some other economic system" (Miller 1995a: 157).

In other places and times, too, the sudden withdrawal of habituated stimuli has underscored how vital certain commodities are to people's sense of living decently. Chinua Achebe's (1973) short story "Sugar Baby" tells the tale of a man with an extraordinary sweet tooth—for whom "sugar is not simply sugar. It is what makes life bearable." The story recounts what happens to him when sugar becomes unavailable for more than a year during the Biafran War. In his desperate search for the sweet crystal, he experiences the indignity of being chastised and chased away by a Catholic relief worker, for begging for sugar while others are starving. He reaches his nadir when he attempts to wrest a dozen smuggled sugar cubes from his girlfriend's clenched fist, gaining the sugar but losing the girl: she throws the stuff in his face and storms out. It is nowhere clearer than with regard to habituating substances that the appeal of commodities nearly always rests to a degree in the sensations of invigoration and comfort that these provide to their consumers.

If space permitted, the historical and cross-cultural range of these comparisons could surely be extended further. Suffice it to say that, in considering these issues, we are dealing with common, if insufficiently theorized, dimensions of the worlds of meaning of industrial societies. From the consumer's point of view, certain outwardly "inessential" forms of consumption may be essential to achieving desired personal and social ends. Consumption of mass-produced commodities may be vital to a woman's sense of living decently, raise a man in the eyes of his fellows, personalize a family's domestic space, convey messages about morality, or provide a focus for valued sociality.

But in making this point I am still left looking at consumption's social consequences and I stand some distance still from a fuller appreciation of the motives that drive it. Mixed up though the anticipated social effects may be with the other, more direct, sensual or psychological satisfactions, part of the appeal of consuming in distinctive ways inheres in the immediate feeling that the consumer hopes to get from it. Already at the turn of the twentieth century, Georg Simmel put forward the thesis that the allure of modern mass entertainments lay in the transient and fleeting stimulation and excitement that these produced in the minds of their audiences. Yet, other than to point out that new and ever faster-paced and more shocking entertainments were needed to entice jaded, blasé consumers, he did not seem inclined to ponder why these experiences should fascinate people so much in the first place. Why expenditure on things more ephemeral than froth might appeal more than investment in resources of lasting substance is a question that Simmel does not take us further toward answering, other than to postulate that these consumption experiences function as a salve for the alienation and anonymity of modern life.

Bataille—who was always interested more in *how* things mean than in what they mean—comes closest perhaps to saying in general terms what I am driving at, when he juxtaposes the *sovereignty* of rulers to the *dignity* of subjects.[1] For Bataille (1991: 198), "What distinguishes sovereignty is the consumption of wealth, as against labor and servitude, which produce wealth without consuming it. The sovereign individual consumes and doesn't labor, whereas at the antipodes of sovereignty the slave and the man without means labor and reduce their consumption to the necessities, to the products without which they could neither subsist nor labor." For ordinary people, a measure of dignity may derive from pure expenditure, permitting them to inhabit the domain of sovereignty, even if only for a fleeting moment: "If I consider the real world, the worker's wage enables him to drink a glass of wine: he may do so, as he says, to give him strength, but he really drinks in the hope of escaping the necessity that is the principle of labor. It's not much, but at least the glass of wine gives him, for a brief moment, the miraculous sensation of having the world at his disposal" (ibid.: 199). I am drawn to this image. I think it is not straying from Bataille's meaning to suggest that what the worker drinking the wine, as well as consumers in Monte Coca, are saying to the world is, "I am neither a slave nor a laborer without means. I have my dignity."

Yet Bataille demands also that we go beyond asking what the sight of the worker drinking might signify to those who observe him, to ponder his inner experience. Recall that for Bataille (1988: 12, 28) the central subject of "general economy" is neither scarcity nor the conservation of resources nor means-ends calculations but the expenditure of the surplus of energy stored on the face of the Earth and in the body of each human being. I have followed Bataille's lead in seeking clues about this experiential dimension of material culture in Monte Coca, first by looking squarely at non-utilitarian consumption and then by tracing expenditure to excess into the domains of eroticism and ritual.

A common source of fascination for the consumer of electronic media, the payday-weekend reveler and the *Rara* procession participant is the experience (or simulation) of super-abundance, ceaseless flux and unbounded kinetic energy. Television draws viewers in with its luminescent glare and holds their attention in large part through the ever-changing flow of images that dance across it and the illusion of ceaseless novelty that these create. Not just exaggerated effects and sensational content but a sense of constant movement holds the audience captive. A wilder abundance surrounds the customer in the midst of a binge at La Yagüita. Multiple distinctive consumption activities and overlapping brute sensations—drinking, smoking, gambling, plugging the juke box, feeling the rhythm of the music, laughing at its double entendres, sharing dances with the prostitutes, displaying male camaraderie and competitiveness and wallowing in the attention of sexually available women—envelop the barroom patron in a sauna of emotionally heightening experiences. By contrast, sudden deprivation made it dramatically clear how habituated Monte Cocans are to the consumer satisfactions that electricity makes possible. When the flow of electronic media was largely stopped during two lengthy suspensions of electrical service, Monte Coca residents fell into a kind of stupor, describing their strangely quiet surroundings as intolerably "cold," a term connoting not just inactivity but ill-health. Metaphors of heat and energetic rocking movement also course through the symbols and song lyrics of the *Rara* festival as well as emerging in its participants' conscious formulations of experience of the festival. Rhythmic drumming and call-and-response chanting and singing drive the *Rara* processions forward. Episodes of ritualized spirit possession bring the festival to a higher, "hotter" level. Carnivalesque transgression of the bounds of propriety and inversion of the social hierarchy are therefore only the most obvious ways in which *Rara* is about meaningful excess. *Rara* glorifies expenditure beyond utility. Its participants not only expend a tremendous amount of their own energy in its processions but strive to shake loose the weight of the real, to indulge in the dream of carrying out a great collective work of the spirit, leaving far behind "the dreary, reiterative demands of necessity" (Deren 1953: 138).

That human beings need to desire beyond satiety and create beyond necessity is where I think a deeper meaning is to be found more specifically in the erotically suggestive dancing that takes place on the perimeter of the *Rara* processions as well as in the sexual innuendo and outright vulgarity of *Rara* 's "*betiz* songs." Bataille identifies Eros as the template of humans' desire for expenditure beyond utility. Ladelle McWhorter (1995: 37) writes, "Throughout his work, Bataille concerns himself with transgression, particularly with events of laceration—that is, moments when the self is torn open and is exposed to what is other to it ... , for example, religious ecstasy, extreme physical suffering, or erotic release." At such moments, the boundary between subject and object dissolves, creating not unity of two wholes but only expenditure and loss, the object of general economy. Eroticism is expenditure of sexual energy, aimed not at reproduction but at pleasure that has no point but its own realization. Thus, eroticism has no meaning without taboo, the refusal of nature and the setting apart of animal impulses as something to be repressed in daily public conduct. Quoting Bataille's *Eroticism*, Paul Hegarty (2000: 108–09) writes, "All that is rejected or distanced [through taboo] is part of the sacred, and can be recalled ... [in] the form of transgression, which is absolutely part of taboo, as it 'suspends a taboo without suppressing it.'" That sacred festivals are commonly also occasions for festive license, especially public erotic play, is a phenomenon that seems not contradictory but entirely expectable in Bataillean perspective, inasmuch as nothing can mark the sacred more clearly than the transgression of its taboos.

This juxtaposition of sacredness and transgression in Bataille's general economy provides a basis for understanding the combination of erotically charged songs and dancing among the perimeter crowd with the sacred work going on at the center of *Rara* processions. *Betiz* songs may well be, as Elizabeth McAlister (2002: 61) suggests, "the last bastion of uncensored speech," and hence an oblique form of political commentary. "When you are not permitted to say anything else," she writes, "at least you can swear, drink, and sing vulgar songs." I think *Rara*'s vulgarity is this and more. I see it also as transgression distilled, expressing the human desire to break out of an existence shackled to ordinary ends, if only for the hiatus in observance of taboos that the festival opens. Inasmuch as these negate the limits of the ordinary, *betiz* songs and the erotically suggestive play that swirls around the *Rara* band merge with the sacred work going on at the festival's core. I am suggesting that we look at the profane and sacred elements of *Rara* not as two, homogeneous parts—relating to each other as a mask to its hidden content—but as mutually constitutive dimensions of a single dimorphic, dynamic balance. For example, the twinning of the erotic and the sacred in the following lyric, recorded by McAlister (2002: 63) in Port-au-Prince, would have made Bataille nod in satisfaction:

Our Lady of Perpetual Help	*Notre Dame de Perpétuel Secours*
Watch over your children	*Veuillez sur vos enfants*
Our Lady of Perpetual Help	*Notre Dame de Perpétuel Secours*
Pray for us	*Priez pour nous toujours.*
If I fuck her I'll get AIDS	*Si'm konyen'l m'ap pran sida*
Your mama's clitoris	
[or, fuck your mother]	*Kou langèt manman-ou*

Though profane and even scatological, the liberation of Eros in *Rara* song and dance partakes of the sacred in Bataille's "heterological" approach. Like the serious spiritual work of *Rara*, Eros is the antithesis of mundane, everyday constraint. Rather than just shielding the spiritual content of the festival from the skeptical or even hostile gaze of non-believers, the letting-go of restraints on the body during *Rara* and the frequent references made in its songs to unquenchable sexual desire—in the form of lyrics about men with penises too large to take in or women with appetites too voracious for one man to satisfy—symbolize humans' desire for satisfaction beyond adequacy.

It is not that the awe of expenditure for expenditure's sake is the only intrinsic source of appeal in distinctive material practices, or even the most important of these. Clearly, the worker of Bataille's "real world" drinks his wine not just to gain prestige in others' eyes or to attain momentary escape from the dead weight of necessity. He also drinks because of the physiologically mediated effects the wine has on his mood and consciousness, its way of relieving anxiety, providing reassurance and relaxing his inhibitions. He may have even learned to like the way the wine tastes. I look at the allure of expenditure for its own sake, then, not to exclude or diminish the importance of other immediate gratifications. Rather, expenditure takes a place in this book second only to the social meanings of material culture because expenditure for its own sake is senseless and thus stands at the furthest remove possible from the ways time, space and commodities enter into people's ways of making sense of the world. The distance between these two conceptualizations of material practice is vast: one approach treats the material world as a source of social meanings or a screen onto which people "project" and "read" human difference; the other conceives of material culture as an arena for practices so flagrantly useless that they can be said to gain their authors nothing but the awe and admiration of the beholder. The distance between these approaches is a measure of the span of how humans attribute meaning to the material world, an indicator of how "over-determined" consumption phenomena are, and a sign of how various and broad the satisfactions derivable from participation in industrial society can be.

To list what kinds of satisfactions non-utilitarian consumption provides would be pedantic, so often have I touched upon the varied social and psychological rewards of distinctive material practices in the preceding pages. Suffice it to add that I think the allure of expenditure for its own sake should join this list of satisfactions. The appeal of expenditure begins with the excitement of disbursing money itself. It can involve the mood-heightening novelty of indulging in ephemeral pleasure, or the reassuring sense of predictability, personal grace and break from monotony to be gained by marking the passage of time through daily, weekly or yearly non-productive ritualized outlays of time, money or energy, small or large. Non-utilitarian consumption responds to a general human desire however fleetingly to exceed the bounds of necessity and soar in a dream of abundance.

In seeking to spread new consumption habits, the agents of advanced capitalism have powerful "allies" in the multiple levels at which novel consumption experiences can appeal to the consumer. How pointless, therefore, to suggest that the poorer three-quarters of the planet's population should or somehow could be diked in against the rising tide of consumerism. If consumer society is winning the hearts of hundreds of millions around the world, it is in part because they are gaining something of value from it; this, even if many of the consumption choices seem wasteful and even as millions of others are harmed by the freeing-up of markets and spreading commoditization that undergird the twenty-first-century consumption boom.

Lest it seem I am attributing a non-rational outlook particularly to low-income workers, it would be apt to consider what human and material resources are being put to waste in the countries of the global north, solely to kill the ennui of the many and attain a higher margin of profit for the few. From birthday balloons and candles, to fireworks displays, X-games, and demolition derbies, from Bergdorf Goodman holiday window displays to those great temples of waste, the shopping malls, U.S. residents spend much of their leisure time and dollars consuming beyond adequacy and pointlessly expending, and even destroying, wealth. Expenditure to excess is more than a defining theme of North American culture, and "Just do it!" more than a credo of the era: the entire economy floats on the froth of non-utilitarian consumption. If North Americans were suddenly to become rigorously rational and utilitarian in their consumption choices, then Wall Street, the U.S. Treasury, and with them the entire world economy would crash. The grace of waste, experienced by the affluent consumers of the world's industrially advanced nations, is thus linked inextricably to the concentration of economic and political might in the United States, Japan, and European Union states.

Richer ground still for an ethnography of excess is surely to be found in the offices of the Pentagon, the World Bank, and Wall Street banks and investment houses. Neo-liberal reform, global flows of capital, and industrialized militarism are together laying waste to material wealth and destroying human lives on a scale of magnitude, brutality and callousness never before seen. The creation of value for investors through the destruction of jobs and fixed capital in older industries and the re-channeling of capital to branches of investment with higher margins of profit comprise the central dynamic of capital restructuring. Built with international capital during the late-nineteenth and early-twentieth centuries, the Ingenio Consuelo now stands on the precipice because capital has been steadily redirected out of and away from it in more recent decades. It would probably be an understatement to say that this type of "creative destruction" of industrial built environments has been repeated a thousand-fold across the world as one outcome of neo-liberal reform.

It is sadly true that, the day it ceases to exist in the form I describe it here, no one will miss Monte Coca much. Life was hard and getting worse already years before neo-liberal reform and global competition sank the Dominican sugar industry into decline and struck batey residents into deeper deprivation, insecurity, uncertainty and despair. Poignant though their struggle to live decently might appear to our eyes, there is really nothing ennobling about misery. To paraphrase Jean-Bertrand Aristide, poverty may permit dignity but misery cannot. Misery is the greatest enemy of freedom and human rights on the planet today. Poverty so deep that it leaves its victims little choice but to accept humiliation, mistreatment and neglect of their needs as the price for holding a job or keeping a shelter turns life into survival, not life as we would choose to live it. It is all the more significant, then, that Monte Cocans still reach for higher things and direct their energy, time and money toward non-utilitarian ends, in spite of living in material poverty verging on misery. That they must overcome severe material constraints, to realize these strivings, suggests that sufficiency of means is never enough, and expenditure to excess, an inalienable part of a life worth living and of what it means to be human and to be free, in the modern age.

Note

1. I thank Lanfranco Blanchetti for drawing my attention to the potential relevance of Bataille's thought to the topic of modernity's material culture.

Works Cited

Abu-Lughod, Lila, 1991 "Writing against Culture." In *Recapturing Anthropology: Working in the Present*. Edited by Richard G. Fox. Pp.137–62. Santa Fe: School of American Research Press.
Achebe, Chinua, 1973 "Sugar Baby." In *Girls at War and Other Stories*. Pp.95–107. New York: Doubleday.
Americas Watch, 1989 *Haitian Sugar-Cane Cutters in the Dominican Republic*. New York: Americas Watch, National Coalition for Haitian Refugees, and Caribbean Rights.
——— 1990 *Harvesting Oppression: Forced Labor in the Dominican Sugar Industry*. New York: Americas Watch, National Coalition for Haitian Refugees, and Caribbean Rights.
——— 1992 *A Troubled Year: Haitians in the Dominican Republic*. New York: Americas Watch and National Coalition for Haitian Refugees.
Appadurai, Arjun, 1986a "Theory in Anthropology: Center and Periphery." *Comparative Studies in Society and History* 28(2): 357–61.
———, ed., 1986b *The Social Life of Things: Commodities in Cultural Perspective*. Cambridge: Cambridge University Press.
——— 1988 "Putting Hierarchy in Its Place." *Cultural Anthropology* 3(1): 37–50.
——— 1996 *Modernity at Large: Cultural Dimensions of Globalization*. Minneapolis: University of Minnesota Press.
Báez Evertsz, Franc, 1986 *Braceros haitianos en la República Dominicana*. Santo Domingo: Instituto Dominicano de Investigaciones Sociales.
Basch, Linda, Nina Glick Schiller, and Cristina Szanton Blanc, 1994 *Nations Unbound: Transnational Projects, Postcolonial Predicaments, and Deterritorialized Nation-States*. Basel: Gordon and Breach.
Bataille, Georges, 1985 *Visions of Excess: Selected Writings, 1927–1939*. Edited and translated by Allan Stoekl. Minneapolis: University of Minnesota Press.
——— 1988 *The Accursed Share: An Essay on General Economy*. Translated by Robert Hurley. Vol. I. New York: Zone Books.
——— 1991 *The Accursed Share: An Essay on General Economy*. Translated by Robert Hurley. Vols. II and III. New York: Zone Books.
Baudrillard, Jean, 1981 *For a Critique of the Political Economy of the Sign*. Translated by Charles Levin. St. Louis: Telos.
Behar, Ruth, 1987 "Sex and Sin, Witchcraft and the Devil in Late-Colonial Mexico." *American Ethnologist* 14(1): 34–54.
Belk, Russell, 1988 "Third World Consumer Culture." *Research in Marketing, Supplement* 4: 103–27.
Benedict, Ruth, 1959[1934] *Patterns of Culture*. Boston: Houghton Mifflin.

Bobea, Lilian, and Ana Rita Guzmán C., 1985 *"Reproducción de la fuerza de trabajo familiar: Bateyes Lechería y Enriquillo." Tesis de licenciatura, Universidad Autónoma de Santo Domingo.*
Bonacich, Edna, 1972 "A Theory of Ethnic Antagonism: The Split Labor Market." *American Sociological Review* 37: 547–59.
Bourdieu, Pierre, 1977 *Outline of a Theory of Practice*. Translated by Richard Nice. Cambridge: Cambridge University Press.
Bourgois, Philippe, 1989 *Ethnicity at Work: Divided Labor on a Central American Banana Plantation*. Baltimore: Johns Hopkins University Press.
Brennan, Thomas, 1988 *Public Drinking and Popular Culture in Eighteenth-Century Paris*. Princeton: Princeton University Press.
Brewer, Toye, et al., 1998 "Migration, Ethnicity and Environment: HIV Risk Factors for Women on the Sugar Cane Plantations of the Dominican Republic." *AIDS* 12: 1879–87.
Brown, Karen McCarthy, 1991 *Mama Lola: A Vodou Priestess in Brooklyn*. Berkeley: University of California Press.
———, 1995 "Serving the Spirits: The Ritual Economy of Haitian Vodou." In *Sacred Arts of Haitian Vodou*. Edited by Donald J. Cosentino. Pp.205–23. Los Angeles: UCLA Fowler Museum of Natural History.
Bryan, Patrick E., 1985 "The Question of Labor in the Sugar Industry of the Dominican Republic in the Late Nineteenth and Early Twentieth Centuries." In *Between Slavery and Free Labor: The Spanish-Speaking Caribbean in the Nineteenth Century*. Edited by Manuel Moreno Fraginals, Frank Moya Pons and Stanley L. Engerman. Pp.235–51. Baltimore: Johns Hopkins University Press.
Calder, Bruce J., 1981 "The Dominican Turn toward Sugar." *Caribbean Review* 10(3): 18–21 and 44–45.
Castells, Manuel, and Jeffrey Henderson, 1987 "Introduction—Techno-economic Restructuring, Socio-political Processes and Spatial Transformation: A Global Perspective." In *Global Restructuring and Territorial Development*. Edited by Jeffrey Henderson and Manuel Castells. Pp.1–17. London: Sage.
Castillo, José del, 1978 *La inmigración de braceros azucareros en la República Dominicana, 1900–1930*. Santo Domingo: CENDIA.
Certeau, Michel de, 1984 *The Practice of Everyday Life*. Translated by Steven F. Rendall. Berkeley: University of California Press.
Chevalier, Jacques, 1982 *Civilization and the Stolen Gift: Capital, Kin, and Cult in Eastern Peru*. Toronto: University of Toronto Press.
Chomsky, Aviva, 1996 *West Indian Workers and the United Fruit Company in Costa Rica, 1870–1940*. Baton Rouge: Louisiana State University Press.
——— and Aldo Lauria-Santiago, eds., 1998 *Identity and Struggle at the Margins of the Nation-State: The Laboring Peoples of Central America and the Hispanic Caribbean*. Durham: Duke University Press.
Chow, Rey, 1993 "Listening Otherwise, Music Miniaturized: A Different Type of Question about Revolution." In *The Cultural Studies Reader*. Edited by Simon During. Pp. 382–99. London: Routledge.
Clifford, James, 1988 *The Predicament of Culture: Twentieth-Century Ethnography, Literature, and Art*. Cambridge: Harvard University Press.
Codere, Helen S., 1950 *Fighting with Property: A Study of Kwakiutl Potlatching and Warfare, 1792–1930*. New York: J. J. Augustin.

Cohen, Lizabeth A., 1985 "Embellishing a Life of Labor: An Interpretation of the Material Culture of American Working-Class Homes, 1885–1915." In *Labor Migration in the Atlantic Economies: The European and North American Working Classes during the Period of Industrialization*. Edited by Dirk Hoerder. Pp.321–52. Westport: Greenwood Press.

Comaroff, Jean, and John L. Comaroff, 1990 "Goodly Beasts, Beastly Goods: Cattle and Commodities in a South African Context." *American Ethnologist* 17(2): 195–216.

———, eds., 1993 *Modernity and Its Malcontents: Ritual and Power in Postcolonial Africa*. Chicago: University of Chicago Press.

——— 1999 "Occult Economies and the Violence of Abstraction: Notes from the South African Postcolony." *American Ethnologist* 26(2): 279–303.

Comaroff, John L., and Jean Comaroff, 1987 "The Madman and the Migrant: Work and Labor in the Historical Consciousness of a South African People." *American Ethnologist* 14(2): 191–209.

Coombe, Rosemary, 1997 "The Demonic Place of the 'Not There': Trademark Rumors in the Postindustrial Imaginary." In *Culture, Power, Place: Explorations in Critical Anthropology*. Edited by Akhil Gupta and James Ferguson. Pp. 249–74. Durham: Duke University Press.

Coplan, David, 1987 "Eloquent Knowledge: Lesotho Migrants' Songs and the Anthropology of Experience." *American Ethnologist* 14(3): 413–33.

Corten, André, 1992 "*La Démocratie ou l'évasion: Les Réfugiés Haïtiens à l'assaut de l'Amérique.*" *Le Monde diplomatique* no. 455 (February): 15.

Cosentino, Donald J., ed., 1995 *Sacred Arts of Haitian Vodou*. Los Angeles: UCLA Fowler Museum of Natural History.

Courlander, Harold,1960 *The Drum and the Hoe: Life and Lore of the Haitian People*. Berkeley: University of California Press.

Crain, Mary M., 1991 "Poetics and Politics in the Ecuadorean Andes: Women's Narratives of Death and Devil Possession." *American Ethnologist* 18(1): 67–89.

D'Andrade, Roy, 2003 "Values." Department of Anthropology Colloquium, University of Connecticut, 19 May 2003.

Deren, Maya, 1953 *Divine Horsemen: The Living Gods of Haiti*. London: Thames and Hudson.

Desmangles, Leslie G., 1992 *The Faces of the Gods: Vodou and Roman Catholicism in Haiti*. Chapel Hill: University of North Carolina Press.

Dore Cabral, Carlos, 1987 "*Los dominicanos de origen haitiano y la segregación social en la República Dominicana.*" *Estudios Sociales* 20(68): 57–80.

——— 1995 "*La población dominicana, más antihaitiana que racista.*" *Rumbo* 69: 8–10, 12.

Douglas, Mary, 1966 *Purity and Danger: An Analysis of Concepts of Purity and Taboo*. New York: Praeger.

——— and Baron Isherwood, 1979 *The World of Goods: Towards an Anthropology of Consumption*. New York: Basic Books.

Drucker, Philip, and Robert F. Heizer, 1967 *To Make My Name Good: A Reexamination of the Southern Kwakiutl Potlatch*. Berkeley: University of California Press.

Du Bois, W. E. B., 1935 *Black Reconstruction: An Essay toward a History of the Part Which Black Folk Played in the Attempt to Reconstruct Democracy in America, 1860–1880*. New York: Harcourt Brace.

Edelman, Marc, 1994 "Landlords and the Devil: Class, Ethnic, and Gender Dimensions of Central American Peasant Narratives." *Cultural Anthropology* 9(1): 58–93.

Ferguson, James, 1991 Review of *Bitter Money*, by Parker Shipton. *American Ethnologist* 18(3): 620–21.

——— 1999 *Expectations of Modernity: Myths and Meanings of Urban Life on the Zambian Copperbelt*. Berkeley: University of California Press.

FLACSO (*Facultad Latinoamericana de Ciencias Sociales*), 2002 *Efectos de la privatización en tres ingenios de la Provincia de San Pedro de Macorís: Porvenir, Quisqueya y Santa Fé*. Santo Domingo: Centro Cultural Domínico-Haitiano and Action AID.

Foster, George M., 1967 *Tzintzuntzan: Mexican Peasants in a Changing World*. Boston: Little, Brown.

Foucault, Michel, 1970 *The Order of Things*. Translated by Alan Sheridan-Smith. New York: Random House.

Friedman, Jonathan, 1994 *Cultural Identity and Global Process*. London: Sage.

Gallardo, Gina, 2001 *Camino a construir un sueño: Sistematización de experiencia Programa Legal y Derechos Humanos*. Santo Domingo: MUDHA, *Movimiento de Mujeres Domínico-Haitianas*.

Gaspar, David Barry 1993 "Sugar Cultivation and Slave Life in Antigua before 1800." In *Cultivation and Culture: Labor and the Shaping of Slave Life in the Americas*. Edited by Ira Berlin and Philip D. Morgan. Pp.101–23. Charlottesville: University Press of Virginia.

Geertz, Clifford, 1973 *The Interpretation of Cultures*. New York: Basic Books.

Geschiere, Peter, 1997 *The Modernity of Witchcraft: Politics and the Occult in Postcolonial Africa*. Charlottesville: University Press of Virginia.

Gill, Lesley, 2000 *Teetering on the Rim: Global Restructuring, Daily Life, and the Armed Retreat of the Bolivian State*. New York: Columbia University Press.

Gitlin, Todd, 2001 *Media Unlimited: How the Torrent of Images and Sounds Overwhelms Our Lives*. New York: Metropolitan Books.

Gordillo, Gastón, 2002 "The Breath of the Devils: Memories and Places of an Experience of Terror." *American Ethnologist* 29(1): 33–57.

Gottdiener, M., 2000 "Approaches to Consumption: Classical and Contemporary Perspectives." In *New Forms of Consumption: Consumers, Culture, and Commodification*. Edited by Mark Gottdiener. Pp.3–31. Lanham: Rowman and Littlefield.

Gregory, C. A., 1986 "On Taussig on Aristotle and Chevalier on Everybody." *Social Analysis* no. 19: 64–69.

Gross, Daniel R., 1983 "Fetishism and Functionalism: The Political Economy of Capitalist Development in Latin America: A Review Article." *Comparative Studies in Society and History* 25(4): 694–702.

Gupta, Akhil, and James Ferguson, 1992 "Beyond 'Culture': Space, Identity, and the Politics of Difference." *Cultural Anthropology* 7(1): 6–23.

Hall, Douglas, 1978 "The Flight from the Estates Reconsidered: The British West Indies, 1838–42." *Journal of Caribbean History* 10–11: 7–24.

Hecht, Jennifer Michael, 2003. *Doubt, A History: The Great Doubters and Their Legacy of Innovation, from Socrates and Jesus to Thomas Jefferson and Emily Dickinson*. New York: HarperSanFrancisco.

Hegarty, Paul, 2000 *Georges Bataille*. London: Sage Publications.

Higman, B. W., 2001[1988] *Jamaica Surveyed: Plantation Maps and Plans of the Eighteenth and Nineteenth Centuries*. Kingston: University of the West Indies Press.

——— 1998 *Montpelier, Jamaica: A Plantation Community in Slavery and Freedom, 1739–1912*. Mona: University of the West Indies Press.

Hoffman, Susannah M., Richard Cowan, and Paul Aratow, 1973 *Kypseli: Women and Men Apart, A Divided Reality*. Videorecording. Berkeley: University of California Extension Media Center.

Howard, David, 2001 *Coloring the Nation: Race and Ethnicity in the Dominican Republic*. Boulder: Lynne Rienner.

Hufford, David J., 1982 "Traditions of Disbelief." *New York Folklore Quarterly* 8: 47–55.

Human Rights Watch, 2002 *'Illegal People': Haitians and Dominico-Haitians in the Dominican Republic*. http://www.hrw.org/reports/2002/domrep/

Humphrey, Caroline, 1995 "Creating a Culture of Disillusionment: Consumption in Moscow, A Chronicle of Changing Times." In *Worlds Apart: Modernity through the Prism of the Local*. Edited by Daniel Miller. Pp. 43–68. London: Routledge.

Jansen, Senaida, and Cecilia Millán, 1991 *Género, trabajo y etnia en los bateyes dominicanos*. Santo Domingo: Instituto Tecnológico de Santo Domingo, Programa Estudios de la Mujer.

Jayawardena, Chandra, 1968 "Ideology and Conflict in Lower Class Communities." *Comparative Studies in Society and History* 10(4): 413–46.

Jopling, Carol F., 1988 *Puerto Rican Houses in Sociohistorical Perspective*. Knoxville: University of Tennessee Press.

Kan, Sergei, 1986 "The 19th-Century Tlingit Potlatch: A New Perspective." *American Ethnologist* 13(2): 191–212.

Kane, Stephanie, 1994 *The Phantom Gringo Boat: Shamanic Discourse and Development in Panama*. Washington, D.C.: Smithsonian Institution Press.

Kapferer, Bruce, 1991 *A Celebration of Demons: Exorcism and the Aesthetics of Healing in Sri Lanka*. 2nd ed. Providence and Washington, D.C.: Berg and Smithsonian Institution Press.

——— 1997 *The Feast of the Sorcerer: Practices of Consciousness and Power*. Chicago: University of Chicago Press.

Kuhn, Thomas S., 1970 *The Structure of Scientific Revolutions*. Chicago: University of Chicago Press.

Kunstler, James Howard, 1993 *The Geography of Nowhere: The Rise and Decline of America's Man-Made Landscape*. New York: Simon & Schuster.

Lawyers Committee for Human Rights, 1991 *A Childhood Abducted: Children Cutting Sugar Cane in the Dominican Republic*. New York: Lawyers Committee for Human Rights.

Lee, Richard, 2000[1969] "Eating Christmas in the Kalahari." In *Conformity and Conflict: Readings in Cultural Anthropology*. 10th ed. Edited by James Spradley and David W. McCurdy. Pp.27–34. Boston: Allyn and Bacon.

Lefebvre, Henri, 1991 *The Production of Space*. Translated by Donald Nicholson-Smith. Oxford: Blackwell.

——— 2002 *Critique of Everyday Life, Volume II: Foundations for a Sociology of the Everyday*. Translated by John Moore. London: Verso.

Low, Setha M., 1992 "Symbolic Ties That Bind: Place Attachment in the Plaza." In *Place Attachment*. Edited by Irwin Altman and Setha M. Low. *Human Behavior and Environment: Advances in Theory and Research*, Vol. 12. Pp.165–85. New York: Plenum Press.

Lowenthal, Ira P., 1984 "Labor, Sexuality and the Conjugal Contract in Rural Haiti." In *Haiti—Today and Tomorrow: An Interdisciplinary Study*. Edited by Charles R. Foster and Albert Valdman. Pp. 15–33. Lanham: University Press of America.

Marcus, George E., 1998 *Ethnography Through Thick and Thin*. Princeton: Princeton University Press.

Martínez, Samuel, 1995 *Peripheral Migrants: Haitians and Dominican Republic Sugar Plantations*. Knoxville: University of Tennessee Press.

——— 1996 "Indifference within Indignation: Anthropology, Human Rights, and the Haitian Bracero." *American Anthropologist* 98(1): 17–25.

——— 1999 "From Hidden Hand to Heavy Hand: Sugar, the State, and Migrant Labor in Haiti and the Dominican Republic." *Latin American Research Review* 34(1): 57–84.

——— 2003 "Identities at the Dominican and Puerto Rican International Migrant Crossroads." In *Marginal Migrations: The Circulation of Cultures in the Caribbean*. Edited by Shalini Puri. Pp.141–64. London: Macmillan.

McAlister, Elizabeth, 2002 *Rara! Vodou, Power, and Performance in Haiti and Its Diaspora*. Berkeley: University of California Press.

McCracken, Grant, 1988 *Culture and Consumption*. Bloomington: Indiana University Press.

McEachern, Charmaine, and Peter Mayer, 1986 "The Children of Bronze and the Children of Gold: The Apolitical Anthropology of the Peasant." *Social Analysis* no. 19: 70–77.

McWhorter, Ladelle, 1995 "Is There Sexual Difference in the Work of Georges Bataille?" *International Studies in Philosophy* 27(1): 33–41.

Méndez B., José Ernesto, 2001 *El mercado mundial de azúcar y los bateyes dominicanos*. Santo Domingo: Centro de Estudios P. Juan Montalvo s.j.

Métraux, Alfred, 1959 *y7 in Haiti*. Translated by Hugo Charteris. New York: Oxford University Press.

Miller, Daniel, 1987 *Material Culture and Mass Consumption*. Oxford: Basil Blackwell.

——— 1988 "Appropriating the State on the Council Estate." *Man* (N.S.) 23(2): 353–72.

——— 1995a "Consumption and Commodities." *Annual Review of Anthropology* 24: 141–61.

——— 1995b "Consumption Studies as the Transformation of Anthropology." In *Acknowledging Consumption: A Review of New Studies*. Edited by Daniel Miller. Pp.264–95. London: Routledge.

Mintz, Sidney W., 1974 "The Rural Proletariat and the Problem of Rural Proletarian Consciousness." *Journal of Peasant Studies* 1(3): 291–325.

——— 1977 "The So-Called World System: Local Initiative and Local Response." *Dialectical Anthropology* 2(4): 253–70.

——— 1979 "Slavery and the Rise of Peasantries." *Historical Reflections* 6(1): 213–42.

——— 1985 *Sweetness and Power: The Place of Sugar in Modern History*. New York: Viking.

——— 1996 "Enduring Substances, Trying Theories: The Caribbean Region as *Oikoumenê*." *Journal of the Royal Anthropological Institute* 2(2): 289–311.

——— and Eric R. Wolf, 1950 "An Analysis of Ritual Co-Parenthood (Compadrazgo)." *Southwestern Journal of Anthropology* 6(4): 341–68.

Moberg, Mark, 1997 *Myths of Ethnicity and Nation: Immigration, Work, and Identity in the Belize Banana Industry*. Knoxville: University of Tennessee Press.

Moore, Henrietta L., and Todd Sanders, eds., 2001 *Magical Interpretations, Material Realities: Modernity, Witchcraft and the Occult in Postcolonial Africa*. London: Routledge.

Moya Pons, Frank, et al., 1986 *El batey: Estudio socioeconómico de los bateyes del Consejo Estatal del Azúcar.* Santo Domingo: Fondo para el Avance de las Ciencias Sociales.

MUDHA, 2003 "Solidarity with the Struggle of the Dominican Minority of Haitian Descent for Citizenship and Justice," by Movimiento de Mujeres Domínico-Haitianas, *GSC Quarterly* 5. http://www.ssrc.org/programs/gsc/gsc_quarterly/newsletter5/

Munck, Ronaldo, 2005 *Globalization and Social Exclusion: A Transformationalist Perspective.* Bloomfield: Kumarian Press.

Murphy, Martin F., 1986 "Historical and Contemporary Labor Utilization Practices in the Sugar Industries of the Dominican Republic." Ph.D. dissertation, Columbia University.

——— 1991 *Dominican Sugar Plantations: Production and Foreign Labor Integration.* New York: Praeger.

Nash, June, 1994 "Global Integration and Subsistence Insecurity." *American Anthropologist* 96(1): 7–30.

Newton, James R. 1980 "The People of Batey Mosquitisol: Workers on a Sugar Cane Plantation in the Dominican Republic." Ph.D. dissertation, New School for Social Research.

Nexö, Martin Anderson, 1930 *Pelle the Conqueror.* New York: Peter Smith.

Nutini, Hugo G., and John M. Roberts, 1993 *Bloodsucking Witchcraft: An Epistemological Study of Anthropomorphic Supernaturalism in Rural Tlaxcala.* Tucson: University of Arizona Press.

Ong, Aihwa, 1987 *Spirits of Resistance and Capitalist Discipline: Factory Women in Malaysia.* Albany: State University of New York Press.

Osgood, Charles E., 1976 *Focus on Meaning.* The Hague: Mouton.

Parish, Jane, 2000 "From the Body to the Wallet: Conceptualizing Akan Witchcraft at Home and Abroad." *Journal of the Royal Anthropological Institute* 6(3): 487–500.

Parry, J., and M. Bloch, eds., 1989 *Money and the Morality of Exchange.* Cambridge: Cambridge University Press.

PBS, 2003 *A State of Mind.* Producer: John Battsek. Director: Dan Gordon. Wide Angle. PBS, 11 Sept. 2003.

Pellow, Deborah, 1992 "Spaces that Teach: Attachment to the African Compound." In *Place Attachment.* Edited by Irwin Altman and Setha M. Low. *Human Behavior and Environment: Advances in Theory and Research,* Vol. 12. Pp. 187–210. New York: Plenum Press.

Pérez de la Riva, J., 1975 *El barracón y otros ensayos.* Havana: Editorial de Ciencias Sociales.

Piddocke, Stuart, 1965 "The Potlatch System of the Southern Kwakiutl: A New Perspective." *Southwestern Journal of Anthropology* 21(3): 244–64.

Plant, Roger, 1987 *Sugar and Modern Slavery: A Tale of Two Countries.* London: Zed Books.

Pred, Allan, and Michael John Watts, 1992 *Reworking Modernity: Capitalisms and Symbolic Discontent.* New Brunswick: Rutgers University Press.

Rabinow, Paul, 1977 *Reflections on Fieldwork in Morocco.* Berkeley: University of California Press.

Richardson, Bonham C., 1975 "Plantation Infrastructure and Labor Mobility in Guyana and Trinidad." In *Migration and Development: Implications for Ethnic Identity and Political Conflict.* Edited by Helen I. Safa and Brian M. duToit. Pp.205–24. The Hague: Mouton.

Ricoeur, Paul, 1971. "The Model of the Text: Meaningful Action Considered as a Text." *Social Research* 38: 529–62.

Robben, Antonius C. G. M., 1989 "Habits of the Home: Spatial Hegemony and the Structuration of House and Society in Brazil." *American Anthropologist* 91(3): 570–88.

Roberts, Robert, 1973 *The Classic Slum: Salford Life in the First Quarter of the Century*. Harmondsworth: Penguin.

Robertson, Roland, 1992 *Globalization: Social Theory and Global Culture*. London: Sage.

Roediger, David R., 1991 *The Wages of Whiteness: Race and the Making of the American Working Class*. London: Verso.

Roseberry, William, 1989 *Anthropologies and Histories: Essays in Culture, History, and Political Economy*. New Brunswick: Rutgers University Press.

Rosenberg, June C., 1979 *El Gagá: Religión y sociedad de un culto dominicano*. Santo Domingo: Universidad Autónoma de Santo Domingo.

Rouse, Roger, 1995 "Thinking through Transnationalism: Notes on the Cultural Politics of Class Relations in the Contemporary United States." *Public Culture* 7: 535–602.

Rowlands, Michael, 1996 "The Consumption of an African Modernity." In *African Material Culture*. Edited by Mary Jo Arnoldi, Christraud M. Geary and Kris L. Hardin. Pp.188–213. Bloomington: Indiana University Press.

Rutz, Henry J., and Benjamin S. Orlove, eds., 1989 *The Social Economy of Consumption*. Monographs in Economic Anthropology, No. 6. Lanham: University Press of America.

Ryan, William, 1976 *Blaming the Victim*. New York: Vintage Books.

Sabbagh Khoury, Yvette Teresa and Dinorah Tavárez García, 1983 *"La reproducción social de la fuerza de trabajo azucarera: Caso del Ingenio Barahona."* Tesis de licenciatura, Universidad Autónoma de Santo Domingo.

Sachs, Jeffrey, 2005 "The End of Poverty: Economic Possibilities for Our Time." Books for Breakfast Lecture, Carnegie Council on Ethics and International Affairs, 5 March 2005.

Sahlins, Marshall, 1972 *Stone Age Economics*. New York: Aldine.

——— 1976 *Culture and Practical Reason*. Chicago: University of Chicago Press.

——— 1994 "Goodbye to Tristes Tropes: Ethnography in the Context of Modern World History." In *Assessing Cultural Anthropology*. Edited by Robert Borofsky. Pp.377–94. New York: McGraw-Hill.

——— 1999 "Two or Three Things That I Know about Culture." *Journal of the Royal Anthropological Institute* 5(3): 399–421.

Sánchez, Juan J. 1976[1893] *La caña en Santo Domingo*. Santo Domingo: Editora Taller.

Sanders, Todd, 1999 "Modernity, Wealth and Witchcraft in Tanzania." *Research in Economic Anthropology* 20: 117–31.

——— 2003 "Reconsidering Witchcraft: Postcolonial Africa and Analytic (Un)Certainties." *American Anthropologist* 105(2): 338–52.

Scheper-Hughes, Nancy, 2002 "Min(d)ing the Body: On the Trail of Organ-Stealing Rumors." In *Exotic No More: Anthropology on the Front Lines*. Edited by Jeremy MacClancy. Pp.33–63. Chicago: University of Chicago Press.

Shaw, Rosalind, 1997 "Production of Witchcraft, Witchcraft as Production: Memory, Modernity, and the Slave Trade in Sierra Leone." *American Ethnologist* 24(4): 856–76.

Shipton, Parker, 1989 *Bitter Money: Cultural Economy and Some African Meanings of Forbidden Commodities*. Washington, D.C.: American Anthropological Association.
Silverblatt, Irene, 1987 *Moon, Sun, and Witches: Gender Ideologies and Class in Inca and Colonial Peru*. Princeton: Princeton University Press.
Simmel, Georg, 1957[1904] "Fashion." *American Journal of Sociology* 62(6): 541–58.
—— 1990[1907] *The Philosophy of Money*. London: Routledge.
—— 1991. "The Berlin Trade Exhibition." *Theory, Culture and Society* 8(3): 119–23.
Slater, Don, 1997 *Consumer Culture and Modernity*. Cambridge: Polity Press.
Smith, Daniel Jordan, 2001 "Ritual Killing, 419, and Fast Wealth: Inequality and the Popular Imagination in Southeastern Nigeria." *American Ethnologist* 28(4): 803–26.
Smith, Jennie M., 2001 *When the Hands Are Many: Community Organization and Social Change in Rural Haiti*. Ithaca: Cornell University Press.
Suttles, Wayne Prescott, 1960 "Affinal Ties, Subsistence, and Prestige Among the Coast Salish." *American Anthropologist* 62: 296–305.
Sweezy, Paul Marlor, 1968 *The Theory of Capitalist Development: Principles of Marxian Political Economy*. New York: Monthly Review Press.
Taussig, Michael T., 1980 *The Devil and Commodity Fetishism in South America*. Chapel Hill: University of North Carolina Press.
Tejada Yangüela, Argelia, 2001 *República Dominicana, bateyes del estado: Encuesta socioeconómica y de salud de la población materno-infantil de los bateyes agrícolas del CEA, diciembre 1999*. Santo Domingo: USAID.
Torres-Saillant, Silvio, 1998 "The Tribulations of Blackness: Stages in Dominican Racial Identity." *Latin American Perspectives* 25(3): 126–46.
Trouillot, Michel-Rolph, 1986 "The Price of Indulgence." *Social Analysis* no. 19: 85–90.
—— 1992 "The Caribbean Region: An Open Frontier in Anthropological Theory." *Annual Review of Anthropology* 21: 19–42.
Turner, Victor, 1977 *The Ritual Process: Structure and Anti-structure*. 2nd ed. Ithaca: Cornell University Press.
UNDP (United Nations Development Programme), 1998 *Human Development Report 1998: Consumption for Human Development*. http://hdr.undp.org/reports/global/1998/en/
Veblen, Thorstein, 1899 *The Theory of the Leisure Class*. New York: New America Library.
Verdery, Katherine, 1996 *What Was Socialism, and What Comes Next?* Princeton: Princeton University Press.
Verrijp, Annemieke, 1997 *Respiramos el mismo aire: Salud, nacionalidad y descendencia de la mujer en siete bateyes dominicanos*. Santo Domingo: Movimiento de Mujeres Domínico-Haitianas, MUDHA.
Wagley, Charles, 1957 "Plantation-America: A Culture Sphere." In *Caribbean Studies: A Symposium*. Edited by Vera Rubin. Pp.3–13. Mona: Institute of Social and Economic Research, University College of the West Indies, Jamaica.
Wallerstein, Immanuel Maurice, 1974 *The Modern World-System, Volume I: Capitalist Agriculture and the Origins of the European World-Economy in the Sixteenth Century*. New York: Academic Press.

Wardlaw, Cecelia, 1988 "Dream Turned Nightmare." In *Sex Work: Writings by Women in the Sex Industry*. Edited by Frédérique Delacoste and Priscilla Alexander. Pp.108–12. London: Virago.

Wardlow, Holly, 2002 "Headless Ghosts and Roving Women: Specters of Modernity in Papua New Guinea." *American Ethnologist* 29(1): 5–32.

Watts, Michael, 1992 "Capitalisms, Crises, and Cultures I: Notes toward a Totality of Fragments." In *Reworking Modernity: Capitalisms and Symbolic Discontent*, by Allan Pred and Michael John Watts. Pp. 1–19. New Brunswick: Rutgers University Press.

Werbner, Pnina, 1990 "Economic Rationality and Hierarchical Gift Economies: Value and Ranking among British Pakistanis." *Man* (N.S.) 25(2): 266–85.

West, Harry, 2001 "Sorcery of Construction and Socialist Modernization: Ways of Understanding Power in Postcolonial Mozambique." *American Ethnologist* 28(1): 119–50.

White, Luise, 1990 *The Comforts of Home: Prostitution in Colonial Nairobi*. Chicago: University of Chicago Press.

——— 2000 *Speaking with Vampires: Rumor and History in Colonial Africa*. Berkeley: University of California Press.

Wilk, Richard, 1990 "Consumer Goods as Dialogue about Development." *Culture & History* 7: 79–100.

——— 1993 "'It's Destroying a Whole Generation': Television and Moral Discourse in Belize." *Visual Anthropology* 5(3–4): 229–44.

——— 1995 "Learning to Be Local in Belize: Global Systems of Common Difference." In *Worlds Apart: Modernity through the Prism of the Local*. Edited by Daniel Miller. Pp. 110–33. London: Routledge.

Wilson, Peter J., 1995[1973] *Crab Antics: A Caribbean Case Study of the Conflict between Reputation and Respectability*. Prospect Heights: Waveland Press.

Wolf, Eric R., 1966 *Peasants*. Englewood Cliffs: Prentice-Hall.

——— and Sidney W. Mintz, 1957 "Haciendas and Plantations in Middle America and the Antilles." *Social and Economic Studies* 6: 380–412.

Index

baseball, 151
Bataille, Georges, 15, 50–51, 166–69
Baudrillard, Jean, 52–53
bodega (dry-goods store), 105–06, 139
brothel, 106, 139–40, 162–64, 204–05

ceremony, 129–38
children, 89–90, 105
community initiatives, 125
   vs. "top-down" approach (e.g., feeding center, SSID house), 107–08, 143–44, 155n1
consumption. *See also* expenditure; globalization; material world; sharing; sign value; Simmel; Veblen
   alcohol, 140–41, 161–62
   anthropological studies of, 53–54, 201–02
   as display, 51, 106, 122–23, 132, 201
   electricity and electrical appliances, 148–50, 157–59, 208. *See also* radio and television
   among enslaved workers, 35
   global trends, 7–9
   in Marxist theory, 49
   non-utilitarian, 47, 203–04, 210–11
   among peasants, 130–32
   and "socially defined needs" of low-income workers, 48–49, 129, 204–06
   trends in the Dominican Republic, 44–45
culture
   and in/authenticity, 202–03
   and judgment, ix–xi

decency
   and the home environment, 84–85, 120–24, 201
   versus "indecency," in leisure activities, 141–42, 204
   versus "indecency" of the *braceros*, 5–6, 12, 72, 76–77, 110, 124, 148, 197–200
difference, 19n4, 64
Evangelicals, 141–42
"structures of common" (Wilk), 150–51, 196

envy, 3, 27–28, 132, 146–47, 152
eroticism, 164, 186–88, 208–09
ethnic division of labor
   in subsistence gardens (*conucos*), 67
   in sugar industry, 22–23, 30n5, 61–64
ethnicity, 68
   and conjugal unions, 70–71
   stereotypes of Haitians and Dominicans, 77–79
ethnography. *See also* Potlatch and "Witchcraft critiques modernity"
   functionalism, 164–66
   and globalization, ix, 59–60
   holism, 17
   multi-sited, 57–59
   of neo-liberal reform, 7, 9, 19n2
   of plantations, 21–24
expenditure, 15, 51, 160–70, 181–82, 184, 186, 207–11
   and metaphors of "heat/cold," 157, 159, 164, 170, 176, 181, 190–94, 208
exploitation. *See also* sugar industry, labor conditions
   from fellow workers, 81–82
   sexual, 81–83, 87. *See also* gender, violence

feeding center (SSID house). *See* community initiatives

gender
  division of labor, 62–63,
  in domestic unit, 120–22
  violence, 82–83, 86–88, 91n10
globalization, 54–55,
  and cultural diversity, 55–56, 202
  and international awareness, 154–55, 200–01,

housing, 119, 123–24
  modifications by residents, 95, 113–23, 183
human rights, 40, 87–88. *See also* "new slavery" and women, trafficking of
hunger, 138

Inequality, intra-community, 22, 57, 203

Jayawardena, Chandra, 21–22

Marcus, George, 57–58
material world, 12–14
McAlister, Elizabeth, 180–81
meaning
  social, 10–11, 19n3, 195–96
  studying the "how" (vs. the "what") of, 133, 169, 181
migration, seasonal. *See also* prejudice
  history, Dominican Republic, 22–23, 38, 61
  present-day, Dominican Republic, 39–40, 45n3, 79–82, 176
Mintz, Sidney, 21–22, 53–54

"Nacirema," 168
neo-liberal reform, 46n7, 211
  impact on Dominican sugar industry, 42–44
  and inequality, 7–9, 125–26
"new slavery" allegations, 40, 113

Osgood, Charles, 11

"pendular synergism," 18, 181–82, 189, 194

photography, portrait, 3, 28, 94–95, 202
plantations (see also sugar industry),
  architecture (see also Housing), 36–37, 103–04, 108–110
  geography, 35–37, 45n1, 97–102
  and modernity, 33–34, 96
  organizational structure, 64–65
  place attachment, 34–36, 112
popular music, 150, 155n2
possession, spirit, 190–93
potlatch, anthropological interpretations of, 165–67
prejudice, 155
  anti-Haitian, 68–70, 73, 77, 90n3, 153, 199
  against Dominican peasants, 151–52
  against seasonal migrants from Haiti (*congoses*), 70–79
"psychological wage" of whiteness (DuBois), 6, 198

radio and television, 148–50, 154, 159–60, 207
  political campaign advertisements, 151–52, 196
Rara (Lenten festival), 168–94, 207–09
reductionism, 50
religion, anthropology of, 168–69
residents, permanent, 40–41
  Haitian (*viejos*), 45n3, 72
  living conditions on the Dominican sugar estates, 41, 113–14
Rosenberg, June, 179–81

selfishness (*comparón/a*), 144
sensation, 14–15, 204, 206–07
sex work, 81–85, 91n12, 106, 140–41, 162–64
sharing
  of commodities and consumption activities, 133, 148–49, 201
  of food, 136–37
  at holidays, 135–36
Simmel, Georg, 51–52
sign value, 27, 52
social binarization, 11–12
"sovereignty," 50, 207
space, 13, 93
  Batey Monte Coca, 102–111

flows/places, 96–97
"nowhere," the geography of, 33
and power, 110–11, 126
"practical" (Bourdieu), 104
"social" (Lefebvre), 112–13
for socializing, 116–17
subsistence gardens (*conucos*), 66–67, 102
sugar industry, Dominican Republic, 37–39. *See also* ethnic division of labor, plantations, and space
clientelism and corruption, 65–66, 76, 82–83, 85, 87–88, 107, 147, 153
Consejo Estatal del Azúcar (CEA), 39, 124–25, 147, 183–85
labor conditions in the sugarcane fields, 74–76, 98–100
management, 64–66, 100
neglect of workers' human needs, 41–44, 111–14, 124, 158

Taussig, Michael, 24–27, 31–32n16
time
holidays, 134–36
and industrial slavery, 34
leisure, 75, 138–40
and yearly cycle of work in the cane sugar industry, 39

UNDP Human Development Report (1998), 7–9

vodou (see also Possession, spirit), 2, 90, 137–38, 170–71, 176–78, 183, 184, 189–90, 193
Veblen, Thorstein, 51

Wagley, Charles, 21
Wallerstein, Immanuel, 56
witchcraft
and acquisition of wealth, 2, 132, 144–47, 152
"critiques modernity thesis," 2–3, 25
ethnographic analyses of, 24–27, 29, 30–31nn8–14
Wolf, Eric, 21–22, 129, 131
women. *See also* exploitation, sexual and gender
health status, 88
and ritual, 137–38, 175–76
sources of income on the Dominican sugar estates, 41, 79, 88–89. *See also* sex work
trafficking to sugar estates from Haiti, 79–82

About the Author

Samuel Martínez is associate professor of anthropology and Latin American and Caribbean studies at the University of Connecticut and has served as chair (2003–04) of the American Anthropological Association's Committee for Human Rights. He is the author of one earlier ethnographic monograph and several peer-reviewed articles on the situation of Haitian nationals and people of Haitian ancestry in the Dominican Republic, and is editing a contributory volume, *National Security and International Migration: The Global Repercussions of US Policy*. With funding from the Social Science Research Council's Program on Global Security and Cooperation, he is now doing a comparative study of the substantive agenda, information practices, and advocacy strategies of international human rights organizations and Haitian-Dominican community-based organizations.